The Changing Institutional Face of British Employment Relations

Studies in Employment and Social Policy

In the series Studies in Employment and Social Policy this book
The Changing Institutional Face of British Employment Realtions, is the
thirty-first title.

The titles published in this series are listed at the end of this volume.

Studies in Employment and Social Policy

The Changing Institutional Face of British Employment Relations

Edited by
Linda Dickens and Alan C. Neal

KLUWER LAW
INTERNATIONAL

A C.I.P. catalogue record for this book is available from the Library of Congress.

ISBN 90 411 2541 8

Published by:
Kluwer Law International
P.O. Box 316
2400 AH Alphen aan den Rijn
The Netherlands

Sold and distributed in North, Central and South America by:
Aspen Publishers, Inc.
7201 McKinney Circle
Frederick, MD 21704
USA

Sold and distributed in all other countries by:
Turpin Distribution Services Ltd
Stratton Business Park
Pegasus Drive
Biggleswade
Bedfordshire SG18 8TQ
United Kingdom

Printed on acid-free paper

© 2006 Kluwer Law International

Printed in the Netherlands

This volume is dedicated to Jon Clark
1st June 1949 – 21st October 2005

TABLE OF CONTENTS

PREFACE

This volume has been prepared to mark thirty years of Acas activity at the heart of British employment relations.

The idea was conceived during the course of discussions between Alan Neal and John Taylor, while working together in Beijing on a technical assistance project to develop a Labour Arbitration Court for China. Thereafter, the book gradually took shape under the guiding hand and editorship of Linda Dickens, in collaboration with Alan Neal, at the University of Warwick.

The editors wanted to provide a contemporary picture of the institutional landscape of British employment relations. Much of the available literature (which, in any event, covered only some of the relevant institutions) was significantly out of date. We felt that public policy debate, as well as researchers, students and other readers, would benefit from a comprehensive, expert presentation of the current 'state of play', along with a discussion of developments and current challenges

The invited contributors to the volume are a mixture of highly regarded academics and senior practitioners, notably those most closely associated with particular institutions. The academic/practitioner distinction is a blurred one, however. Some authors have been both at different times; many of the academics involved in the project also have experience in practitioner/institutional roles, and the 'non-academics' are what are sometimes termed 'reflective practitioners'. We felt that this combination would provide a valuable mix of expert independent discussion with additional personal insights gained from direct involvement with the operation of various bodies. We hope that, as a result, the book will be of interest not only in terms of the substantive topics covered, but also as regards what those writing about them have to say. To this end, the editors have refrained from intrusion into authors' personal contributions and views.

Invitations to contribute were taken up enthusiastically, and we are grateful to the contributors for giving up valuable time to meet and discuss their areas and approaches, and to develop their contributions within our general framework.

The volume is dedicated to Professor Jon Clark who, as both an academic observer and active participant, contributed much to some of the institutions included here, and to our critical understanding of them.

The final presentation (unless otherwise indicated) reflects the institutional face of British employment relations as of 1st January 2006.

Linda Dickens
Alan C. Neal

Linda Dickens & Alan C. Neal (eds), The Changing Institutional Face of British Employment Relations, ix
© 2006 Kluwer Law International. Printed in the Netherlands

ABOUT THE AUTHORS

WILLIAM BROWN, CBE, is Professor of Industrial Relations and Master of Darwin College at the University of Cambridge. He is an experienced arbitrator and has been a member of the Low Pay Commission since it was established.

SIR MICHAEL BURTON practised as a barrister from 1970, was a QC from 1984 and Head of Littleton Chambers from 1991. In November 1998 he was appointed a High Court Judge (Queen's Bench Division). He has been Chairman of the Central Arbitration Committee since April 2000 and was President of the Employment Appeal Tribunal between 2002 and 2005.

BILL CALLAGHAN is Chair of the Health and Safety Commission. He was previously the Chief Economist and Head of the Economic and Social Affairs Department at the TUC. He served on the Low Pay Commission from 1997-2000.

PETER CLARK practised at the bar from Devereux Chambers from 1971-75, specialising in employment and personal injury law. Since his appointment to the bench in October 1995 he has been the resident Circuit Judge at the Employment Appeal Tribunal. He also sits in the High Court (Queen's Bench Division) and on Circuit.

DAVID COCKBURN was appointed as the Certification Officer for Trade Unions and Employers' Associations in 2001. He is also a part-time Chairman of Employment Tribunals. He had previously practised as a solicitor specialising in employment and trade union law for 29 years.

LINDA DICKENS, MBE, is Professor of Industrial Relations at Warwick Business School, University of Warwick, and a member of its Industrial Relations Research Unit. She has been a disputes mediator and arbitrator on the Acas panel since 1989 and a Deputy Chairman of the CAC since 1994.

MARK FREEDLAND, FBA, is Professor of Employment Law at the University of Oxford and a Law Fellow at St John's College, Oxford. He is currently engaged on a three-year project of research and writing as the holder of a Leverhulme Major Research Fellowship.

Linda Dickens & Alan C. Neal (eds), The Changing Institutional Face of British Employment Relations, xi-xii
© 2006 Kluwer Law International. Printed in the Netherlands

JANET GAYMER, CBE, is the Senior Partner of Simmons and Simmons. She is Life Vice-President and Honorary Chairman of the UK and European Employment Lawyer Associations respectively.

SIMON GOULDSTONE is Director of Policy and Operations at the Central Arbitration Committee.

SIR BOB HEPPLE, QC, FBA, a Barrister at Blackstone Chambers, is Emeritus Master of Clare College and Emeritus Professor of Law at the University of Cambridge. He is a former Chairman of Industrial Tribunals and a former Commissioner for Racial Equality. EWART KEEP is Professor and Deputy Director of the ESRC Centre on Skills, Knowledge and Organisational Performance at the University of Warwick.

NICOLA KOUNTOURIS is a Post-Doctoral Research Fellow in European and Comparative Law at the Research Centre of St John's College, University of Oxford.

GOOLAM MEERAN is President of the Employment Tribunals of England and Wales.

GILLIAN MORRIS is former Professor of Law, now Professor Associate, at Brunel University, a barrister at Matrix Chambers, and a Deputy Chairman of the Central Arbitration Committee.

ALAN C. NEAL, a Barrister at Cloisters Chambers, is Professor of Law at the University of Warwick, and a part-time Chairman of Employment Tribunals. He is the Convenor of the European Association of Labour Court Judges, and was the Founding Editor of *The International Journal of Comparative Labour Law and Industrial Relations*.

KEITH SISSON is Emeritus Professor of Industrial Relations in Warwick Business School's Industrial Relations Research Unit (IRRU), having previously been its Director for many years. He has just stepped down after two and a half years as the Acas Head of Strategy Development.

JOHN TAYLOR joined Acas in 2001 as its first Chief Executive, having been part of the team which set up the modern service in the mid-1970s. His background is primarily in the public sector, where he has been involved in training, economic development and employment relations.

Linda Dickens & Alan C. Neal

CHANGING TIMES, CHANGING NEEDS

Institutional Development Through Three Decades

INTRODUCTION

The catalyst for this volume is the 30th anniversary of the Advisory Conciliation and Arbitration Service (Acas). Acas shares its birth decade with a number of other institutions featured in this collection. This introductory chapter, which draws, in part, on previous work published by the authors (including Neal 2000; 2004, and, particularly, Dickens 2002; Dickens & Hall 1995, and 2003), considers political, employment relations and legislative developments over the past three decades as a context and institutional map for the contributions which follow. This is no easy task, given the dramatic changes and volatility of trends of that period.

These changes include: the end of 'voluntarism' and increasing juridification of the employment relationship; greater supra-national influence on British legislative policy; considerable decline of union membership and strength; the 'withering away' of strike action; the decentralisation and shrinking coverage of collective bargaining; political differences on how best to manage the British economy in the face of increasing global competition; shifts in the structure and composition of the labour force with, among other features, increased feminisation, more 'non-standard' workers, a growth in the service sector and decline in manufacturing, and restructuring of the public sector. Some of these macro-changes are reflected in the changes which have taken place in Acas as an institution which survived three turbulent decades. Elsewhere in the landscape are ruins or fragments of institutions past. Those which do survive – rather like British pubs – generally have undergone re-modelling, conversion and extensions, and changes in use or emphasis. The sign outside may appear familiar, but a look inside can reveal major transformations.

This book provides a look inside key institutions in British employment relations. Contributors locate their institution(s) in terms of its purpose, origins, and context; discuss its structure, governance and composition, and assess its operation, considering current challenges and future direction. In so doing, they illuminate various issues relating to institutional choice and role which are outlined later in this chapter.

Linda Dickens & Alan C. Neal (eds), The Changing Institutional Face of British Employment Relations, 1-12
© 2006 Kluwer Law International. Printed in the Netherlands

Linda Dickens & Alan C. Neal

THE INHERITANCE OF VOLUNTARISM

To understand the changes in the last thirty years, we need to start a little earlier. In Britain, for most of the twentieth Century, the regulation of the employment relationship by means of collective bargaining between employers and unions (and, where absent, by employers acting unilaterally) was far more important than legal regulation through Acts of Parliament. In turn this system of self-regulation was largely free of State control. 'Voluntarism' (or, to use Kahn-Freund's phrase 'collective laissez-faire'), as this approach is termed, was supported by both sides of industry. Unions saw the main role of legislation as preventing hostile intervention by the courts in industrial disputes. Employers were keen to avoid legislation that constrained their freedom to manage. Looking at it from the point of view of the State, 'one might say the State had delegated the task of ordering working life to the social institutions created by employers and workers, whilst according those social institutions a very substantial degree of freedom of action' (Davies & Freedland 1993:10).

Voluntarism was not only about a minimal role for legal regulation permitting the free play of collective forces. It also encompassed the extension and support of regulation provided through collective bargaining between organised labour and employers and their associations. Nor did it imply the complete absence of statutory intervention. Legislation was necessary in the late nineteenth and early twentieth Centuries to legalise trade union activity; a number of auxiliary measures were introduced (e.g. the provision of dispute settlement services by the Ministry of Labour), and regulatory measures were enacted governing the terms and conditions of employment for certain groups, notably those not covered by collective bargaining – as in the Wages Council industries (see Chapter 6). There were also health and safety laws (Factory Acts) covering various occupations and industries. Nevertheless, set alongside other industrialised countries, a crucial and distinguishing characteristic of British employment law from 1870 to the 1960s was its limited role. What formal regulation there was, assumed the desirability of voluntary collective regulation.

In such a context, the main institutions of employment relations were the so-termed 'institutions of collective bargaining': trade unions and employers and their associations, with auxillary support from the State. These institutions were lightly regulated, if at all. Thus, for example, trade unions were regulated through the constitutions established in their own rule books rather than by more interventionist legal regulation, despite the existence of a Registrar of Friendly Societies, a forerunner to the Certification Officer (see Chapter 8). Collective bargaining arrangements involving national or industry level agreements created other institutions – such as Joint Industrial Councils or National Joint Committees, which could be standing bodies with their own secretariats. The bulk of the *Industrial Relations Handbook,* produced by Acas in 1980, is given over to a description of such collective bargaining arrangements and institutions, many of which were soon to disappear, along with a number of the unions and associations of employers involved in them. Today, reading through the institutions, is rather like reading the names on a war memorial.

INSTITUTIONAL GROWTH AND JURIDIFICATION IN THE 1960S AND 1970S

Signs of a shift to greater legal regulation emerged in the 1960s with the introduction of minimum periods of notice of termination of employment and written particulars of terms and conditions of employment, and redundancy compensation to be paid to workers losing their jobs for economic reasons. These statutory rights produced new jurisdictions for the fledging Industrial Tribunals, originally set up to hear appeals about the imposition of training levies. From such beginnings has grown the (re-named in 1996) Employment Tribunal system (explored in Chapters 10, 11 and 12).

The Royal Commission on Trade Unions and Employers' Associations (the Donovan Commission) was established in 1965 partially in response to growing pressure for the greater legal regulation of industrial relations, particularly strikes – seen as a major problem. Its Report (Donovan 1968:47) however argued against 'destroying the British tradition of keeping industrial relations out of the courts'. The remit of the Commission on Industrial Relations (CIR), set up in 1969 in keeping with a recommendation of the Donovan Commission, was in the voluntary tradition, including the promotion (and reform) of collective bargaining and inquiring into and advising on the state of industrial relations. The political climate within which the CIR began its work, however, was changing significantly, and it operated only a few years on a voluntary basis, with the power, among other things, to hear recognition disputes and make recommendations for their settlement, before becoming part of the statutory arrangements of the Industrial Relations Act 1971. It disappeared in 1974 when Acas was created.

Despite Donovan, both the Labour government's 1969 white paper *In Place of Strife* and the subsequent Conservative government's Industrial Relations Act 1971 accorded a central role to legal intervention in the reform of industrial relations. The 1971 Act, in particular, represented an ambitious attempt at the comprehensive legal regulation of industrial relations, with a National Industrial Relations Court (NIRC) (Weekes *et al* 1975). However, this controversial legislation was given little chance to operate as the drafters envisaged. Its operation depended to a large extent on union registration (see Chapter 8), but most unions opposed this, and the Act had little impact on day-to-day industrial relations in most workplaces before its repeal in 1974. Only its statutory protections against unfair dismissal, originally proposed by the Donovan Commission, were re-enacted. Appeals from tribunals in such cases, which had been heard by the NIRC, were soon entrusted to a new body, the Employment Appeal Tribunal (see Chapter 12) as the NIRC, discredited by association with the Industrial Relations Act, was abolished.

By the time of our starting point of the mid-1970s, there was a return to a modified, supplemented form of voluntarism under the Labour governments of 1974-1979. The traditional framework for immunities for industrial action was reinstated and various auxiliary measures to support collective bargaining were enacted. A mass of piecemeal legislation in the Factory Acts gave way to a more comprehensive system following the Robens Report which led to the Health and Safety at Work Act 1974. This set up the Health and Safety Commission (HSC), emphasising self-regulation within a framework of State inspection and enforcement (see Chapter 4). Equal pay and anti-discrimination legislation covering sex and race was enacted, requiring new institutions – the Equality Commissions (discussed in Chapter 9).

The Employment Protection Act 1975 restructured much of the institutional framework of the industrial relations and employment law system, providing a statutory basis for the activities of Acas (see Chapter 3), which took over dispute settlement functions from the government, and a role in statutory recognition from the CIR; and for the Central Arbitration Committee (CAC) which superseded the inappropriately named Industrial Court (primarily an arbitration body and briefly renamed the Industrial Arbitration Board) to carry out statutory functions, including generalising collectively agreed terms of employment (see Chapter 7). It also introduced important new individual employment rights and strengthened others as the previous gap-filling role of the law gave way to a more 'universal floor of rights'. Although core areas of the employment relationship remained untouched, still resting on regulation by collective bargaining where it existed, there was a clear move towards the increasing juridification of the individual employment relationship.

Institutions established in the 1970s (under both Labour and Conservative governments) such as Acas, HSC, and the Manpower Services Commission (see chapter 5) sought to involve the social partners (as we would now term employers and trade unions) in the tripartite, co-operative administration of labour market and employment relations issues. In this they echoed the National Economic Development Council (NEDC) set up by a Conservative government in 1961: a 'corporatist' institution seeking to integrate business and trade union peak organisations into the conduct of economic policy (Crouch 2003). Acas, HSC and MSC performed roles previously within the remit of the Department of Employment, a development which both reflected and affected the development of that institution (Freedland 1992; and see below, Chapter 2). Developments at this time – notably, perhaps, the setting up of the Bullock Committee of Inquiry on Industrial Democracy in 1977 to report on how trade union representation on company boards might be achieved – were unthinkable less than a decade later.

1979 – 1997 AND THE RUPTURE WITH THE PAST

A major break with the past came with the employment law, economic and institutional reforms introduced by Conservative governments under Prime Ministers Thatcher and Major between 1979 and 1997. The long-standing public policy view that joint regulation of the employment relationship through collective bargaining was the best method of conducting industrial relations was accepted no longer. The change of Acas' terms of reference symbolised the shift away from the ethos of collectivism. It was no longer charged with 'the general duty of promoting the improvement of industrial relations, and in particular encouraging the extension of collective bargaining and the development and, where necessary, reform of collective bargaining machinery'.

Law was used to curb union strength, reduce collective bargaining (but not to replace it with legal protection) and to restrict industrial action. Reforms introduced on an incremental basis curtailed the scope of individual legal rights; enhanced employer freedom of action and reduced union autonomy. In pursuit of this last objective, the government departed from its general preference for minimising the scope of legal regulation and even set up a new institution – the Commissioner for the Rights of Trade Union Members (see Chapter 8), the sparse use of which before its abolition in 1999 indicated it had more symbolic than practical value.

The post-1979 legislative agenda was strongly influenced by the Conservative government's neo-liberal economic and social objectives, with statute law being utilised as a key instrument facilitating labour market restructuring. Neo-liberalism emerged as the political response to the problems of collective bargaining under full employment (wage militancy, inflation and poor adaptation to change), especially where they were exacerbated by growing international competition (Ludlam *et al* 2003).

Keynesian demand management became increasingly incapable of coping with the inflationary tendencies of the world economy during the 1970s, and co-ordination of the labour market through neo-corporatism did not appear to offer a solution. Post second world war attempts to tackle recurrent periods of inflation through incomes policy, whether statutory or voluntary, had produced at best wage restraint for only relatively short periods and institutions had come and gone. Among them was the National Board for Prices and Incomes established in 1964, given statutory status in 1966 and abolished by the incoming Conservative government in 1970 who then set up a Pay Board and a Price Commission. The former was abolished when Labour returned to power in 1974 with its 'Social Contract' understanding with the trade unions whereby the TUC would co-operate in tackling the economic problems, including through wage restraint, in return for a wide programme of measures in industrial relations (including supportive legislation outlined above) and in other social and economic spheres. It ended with the 1978/79 'Winter of discontent' and the election of a radical Conservative administration.

Institutions which had been set up as part of the previous approach (notably a Standing Commission on Pay Comparability) were no longer required after 1979. Institutional arrangements seen as underpinning institutionalised structured collective bargaining and/or imposing rigidities on the operation of the free market (such as Wages Councils) were eroded or ended. Widespread use had been made of voluntary unilateral arbitration arrangements in the public sector following its massive expansion from the 1940s, but most such arrangements were disposed of by the Conservative government on grounds they were inflationary. The public sector was restructured through privatisation and compulsory competitive tendering; determination of the pay and conditions of certain public sector groups was removed from collective bargaining as normally understood and entrusted to Pay Review Bodies, which provide for 'bargaining' at arm's length or one remove (Burchell 2000:147). Also ended was the United Kingdom's adherence to certain international conventions (e.g. ILO Convention No. 94) which stood in the way of dismantling multi-employer collective bargaining.

Collective bargaining in the private sector was increasingly conducted at a decentralised, company or workplace level where it took place at all. In the 1970s, around 80% of employees were covered by collective bargaining for wage fixing, and for over half of them the principal level was multi-employer (industry level) bargaining. By 1998, collective bargaining coverage had slumped to around 40% of the workforce, only 14% of which was multi-employer (Brown *et al* 2003).

Monetarist economic policies cast unions as an obstacle rather than potential partner of the State in economic management. Neo-liberalism involved a rejection of corporatism in principle, and of limited experiments with forms of tripartism in practice such as the NEDC, abolished in 1992. Industrial Training Boards were dismantled; the union role within the MSC was reduced in 1987, and the Commission itself abolished in 1989 (see Chapter 5). Many so-called 'quangos' faced extermination or were put on meager rations with budgets repeatedly cut in real terms. A low profile and caution were the price some paid for survival.

The deregulation and de-rigidification of the United Kingdom labour market during this period conflicted with the approach being taken at European level. Particularly from the 1980s on, legal intervention in the employment relationship has reflected not only national concerns but also the increased supra-national influence of the European Economic Community (later to become the European Union) which the United Kingdom joined in 1973. European legal instruments (usually, in the form of legally binding Directives) were used as a way of addressing disparities between levels and costs of employment protection legislation in different Member States, and as part of the social dimension of the single European market. The unions, frozen out at home, saw the European Community as a source of assistance: providing a competing model, a source of minimum labour standards, and an opportunity to engage in social dialogue. This pro-Europe union stance was a marked reversal from their previous hostility. The Conservative government, meanwhile, was moving in the opposite direction, becoming increasingly hostile to the social dimension of the European Community.

POST 1997 – NEW LABOUR

By the time a Labour government was returned to office in 1997, the debate within the Labour party had switched from whether the law should play a role in British industrial relations to what role it should play. Under the Labour government, re-elected in 2001 and 2005, the trend toward the legislative regulation of industrial relations and the juridification of the employment relationship continued. There are some clear differences in approach, but also underlying continuities with the preceding period.

The Labour government retained large parts of the Conservatives' industrial relations legislation, notably restrictions on industrial action and the control of internal union affairs, while in other areas, such as minimum wages to tackle low pay, there was new statutory intervention, as called for by both the Labour Party and the TUC. Unions had learned to live with the law and, at a time of greatly reduced membership density after the neo-liberal onslaught, came to see it as a potential source of support and renewal. The peak union density of 56% in 1979 was followed by the longest period of continuous annual union membership decline since records began in 1892 (Waddington 2003:219). By 1997, unions organised only 3 in 10 of the British labour force, and union recognition became predominantly a public sector phenomenon (Cully *et al* 1999:93). Applications to Employment Tribunals, rather than strikes, emerged as a measure of 'workplace well being' (Cully *et al* 1999), and it is no mere co-incidence that the rise in the number of such applications corresponded to the growth in the proportion of workplaces without union recognition.

Access to statutory rights was increased and legal regulatory norms were extended into areas of the employment relationship which had until then remained largely a matter for voluntary determination such as pay and working time. By the late 1990s, Employment Tribunal applications were exceeding 100,000 a year. The pubic cost of running the ETS is currently around £52 million. So overwhelming has the activity of the Tribunals now become, with over 70 different areas of law covered where rights have been granted by nineteen different Acts and regulations, that a self-contained institution – the Employment Tribunals Taskforce – has been established to review the arrangements, and to develop recommendations for reform and future evolution of the specialised individual employment relations judicial system (see Chapter 10).

The New Labour government reversed the Conservative government's United Kingdom opt-out from the 1992 social policy agreement negotiated at Maastricht and its associated 'social dialogue' Directives. This led to significant legislative development (not all of it welcomed by the government), and institutional knock-on. For example, the commitment to a 'general framework' of regulation in the area of anti-discrimination and equality, and a unitary regulatory model at the European level, has forced the British legislator to abandon the earlier variegated approaches to sex, race, or disability etc. and, coupled with Human Rights developments, is leading to a single Commission for Equality and Human Rights (see Chapter 9).

European Union employment law developments since the modest platform of the first Social Action Programme in 1974 have had a growing significance in shaping or constraining the domestic legislative agenda (as shown, for example, in Chapters 4 and 9). They have also placed novel pressures upon the institutions charged with supervision of the consequent rule system or delivery of rights enshrined in those frameworks. Thus, Chairmen of Employment Tribunals, when dealing with matters whose regulatory objectives increasingly reflect the demands of European Union Law, have learned to play the role of 'Community judges', as required by the European Court of Justice.

In giving effect to European Law in areas such as consultation on collective dismissals and transfer of undertakings, the government resisted institution building at the workplace and took more ad hoc approaches to implementation. However, the implementation of recent Directives in the area of information and consultation at transnational and national level have led to novel institutional features in British employment relations, in the form of something akin to 'works councils'.

The map and operation of institutions have been shaped not only by such supranational influences, but also by changes to 'the State' at national level through devolution and regionalisation, which have added a further dimension to long standing geographic diversity (see, for example, the observations in Chapter 3). The geographical coverage of the institutions dealt with in this volume varies. For pragmatic reasons of space we have not been able to encompass all institutions where separate ones exist for the different countries which make up the United Kingdom. The existence of separate institutional structures for Northern Ireland led us to restrict our attention to Britain. The legal system in England and Wales differs from that in Scotland, and this is reflected in the scope of judicial institutions (such as the Employment Tribunals, as shown in Chapter 11), but not necessarily other institutions with judicial functions (such as the CAC, see Chapter 7).

Some of the new legislative initiatives after 1997 spawned a new institution, the Low Pay Commission (LPC) responsible for the national minimum wage (see Chapter 6) and reshaped other institutions, including the CAC which effectively had been 'mothballed' during the years of Conservative government (Rideout 2002; and see below Chapter 7).

INSTITUTIONAL CHOICE, NATURE AND FUNCTION

As Janet Gaymer points out in her contribution to this volume (see Chapter 10), at the time the Industrial (now Employment) Tribunals were set up there was no serious parliamentary debate about their constitution or long term purpose. The incremental growth of statutory regulation of the employment relationship occurred without any strategic decision as to the kind of institution needed. There was a rough adherence to the proposal of the Donovan Commission (1968:573) that the jurisdictions of the labour tribunals (its suggested name for the Employment Tribunals) should include 'all disputes arising between employers and employees from their contractual employment or from any statutory claims they may have against each other as employer and employee', with matters arising between trade unions and their members being excluded. Donovan (para. 576) argued that disputes between employers and groups of workers or trade unions 'must be settled by procedures of, or agreed through, collective bargaining'.

The distinction between collective and individual disputes is in practice difficult to draw and the proposal to leave collective issues to be resolved through procedures of collective bargaining assumes the existence and health of collective bargaining – something which, as described above, has changed dramatically since Donovan reported in the late 1960s. In practice, as Simon Gouldstone and Gillian Morris discuss in this volume (see Chapter 7), the CAC has emerged as the repository for rights given to trade unions (such as union recognition), or employees acting collectively (information and consultation). Yet, collective disputes involving industrial action still may involve the ordinary courts. As David Cockburn discusses (see Chapter 8), the Certification Officer handles (most, but not all) issues concerning unions and their members. Both institutions provide interesting examples of non-court bodies with judicial as well as non judicial functions.

The post-1997 legislative agenda added yet further to the jurisdictions of the Employment Tribunals, whether as institution of choice or a matter of expediency. Institutional choice in part reflects how the 'problem' – and thus the 'solution' – is perceived by policy makers. 'Employment protection', once seen as resting on collective bargaining supported by public policy, is increasingly framed in terms of individual legal rights, which then are enforceable before judicial forums.

Despite its title, the Conservative government's 1994 Green Paper, *Resolving Employment Rights Disputes – Options for Reform,* did not herald a fundamental reconsideration of how employment rights disputes might be resolved. The terms of reference for the Green Paper were concerned with examining options for cost-saving through increased efficiency rather than any radical rethink of approach to the enforcement of individual employment rights. This arguably was a missed opportunity to take a strategic overview and was not remedied by the 1997 incoming Labour government. As has been argued elsewhere (Dickens 2000), a more radical re-consideration might have included discussion of whether some of the jurisdictions given to tribunals more appropriately might go elsewhere, perhaps to other institutions included in this volume.

The Green Paper did lead to a new arbitral route for determining unfair dismissal claims introduced by the Labour government in 2001. This attempt at providing binding arbitration as a voluntary alternative to judicial determination by Employment Tribunals which could be opted for in certain jurisdictions once an application was made, if both parties agreed, has not been a success. Arguably it came too late (at time when the Tribunals are firmly entrenched and familiar); was driven predominantly by concerns for cost-saving through increased efficiency, rather than appreciation or acceptance of the fact that benefits might be gained through differences in process etc. (as highlighted by Lewis & Clark 1993); and was inserted into a context where there are few incentives for key gatekeepers, including Acas conciliation officers and legal representatives, to promote or encourage its use. The 'arbitral alternative' was also constructed in a way likely to erode some key differences between the arbitral and judicial approach (Dickens *et al* 1985: Ch. 9).

The contributions to this book enable consideration of why a particular institution has a particular role, and the factors which have shaped the division of tasks between courts, quasi-courts and non court bodies, and the shifting allocations over time. As the discussion above indicated the institutional map is a reflection of a range of influences, among them historical legacy, political choice and ideology, national and supra-national perceptions of labour market and employment relations 'problems' and their 'solutions', as well as happenstance and expediency.

Issues emerge in a number of chapters concerning overlap and boundaries between institutional remits, together with questions of appropriate and effective enforcement mechanisms and location of enforcement powers. Brown (see Chapter 6) raises the issue of a greater role for enforcement by inspectorates and agencies rather relying primarily on individuals to bring cases to tribunals. He suggests that the most fundamental lesson of the LPC as a regulatory agency may be the value of independent enforcement. Sisson and Taylor (Chapter 3) stress the importance to Acas of no longer having any enforcement role, unlike the Equality Commissions and Health and Safety Commission/Executive, where an enforcement role is combined with other functions.

Brown also characterises the LPC as a social partnership institution, not only in composition but also in its way of operating. Elsewhere however there has been no return under New Labour to corporatist arrangements, tri-partism, nor adoption of the European model of social partnership. As can been seen from various chapters in this volume, the involvement of the social partners in some British institutions currently appears to be more in the guise of one among a number of 'stakeholders' or representatives of stakeholders. This was always so for the Equality Commissions (see Chapter 9), but represents a changed position in others. The purpose of social partner involvement is not always clear and may be expected to vary over time: bringing particular expertise,

9

experience and knowledge, conferring legitimacy on process, assuring acceptability or implementation of outcomes, providing a bulwark against government interference?

As various contributors to this volume record, increasingly unions and employers' organisations have no monopoly when it comes to institutional involvement. Bill Callaghan (see Chapter 4) charts the shift in governance of the HSC from 'bargained corporatism' to 'non-executive board'. There has been a move away from unions and employers' bodies (the source of expertise for the 'industrial jury') as preferred or sole sources of nominations to, or as actors in, a number of institutions in the employment relations field. Partly this reflects new standards in public life (Nolan 1995) including requirements to fill public office by open competition, but it also reflects New Labour's ambivalence towards trade unions; its acceptance of the move away from tripartism which occurred in the Conservative era, and a recognition that the decline of union membership, collective bargaining and the influence of employers' associations, together with the changing nature of employment and labour force composition, raise questions as to the representative nature of the peak bodies. There appears to be a growing acknowledgment and involvement of the – generally non-union – small and medium enterprise (SME) sector which now employs some 46% of the workforce. As noted by Freedland and Kountouris (see Chapter 2), the move away from the peak bodies is not however a move away from business since the Department of Trade and Industry – unlike the old Department of Employment, which was part of the tripartite approach with unions as 'natural clients' – is the 'department for enterprise'.

Institutional autonomy from government and the relationship of the institution with Government Departments is touched upon by various contributors. As noted above, some institutions (e.g. the HSC and Acas) were formed when functions previously performed by government departments were spun off to independent bodies. The relevant department, however, retains mechanisms of influence through funding, appointments, target setting, audit and review. Various chapters note the complexity and fragmentation of departmental responsibilities for, and control over, the different institutions in British employment relations. A key, and internationally distinctive feature of the institutional map noted by Freedland and Kountouris (see Chapter 2), is that 'there is no longer a Government Department dedicated to employment relations, leaving a hole at the core of the institutional set up'.

This volume does not have chapters on the 'institutions of collective bargaining' nor trade unions or employers as institutions. However, as the above discussion indicates, the decline of collective bargaining as an institution (along with the decline of collective organisation of employers and decline in trade union membership) is part of the context for the existence, growth and (changing) nature of those institutions which are included.

The 'de-institutionalisation of industrial relations' (Purcell 1993) clearly has not meant an end to institutions in British employment relations. Yet, in spite of a rich literature on the changes in British employment relations, the political backdrop to reform and change over the past three decades, and detailed exploration of the nature and growing reach of the law (including Cully *et al* 1999; Millward *et al* 2000; Kersley *et al* 2004; Davies & Freedland 1993; and Deakin & Morris 2005), surprisingly little recent attention has been directed to the institutional arrangements which have been emerging or adapting to these dramatic forces. This volume seeks to remedy this, providing an overview and basis for evaluation of the current institutional map, and consideration of the lessons to be drawn from the changing institutional face of employment relations in Britain.

REFERENCES

Brown, W., Marginson, M. & Walsh. J. (2003): 'The Management of Pay as the Influence of Collective Bargaining Diminishes', in Edwards, P. (ed) *Industrial Relations: Theory and Practice*. 2nd edition (Blackwell, Oxford)

Burchell, F. (2000): 'The Pay Review Body System: A comment and a consequence', *Historical Studies in Industrial Relations*, 10, 141-57

Crouch, C. (2003): 'The State, Economic management and Incomes Policy', in Edwards, P. (ed), *Industrial Relations: Theory and Practice*. 2nd edition (Blackwell, Oxford)

Cully, M., Woodland, S. O'Reilly, S. & Dix, G. (1999): *Britain at Work: As depicted by the 1998 Workplace Employee Relations Survey* (Routledge, London)

Davies, P. & Freedland, M. (1993): *Labour Legislation and Public Policy* (Clarendon Press, Oxford)

Deakin, S. & Morris, G. (2005): *Labour Law*. 4th edition (Hart Publishing, Oxford)

Dickens, L. (2000): 'Doing more with less: Acas and individual conciliation', in Towers. B. & Brown, W. (eds), *Employment Relations in Britain: 25 Years of the Advisory Conciliation and Arbitration Service* (Blackwell, Oxford)

Dickens, L. (2002): 'Individual statutory employment rights since 1997: Constrained Expansion', *Employee Relations* 24, 6

Dickens, L. & Hall, M. (1995): 'The State: Labour Law and Industrial Relations', in Edwards, P. (ed), *Industrial Relations: Theory and Practice in Britain* (Blackwell, Oxford)

Dickens, L. & Hall, M. (2003): 'Labour Law and Industrial relations: A New Settlement?', in Edwards, P. (ed), *Industrial Relations: Theory and Practice*. 2nd edition (Blackwell, Oxford)

Dickens, L., Jones, M., Weekes, B. & Hart, M. (1985): *Dismissed: A Study of Unfair Dismissal and the Industrial Tribunal System* (Blackwell, Oxford)

Donovan (1968): *Report of the Royal Commission on Trade Unions and Employers' Associations 1965-1968* (Chairman, Lord Donovan), Cmnd.3623 (HMSO, London)

Freedland, M. (1992): 'The role of the Department of Employment – Twenty Years of Institutional Change' in McCarthy, W. (ed) *Legal Intervention in Industrial Relations: Gains and Losses* (Blackwell, Oxford)

Kersley, B., Alpin, C., Forth, J., Bryson, A., Bewley, H., Dix, G. & Oxenbridge, S. (2004): *Inside the Workplace: First Findings from the 2004 Workplace Employment Relations Survey* (HMSO, London)

Lewis, R. & Clark, J. (1993): *Employment Rights, Industrial Tribunals and Arbitration: The Case for Alternative Dispute Resolution* (Institute of Employment Rights, London)

Ludlam, S. *et al* (2003): 'Politics and Employment Relations', *British Journal of Industrial Relations,* Special Edition (December)

Millward, N., Bryson, A. & Forth, J. (1999): *All Change at Work?* (Routledge, London)

Neal, A. (2000): 'From 'Bad Boy' to European Role Model? The Strange Legacy of United Kingdom Employment Policies Since the Single European Act', in Biagi, M. (ed), *Job Creation and Labour Law: From Protection towards Pro-action* (Kluwer, The Hague)

Neal, A. (2004): *The Evolution of Labour Law (1992-2003): Country Study – United Kingdom* (European Commission, Luxembourg)

Nolan, Lord (1995): *First Report of the Committee on Standards in Public Life,* Cmnd 2850 (HMSO, London)

Purcell, J. (1993): The end of institutional industrial relations', *Political Quarterly*, 64 (1), 6-23

Waddington, J. (2003): 'Trade Union Organisation', in Edwards, P. (ed), *Industrial Relations: Theory and Practice.* 2nd edition (Blackwell, Oxford)

Weekes, B., Mellish, M., Dickens, L. & Lloyd, J. (1975): *Industrial Relations and the Limits of Law: The Industrial Effects of the Industrial Relations Act, 1971* (Blackwell, Oxford)

Mark Freedland & Nicola Kountouris

THE INSTITUTIONAL FACE AT MINISTERIAL LEVEL

Not the Department of Employment

INTRODUCTION

The present work has as its central purpose the surveying of institutional change in the sphere of British employment relations during the thirty-year life of the Advisory, Conciliation and Arbitration Service (Acas). Throughout that thirty-year period, employment or labour law has had a frequently changing but always dominant impact upon employment relations. At the outset of that period, Professor Sir Otto Kahn-Freund bestrode the world of British employment law, and of industrial relations, as they were then called, like a colossus. Some of the contributors to and readers of this work will remember him, and may recall that one of his favourite metaphors, which he used to characterise any remarkable gap or omission at the core of whatever discourse it might be, was that of 'the Play of Hamlet without the Prince of Denmark'.

There can be little doubt that he would have been very quick to apply that idiom to an institutional survey of British employment relations which did not describe the position at the ministerial or departmental level of central government. We can expect that he would have applied it even more vehemently to the current institutional situation itself, in which the British governmental State no longer possesses a Ministry of Labour or Department of Employment as such. He would have regarded that as representing a black hole at the core of the institutional set-up. Hence the negatively expressed sub-title of this chapter; it is about how British employment relations came to be without, and are being managed without, a Department of Employment in the traditional and still, we perceive, internationally typical form.

In 1992, one of the two authors of the present chapter published a chapter in an earlier and somewhat similar symposium; the chapter was entitled 'The role of the Department of Employment – Twenty Years of Institutional Change' (Freedland 1992). The present chapter begins by conducting an up-dating survey and analysis of developments in the succeeding fifteen years, during which the Department of Employment has been abolished, and during which its functions have undergone a dispersal and re-alignment so elaborate that by comparison with it, even the reforms of the previous twenty years seem like mild tinkering. The chapter concludes by offering some general assessment of the significance of these multifarious and quite fundamental changes.

Linda Dickens & Alan C. Neal (eds), The Changing Institutional Face of British Employment Relations 13-24
© 2006 Kluwer Law International. Printed in the Netherlands

Mark Freedland & Nicola Kountouris

REFORMING WITH DISCRETION

The organisation of the machinery of executive government is a delicate and politically sensitive task in which government action is shaped by a variety of policy priorities and considerations. It is commonly accepted that politicians and civil servants involved in the process of remodelling the 'organigram' of the executive need to be able to exercise a considerable level of discretion. The work of Professors Clifford, McMillan and McLean offers a clear analysis of the legal background in which the organisation and restructuring of central government departments takes place in the United Kingdom. The authors of the work remind us that while, historically, most modern departments and non-departmental public bodies have been established by statute, the practice since the adoption of the 1975 Ministers of the Crown Act has been to transfer functions to a new department by the exercise of the prerogative, for instance in the creation of a new department of State with new Secretary of State (Clifford *et al* 1997). Before the end of the Second World War the transfer of ministerial and departmental prerogatives between offices could only be undertaken through the adoption of primary legislation. The 1946 Ministers of the Crown (Transfer of Functions) Act provided that a ministerial order, subject to the negative resolution procedure, was a sufficient legal basis for the purposes of transferring functions across different departments.

Further flexibility in the reform of the government machinery was introduced by the Deregulation and Contracting-out Act 1994 which provided that, subject in this case to the affirmative resolution procedure, certain executive functions could also be transferred and contracted out to the private sector by means of a ministerial order. This extremely flexible regulatory framework provides plenty of discretion to the executive for reforming or reshuffling its central organisation. In the present context, the term 'discretion' emerges as having two meanings. Clearly, and this is the first meaning, the Government is given (as it should be) plenty of leeway in deciding how to structure and reshuffle its machinery. But crucially – and this is the second and less obvious meaning in a world where administrative transparency is commonly recognised to be a virtue – this state of affairs can often result in a number of dissolutions and transfers proceeding stealthily under the negative resolution procedure, by merger, by change of title of minister or department, or simple transfer of functions.

It is against this background of 'discretion' that the current chapter seeks to describe the institutional change in the sphere of British employment relations during the last three decades or so, with a specific focus on the reforms affecting what in Whitehall terminology are defined as the 'employment function', the 'social security function' and the 'industrial relations function' of the government machinery. The remainder of this chapter is subdivided in five sections. The first sections describe three different steps in the reorganisation of these functions within the British executive machinery. The first one provides a brief reconstruction of the changes affecting the Department of Health and Social Security (DHSS) and the Department of Employment (DE) from their formation in 1968 and 1970 until the late 1980s, early 1990s, when a string of radical changes came to affect both departments, albeit in different ways. The second part describes the changes taking place in the last years of Conservative Governments and up to the New Labour victory in the United Kingdom general election of May 1997. The third part of the chapter presents the radical reforms introduced under New Labour Governments since their rise to power in the late 1990s, that effectively led to a merger of some of the main employment and social security functions into a single department, the Department of Work and Pensions (DWP). The fourth part provides a political and analytical assessment of the manifold rationales and dynamics shaping the institutional changes and reforms summarised in the earlier sections, and particularly in the period from 1990 onwards. Lastly, our final section present a concluding snapshot of the main features of the institutional landscape in its current state.

THE EMPLOYMENT, SOCIAL SECURITY AND INDUSTRIAL RELATIONS FUNCTIONS IN THE 1970S AND 1980S

The DE was formally established on 20 October 1970, following the dissolution of the Department of Employment and Productivity. Since its creation, it was effectively subjected to a slow but fairly relentless haemorrhage of functions. Already in 1974 and 1975, some of its job placement and training functions and most of the health and safety function were hived off, respectively, to the Manpower Services Commission and to the Health and Safety Commission and Executive. In 1974, the functions relating to arbitration and conciliation were passed to Acas. Occupational health and safety off-shore was transferred to the Department of Trade and Industry (DTI) in 1987. Responsibilities for economic statistics were transferred to the Central Statistical Office in 1989. In 1992, following the general election, the DTI took responsibility for small firms. But in spite of this slow transfer-out of prerogatives, most of the original functions of the DE still preserved some degree of kinship and functional closeness by appearing under the umbrella notion of the Employment Department Group.

Over the same period of time, the social security function – attributed to the DHSS since its creation in 1968 – had a comparatively less tumultuous life, culminating in the creation of an autonomous Department of Social Security (DSS) in July 1988. The original social security functions of the DHSS included the payment of social security cash benefits under national insurance schemes, industrial injuries insurance and family allowances and, through the Supplementary Benefits Commission, the determination of non-contributory benefits. The main-transfer out of the body occurred in January 1985 when the Transfer of Functions (Social Security Commissioners) Order 1984/1818 effectively attributed to the Lord Chancellor a number of competencies in respect of the Commissioners' offices, administration, procedure and remuneration.

THE 1990S AND THE DISINTEGRATION OF THE EMPLOYMENT, SOCIAL SECURITY AND INDUSTRIAL RELATIONS FUNCTIONS

During the 1990s the DSS continued to have a rather uneventful existence, at least in terms of transfer of functions and internal structural changes. The main transformation was the reconfiguration of a number of its agencies and departments as Executive Agencies. The Social Security Resettlement Agency was the first to become an Executive

15

Agency, in May 1989. The Social Security Information Technology Services followed suit in April 1990. In April 1991 it was the turn of the Social Security Benefits Agency and of the Social Security Contributions Agency. On a more substantive note, in October 1996 the Employment Service transferred some 3,400 non-industrial staff to the Benefits Agency, also transformed into an executive agency of the DSS, due to the introduction of the Job Seekers Allowance. And in July 1998 the Women's Unit was transferred from the DSS to the Cabinet Office.

Back in the early 1990s, the Department of Employment was celebrating the first centenary of its, somewhat tumultuous, life (dated from the first establishment of a section for labour issues within the Board of Trade), probably unaware that there would be no further such celebrations in the years to come. In fact, the 1990s effectively witnessed the end of the DE and the disintegration of a considerable part of its core employment function and, to some extent, its industrial relations function. The result of this process was twofold. The first one was the creation of a new departmental body, the Department for Education and Employment (DfEE). The second was the consolidation of the DTI as a second, but by no means secondary, locus for the performance of a number of ministerial functions in the area of industrial relations and, increasingly, employment.

The major change in the life of the DE was to occur in July 1995 when the Prime Minister John Major undertook a massive cabinet reshuffle. The 1995 restructuring epitomised the end of the 'hemorrhagic' period and the beginning of the 'disintegration' era. The reshuffle effectively abolished the Employment Department Group by merging some of its core functions with the Department of Education to create the new DfEE, while simultaneously transferring a considerable amount of core competencies to the DTI. The main functions of the DE, discharged by some 3,863 permanent and 399 casual staff, and the Employment Service Agency (38,495 permanent and 1,922 casual staff) merged with the much smaller Department of Education (DoE, 2,027 permanent and 68 casual staff) to become the DfEE, with some 44,246 permanent and 2,389 casual staff. The Health and Safety Executive (HSE) went to the Department of the Environment, Acas (602 staff), the Industrial Relations Division (about 746 permanent staff) and the Office for Manpower Economics moved from Employment (Main) to DTI, while the Labour Market Statistics Group went to the Central Statistical Office.

From the 1995 reshuffle onwards, tracking the moves and subsequent transfers of the original executive and ministerial functions and responsibilities of the old DE becomes a real maze. On 30 September 1996, the Teachers Pension Agency (an executive agency of the DfEE) was effectively outsourced to Capita Managed Services Ltd, while the following day, as pointed out above, due to the introduction of the Jobseekers Allowance the Employment Service transferred 3,450 non-industrial staff to the Benefits Agency, an Executive Agency acting under the control of the Department of Social Security. In April 1997, the DfEE transferred its Information Services Division (150 permanent staff) to F1 Group PLC while the Employment Tribunal Service was established as a new agency under the DTI, and this was the last change adopted by a Conservative Government before the May 1997 election victory of New Labour.

NEW LABOUR AND THE MARGINAL MERGER OF THE SOCIAL SECURITY AND EMPLOYMENT FUNCTION

New Labour came into power with a number of precise ideas regarding the changes needed to reform the welfare state and the labour market. These ideas involved to a considerable extent the structure and organisation of the providers of welfare and labour market 'services'. This certainly had a number of implications for the DfEE and the DSS.

The 1998 Green Paper, *New Ambitions for our Country: A New Contract for Welfare*, (DSS 1998), had at its core a welfare reform revolving around the notion of 'work'. As put by Prime Minister Blair, 'the system all too often acts against those who want to work, creating a number of disincentives to move from benefits into the world of work'. The very same idea of 'welfare to work', as developed by the Government under its New Deal programmes, brought social benefits and employment service providers in a 'partnership' relationship, eventually justifying the creation of a single organisational framework for the administration of these programmes.

In July 2000, David Blunkett and Alistair Darling, at that time Secretaries of State for the DfEE and DSS respectively, appeared together before the House of Commons Social Security Select Committee to argue the case for ministerial reorganisation (HC SSSC, 2000). Mr Darling explicitly claimed that the new organisation, bringing together employment services (ES) and benefit agencies (BA)

> 'would not work simply with a sort of classic merger, and you have got people who have always been ES and people who have always been BA, we need to change the whole culture of the organisation, just as we are changing the whole culture of the benefits system and the culture in this country'.

This organisational leap occurred after the 2001 General Election. On the 8th of June the Government announced a number of major changes to its executive machinery. In its statement to the press, the Government announced that

> 'A new Department for Work and Pensions will continue the reform of the welfare state. It will bring together the previous Department of Social Security and the Employment Service to enable the Working Age Agency to be established with a single and clear line of Ministerial accountability. The Department will combine the employment and disability responsibilities, of the former DfEE with the welfare and pensions responsibilities of the DSS'.

What was left of the DfEE was quickly rebranded the Department for Education and Skills (DES), although competencies relating to work-life balance, equal opportunities and pay were transferred to the DTI. As promptly put by one commentator, 'one of the main driving forces behind the creation of the Department for Work and Pensions (DWP) was that the government wanted to create a one-stop shop – first dubbed the Working Age Agency, now called Jobcentre Plus – where people could receive benefits and be offered opportunities to find work. The idea behind this was that, by combining welfare, pensions, employment and disability responsibilities, the agency would be allowed to adopt a much more carrot-and-stick approach to getting people back to work' (Midgley 2001).

17

But there were also other concurrent, albeit possibly secondary, rationales behind the creation of the DWP. Part of the change was also, at least in part, presentational. The term 'work and pensions' was much more in tune with the Government's workfarist agenda as it suggests economic activity, as opposed to the term 'social security' that rings much more like 'old labour' and suggests dependency and inactvity. Also, the DWP effectively laid a heavy gravestone over the last vestiges of a functionally independent Employment Department, traditionally perceived as the actor in Whitehall most sympathetic to the views of trade unions.

In April 2002, within the DWP, the Benefits Agency merged with the Employment Service to form Jobcentre Plus and the Pension Service was also launched. This reshuffle had also a number of internal occupational consequences with additional staff being recruited in Jobcentre Plus, the Child Support Agency, the Early Pensions Centres and in Inland Revenue, to 'backfill' for training and to implement the string of new initiatives arising from the welfare modernisation programmes, such as child support reforms and tax credits. The fate of some of this additional staff appears to be anything but certain, as suggested by information recently leaked to the press (Hencke 2005), possibly contributing to the consolidation of a rather gloomy mood within the DWP's workforce (Millar 2005).

The last few decades have thus witnessed a major overhaul of work-related functions within Whitehall. The slow but steady decline, and eventual termination, of the DE produced what we have termed the fragmentation of the employment function within British government. On the other hand, those areas of the employment function dealing with employment services have eventually come to merge with the old social security function, within what is now the DWP. It is likely, though, that a good deal of the execution of these functions will be increasingly contracted out to the private or public-private market, under initiatives such as the Employment Zones.

Throughout these changes, a major beneficiary in terms of competencies and functions has been the DTI. The 1995 and the 2001 ministerial reshuffles radically altered the Department's organisational structure, that has currently a dedicated Employment Relations Directorate, 'working to develop a framework for employers and employees which promotes a skilled and flexible labour market founded on principles of partnership. It deals with relationships between workers and their employers, including individual rights as well as collective arrangements'. Within the labour movement, in particular, the Department is still very widely perceived as the business-oriented government department shaped by policy documents such as Lord Young's 1988 White Paper *The DTI – the Department for Enterprise*. The 2001 reorganisation, in particular, raised considerable alarm within British unions. As John Monks – then the TUC General Secretary – put it in 2001, 'I find it increasingly difficult to have confidence that the DTI will be even-handed, never mind committed to building a better system of employment relations in this country, which I would expect to be a central tenet of the beliefs of a Labour government. All this looks like favours to business, not fairness' (EIRO 2001). However, rather than contenting ourselves with that understandably partisan assessment, we go on, in two concluding sections, to offer a political and analytical assessment of these rather momentous developments.

THE DYNAMICS OF CHANGE IN THE INSTITUTIONAL STRUCTURE

Having thus re-capitulated upon the main institutional developments at ministerial or departmental level in the period from 1970 to 1990, and having then provided an up-dating account of the changes in the succeeding period down to the present day, we proceed to propose an analysis both *ex ante* and *ex post* of what, from our particular perspective, is the central event of that whole period, namely the abolition of the Department of Employment in 1995. In this section we will offer an account of the dynamics of change in the institutional structure in the period from 1990 onwards and in the next and final section we will present a concluding snapshot of the main features of the institutional landscape in its current state.

To be more precise, in this section we will identify two dynamics of institutional change, a negative one and a positive one, and one vector of change, that is to say a factor which influences the velocity of those dynamics, in this case a vector of acceleration. These three factors may be specified as follows:

(i)   a negative dynamic of de-regulation and curtailing tri-partism,
(ii)   a vector of acceleration contributed by new public management, and
(iii) a positive dynamic towards a workfare system for the labour economy.

We proceed to enlarge upon each of those three factors in turn.

The Negative Dynamic of De-regulation and Anti-tripartism

For much of its history since its establishment in 1916 as the Ministry of Labour, and especially during the post-war years of 'collective laissez-faire' in industrial relations, from 1945 to 1970, the Department of Employment identified itself as the seat and location of a tri-partite approach to the governance of the labour economy. By this we mean the regulation of employment relations by collective bargaining of various sorts and at various levels between employers and organised labour, brokered and supported by the State or government. In the view of many, the Department in that historical phase had the trade unions as its natural clients or interlocutors in the way that, for example, the Ministry of Agriculture might at the same period speak to and with the farming and fishing communities.

It now seems ironical to recall that, at the outset of the period under discussion, that is to say in the early 1970s, the period of the Industrial Relations Act, the Department of Employment was perceived by the trade union movement to have forfeited this mutual trust, and to have become an engine of governmental constraint upon trade unions, therefore serving the interests of employers and allied with them. So the creation of Acas as a free-standing institution in 1975 was designed precisely to ensure that the industrial conciliation, arbitration and advisory services hitherto provided by the Department of Employment would be administered on a basis of independence from the DE under a governance mechanism which would restore the tripartism now perceived to have vanished from the Department itself.

So it may have seemed to the trade unions and to the Labour government of the mid-1970s. But Conservative governments from 1979 had a different perception. Especially during Mr Prior's period of office as Secretary of State for Employment and Productivity in the initial years of Mrs Thatcher's Prime Ministership, the Department re-gained its reputation for complicity with the trade unions – or 'wetness' in the newly emergent terminology of neo-liberalism. At the level of the Secretary of State personally, this balance was redressed, for example by the appointment of the famously anti-trade-union Mr Tebbit from 1981 onwards. However, the stigma remained, and a tendency to marginalise and downgrade the Department characterised the later 1980s and early 1990s, culminating in its abolition during Mr Major's Prime Ministership.

Note that we deploy the rather stark terminology of abolition to describe what happened to the Department in 1995. This consciously challenges the characterisation of this transaction by the government of the day as a merger of the Department with or into the then Department of Education and Science, to create a new Department for Education and Employment. That representation of what had occurred, although of course in a sense technically accurate, conceals the underlying direction of change. For that which was absorbed into the new DfEE was by no means the DE as a going concern, and this was no lock, stock and barrel transfer of an enterprise. Certainly, the very important central administration of employment and training policy was seconded to the new department. But the functions of the former DE were, in a crucial sense, fragmented and de-constructed.

In fact, it is crucial, from the standpoint of this present work, that one big fragment, namely the responsibility for industrial or employment relations, was hived off to the Department of Trade and Industry – to a Department, therefore, of which the natural clients and interlocutors are the representative of the interests of commerce, manufacturing, and private sector service provision. Already prior to the 2001 reshuffle, the DTI was the clear fulcrum of the industrial relations and employment relations functions. Within the DTI these responsibilities were managed and performed by an ad hoc Employment Relations Directorate (ERD) whose mandate was described in the 1998-99 *Civil Service Yearbook* as follows: '[The EDR] advises on policy and legislation concerning: individual employment rights (including redundancy and transfer); trade union and industrial action; pay, working hours and holidays; and conduct of employment agencies. It administers statutory redundancy and insolvency payments; and enforces employment agencies law' (Civil Service Department 1998: 284).

Henceforth, employment legislation would be debated, and processed from within that particular governmental and cultural environment. No less important, it would be within that departmental framework that the responses, whether positive or negative, would be devised to the legislative requirements imposed by European Union social policy Directives in the employment sphere, and it would be largely from that Department that representatives would conduct the corresponding interactions with the European Commission and the EU Council.

The Vector of New Public Management

It might appear from the above analysis that we regard the 1995 abolition of the DE and dispersal of its function as a uniquely or singularly trenchant exercise in Departmental reform and re-organisation, the sudden driving of a coach and horses through an otherwise tranquil governmental village green. That is far from being our view, for, throughout the period under consideration, a vector or accelerating factor of new public management had been almost exponentially increasing the pressure for change in the departmental organisation of central government. By 'new public management' we mean the particular approach to the organisation of government and public service provision which has identified itself more and more clearly during the last twenty or thirty years in the British State, and which consists essentially in the pursuit of governmental or administrative efficiency by means of financial or business-oriented managerialism. A very major feature or expression of the 'new public management' approach consists of organisational re-structuring especially by way of the designation of newly-constituted units or agencies of government, located within newly-structured organisational hierarchies; the 'Next Steps' Agencies initiative of the late 1980s is a prime example.

This new public management approach perfectly harmonises with, and indeed serves to encourage and dynamise, initiatives for governmental re-organisation which are primarily inspired by political factors or policy goals, especially those directed at neo-liberalisation or 'de-rigidification' in any given sphere of governmental activity, and most especially of all in the sphere of employment policy and flexibilisation of employment relations. Hence we find that there has been a notably high degree of organisational churning in the sphere of employment and training policy throughout the period under review. Thus, the hiving off of the manpower policy division and service of the DEP (as it then was) into distinct agencies, later merged into the Manpower Services Commission in the early 1970s, was a fore-runner or harbinger of a plethora of such new public management re-constructions of this particular sphere of activity, as chronicled earlier in this chapter (see also Chapter 5). So the merger of this organisational set-up into the newly formed DfEE in 1995 seemed to fit into a pattern which, by then, had become reasonably normal and accustomed; and the disappearance of the DE itself could thus pass comparatively unnoticed.

The Dynamic of the 'New Deal' and of 'Workfare'

As in certain other spheres, but most conspicuously in the area of employment relations, post-1997 New Labour governments travelled further and more willingly down organisational or managerial roads which had been opened up by their Conservative predecessors than had been generally predicted. Thus, the dynamic of anti-tripartism accelerated by the vector of new public management, turned out to suit their purposes and policy directions. But if the dynamic of anti-tripartism had been essentially a negative one, entailing the dismantling of older organisational and political structures, post-1997 governments would add a fresh and positive dynamic, though by no means an incompatible one, namely that of the 'New Deal' and of the elaboration of 'workfare' arrangements in the sphere of employment and social security policy.

Explaining that proposition more fully, we suggest that it is appropriate to think of the New Labour government's 'New Deal' as a plan for social welfare provision which would be on the one hand enhanced but on the other hand more tightly linked to the acceptance of corresponding social responsibilities by the citizens benefiting from that provision. More specifically, the 'New Deal' in the sphere of employment and social security policy envisages 'workfare' arrangements whereby social welfare provision in the nature of replacement or supplementation of income from work is conditioned strictly upon the willingness of its recipients to seek work and make themselves available for work. This was a strategy which Conservatives had embedded, in the later 1980s and 1990s, most conspicuously by their legislative transformation of Social Security Unemployment Benefit and Supplementary Benefit into the Jobseekers Allowances from 1995 onwards. New Labour governments would elaborate that strategy, for example by the creation of Employment Zones within which specially positive but stringent workfare arrangements applied; and the government continues to build up and extend such dispositions at the time of writing.

This third factor of change interacted with the other two to bring about a further bout of institutional re-structuring in the employment sphere, that is to say the creation of the Department of Work and Pensions. Our first, anti-tripartist, factor has operated to ensure that this new Department of State is no phoenix re-born from the ashes of the Department of Employment; trade union representation or client-hood is not remotely in sight in its conception or operation. This is 'Not the Department of Employment'; it is the Department of Social Security and the Employment Service of the DfEE re-cast to the purposes of the New Deal. The vector of new public management has, again, been conducive to this re-structuring so that when Mr Blunkett and Mr Darling described to the Social Security Select Committee of the House of Commons their plans for the setting up of the Working Age Agency, in a sense the immediate precursor of the new DWP, their justificatory rhetoric was very much that of new public management, almost, it must be said, to the point of self-parody at some points (HC SSSC 2000).

CONCLUSION: THE INSTITUTIONAL LANDSCAPE AFTER THE DEPARTMENT OF EMPLOYMENT

Having sought to analyse the factors which brought about or contributed in particular to the abolition of the Department of Employment in 1995, and the creation of the Department of Work and Pensions in 2001, we conclude with a brief survey of the institutional landscape of departmental government in the sphere of employment relations as it looks at the time of writing. The developments which we have described are almost bewildering in the complexity of the institutional convolutions which they represent. Permitting ourselves a mode of depiction which we hope will not seem unduly satirical, we single out for description three parts or features of the institutional landscape at departmental level as it currently presents itself, re-fashioned as it has been by the factors of change which we have previously identified. So we conclude with a fleeting glance at these three topographical locations: the institutional nursery, the institutional graveyard, and the enclaves of government in exile.

The institutional nursery is the location where the new institutions and institutional structures for the governance of employment relations at departmental level are grown. This place bustles with activity. Ministers and civil servants busily plant seeds and tend the new shoots; here a new Department is establishing itself, there a new Agency, over there a young Commission is struggling to cope with the climate. Political advisers and consultancies are brought in as expert grafters and pruners, to create new breeds and trim back older ones. All the plants need constant watering with public resources, which for once are liberally provided, for this is a much-cherished part of the governmental garden. Currently on display here is a new Working Neighbourhoods Programme, the latest product of the Jobcentre Plus part of the Department of Work and Pensions. In a more distant part of the garden, the Department for Education and Skills (as it has become) is preparing to split the tree of the Learning Support and Development Agency into two new shrubs, the Quality Improvement Agency for Lifelong Learning and the Learning and Skills Network.

Then there is the institutional graveyard. This is a sad and neglected place, in a permanently fogbound part of the territory. Each time a new display of flowering plants is laid on in the institutional nursery, there have to be some quiet interments of defunct ancestors in the institutional graveyard. Small burial parties of civil servants are dispatched to these tasks, often doing their work at night, and always avoiding the public gaze. Often the institutional graves are unmarked, and it quickly becomes hard to discover or remember when the defunct institutions were born and died. To revert to our Hamlet metaphor, one stumbles across the remains of old friends – 'Alas, poor Yorick, I knew him … a fellow of infinite jest', one might say of the Benefits Agency of the Department of Social Security, absorbed into the Department of Work and Pensions in 2001. Some have had quite long lives by current Whitehall standards – the Manpower Services Commission, 1976-1987; other have the pathetic graves of still-born or very short-lived children – the Department of Energy, Productivity and Industry, the DTI as 're-branded' by the Prime Minster after the General Election of 2005, survived for only one week. In one part of the graveyard, a forest of crosses, as for a battalion of the fallen in the Great War, marks the resting place of 76 Training and Enterprise Councils – quite elaborate research is needed to discover that they were wound up, again in 2001. However, saddest of all, of course, from a traditionalist viewpoint at least, is the looming family mausoleum of the principal Department of State itself, the Ministry of Labour/ Department of Employment/ Department of Employment and Productivity 1916-1995.

Finally, there are the enclaves of government in exile. These are the distant places to which groups of civil servants have been banished as they struggle to carry on the governance functions of the former and widely discredited Department of Employment. These relics of the *ancien regime* are found in odd and unexpected places. The employment relations unit is, as we have remarked, housed in the Department of Trade and Industry. More egregiously, the Wages Inspectors, now the National Minimum Wage Compliance Officers, have their institutional home in the (itself newly merged) HM Revenue and Customs department. When, in the aftermath of the tragedy which befell the Chinese cockle-pickers in Morecombe Bay, the government resolved to introduce a system of licensing of the gangmasters employing such workers, the institutional base for the running and policing of that system was located in the Department for Food, Environment and Rural Affairs.

That account of those outplacings of the functions of governance of employment relations leads on to what ought to be a serious end-note to this little essay in satire. The weighty and as yet unresolved question is whether the vocation and mission of government to secure decent conditions of work and life for our national labour force and its dependents is as well served and carried out under our present and evolving institutional structure as it was during the period when there was a department of government essentially if imperfectly dedicated to it. We do not presume to suggest or imply an answer to that question; but we hope to have posed the question as one of the utmost gravity and importance.

REFERENCES

Civil Service Department (1998): *Civil Service Yearbook 1998-99*

Clifford, C., McMillan, A. & McLean, I. (1997): *The Organisation of Central Government Departments: A History 1964-1992. Volume I: Project Synopsis* (Nuffield, Oxford)

Department of Social Security (1998): *New ambitions for our country: A New Contract for Welfare* (HMSO, London)

European Industry Relations Observatory Online – EIROnline (2001): 18 December 2001. *Planned restructuring of DTI angers unions.* Accessed 29 October 2005 at: http://www.eiro.eurofound.eu.int/2001/12/feature/uk0112132f.html

Freedland, M. (1992): 'The role of the Department of Employment – Twenty Years of Institutional Change', in McCarthy, W. (ed), *Legal intervention in industrial relations: gains and losses* (Blackwell Business, Oxford)

Hencke, D. (2005): 'Secret Plan to put 60,000 jobcentre posts out to tender', *The Guardian*, 12 September 2005

HS SSSC (2003): House of Commons Social Security Select Committee, 3 July 2003. *Minutes of Evidence.* Accessed 29 October 2005 at: http://www.parliament.the-stationery-office.co.uk/pa/cm199900/cmselect/cmsocsec/662/0070302.htm

Midgley, S. (2001): 'It's over!', *The Guardian*, 19 June 2001

Millar, M. (2005): 'Survey Reveals extent of unrest at Department of Work and Pensions', *Personnel Today*, 15 February 2005

Keith Sisson & John Taylor

THE ADVISORY, CONCILIATION AND ARBITRATION SERVICE

Origins and Early Development

The Advisory, Conciliation and Arbitration Service (Acas) was set up in September 1974, following several years of industrial relations and legislative turmoil, during which the role of the then Department of Employment had come in for considerable criticism (Hawes 2000). The Department, critics argued, was not only ill-equipped to deal with the changing realities of workplace industrial relations; its conciliation role was compromised in times of incomes policy and, more generally, in the public sector where government was the employer. A body was needed that was independent of government. Acas was established to meet this need. Although publicly funded, it was to be run by a tri-partite council involving management, trade union and independent members. Its terms of reference, which were initially set out in a letter on September 1975 from the then Secretary of State, Michael Foot, gave it a wide remit:

'To provide conciliation and mediation as a means of avoiding and resolving disputes, to make facilities available for arbitration, to provide advisory services to industry on industrial relations and related matters and to undertake investigations as a means of promoting the improvement and extension of collective bargaining.'

The special independent status of Acas was confirmed in the Employment Protection Act 1975, which stated that,

'…the Service shall not be subject to directions of any kind from any Minister of the Crown as to the manner in which it is to exercise any of its functions under any enactment' (Para.11(i), Schedule 1)

Under this Act, Acas – whose remit covers Great Britain, there being a separate Labour Relations Agency in Northern Ireland with similar responsibilities – was charged with a general duty to promote improvement in industrial relations and given two specific obligations: the resolution of disputes and the extension of collective bargaining. Both had significant statutory as well as voluntary dimensions. In terms of dispute resolution, Acas was under a statutory duty to provide conciliation in individual rights cases, whereas, in collective cases, it was permitted but not required to become involved. In the second area, Acas had a role not only in conciliating trade union recognition disputes, but

Linda Dickens & Alan C. Neal (eds), The Changing Institutional Face of British Employment Relations, 25-36
© *2006 Kluwer Law International. Printed in the Netherlands*

also in operating a statutory recognition process that was inherited from the Commission on Industrial Relations.

This role proved controversial and difficult. There were some high profile recognition disputes and legal challenges in the courts. Most famous was the bitter recognition dispute involving a photo-processing company by the name of Grunwick: the House of Lords effectively ruled that, where the employer did not co-operate, Acas had to carry out its enquiries by other means and, if it could not do this, it was in no position to make a recommendation. The greater difficulties posed by the way the law was being interpreted in the courts, and concerns that Acas' reputation for independence and impartiality risked being compromised, led the Acas Council to write to the Secretary of State in 1979 saying that Acas could not operate the statutory procedure under the prevailing arrangements. The new Conservative Government formally terminated the statutory recognition procedure in the Employment Act 1980.

The remit to encourage the extension of collective bargaining was removed from Acas' statutory duties in 1993. The Trade Union Reform and Employment Relations Act 1993 charged Acas 'to promote the improvement of industrial relations in particular by exercising its functions in relation to the settlement of trade disputes'. Acas itself expressed its mission as 'to improve the performance and effectiveness of organisations by providing an independent and impartial service to prevent and resolve disputes and build harmonious relationships at work'.

A book published to mark the first quarter century of Acas (Towers & Brown 2000) provides detailed accounts of the work of Acas and expert reflections upon it. This chapter makes no attempt to summarise or duplicate that work. Rather, it outlines the organisation and structure of Acas, considers areas of continuity and change and discusses the ways in which Acas is seeking to maximise its contribution in a very changed environment from that in which it was created, and the challenges it faces.

ORGANISATION AND STRUCTURE

Acas continues to be run by a council comprising representatives of employers and trade unions along with independent employment relations experts. Since 1998, however, appointments have been the subject of open competition rather than nomination, reflecting the Nolan Committee's recommendations on public office. Up until 2000, the Chair of Acas was also its Chief Executive. In that year, the job was split – Acas now has a part-time Chair and a full-time Chief Executive. The Chief Executive post, along with those of the three senior directors, are senior civil service appointments. Together with seven Regional Directors, a Director of Human Resources and a Director of Finance, their occupants make up the Management Board of Acas, responsible for running the organisation's day-to-day activities. The option of selective open recruitment was introduced in 2003, whereas previously, all posts had been filled by recruitment from the civil service.

The main activities of Acas are reflected in the organisation of its operational staff. The largest group, accounting for just over half of the overall budget of Acas, is involved in delivering individual conciliation. Two groups of advisers make up the balance. Just over one hundred are employed in giving information and answering questions over the Helpline telephone. In addition, slightly fewer than one hundred senior advisers are involved in collective conciliation and in-depth advisory work.

Acas maintains a panel of suitable, independent people to undertake collective dispute mediation and arbitration which it may provide; another panel to decide individual rights cases under the arbitration alternative to the Employment Tribunals (see Chapter 12), and a third panel of people who are equal pay experts. None of these is an Acas employee; payment is on a *per diem* basis.

Since its inception, Acas has been a national organisation with a regionally-based structure. Acas National, as the headquarters is now known, houses specialist support staff in delivery, information technology, digital solutions, finance, human resources, communications, policy, and research and evaluation. Apart from a small national conciliation team, all operational staff are employed in the regions. These include the advisers who work on the helpline and who, since the end of 2002, have been linked together in a virtual call centre by a national telephone number.

The details of the present regional structure reflect the political and administrative units into which the country has been divided since the late 1990s. The new Labour Government's introduction of a Scottish Parliament, Welsh Assembly and nine English Regional Assemblies/Regional Development Agencies is very important in understanding recent developments. Administratively, Acas is divided into seven 'regions'. Acas Scotland and Acas Wales operate from main offices in Glasgow and Cardiff respectively. In England, two of the five Acas regions, London and the North West, correspond directly to the coverage of their relevant Regional Development Agency. The remaining three are sub-divided into Areas that similarly match the Regional Development Agency coverage.

Continuity and change

Superficially, there has been little change in the overall portfolio of Acas activities, with information and advice sitting side by side with dispute resolution from the very beginning. The balance has changed significantly, however, both within and between the main categories of activity.

Two main considerations have been important here. The first is the increase in the number of individual statutory employment rights, helping to explain both the shift in emphasis from collective dispute conciliation to individual conciliation, and the increase in demand for Acas' information and advisory services. The second is the changing context of employment relations, fuelling the increase in demand for Acas' information and advisory services. In this case, competitive pressures in both product and labour markets mean that employers are looking for help in managing their human resources more effectively. For example, as well as pressures to maximise performance, many are faced with acute labour shortages and/or the need to draw on, what for them, are new sources of supply such as women 'returners' and ethnic minority groups.

Conciliation Services

Most notable here is the decline in collective conciliation (and any subsequent mediation or arbitration) and rise in individual conciliation.

There is no requirement that parties refer a collective dispute to Acas. However, the demand for collective conciliation rose dramatically after Acas' formation, rising to more than 3,000 cases in each of 1976, 1977 and 1978. In the early 1980s, it declined year on year to just over 1,100 in 1988 and 1989. Throughout the 1990s, it hovered between 1,200 and 1,300, staying at, or slightly below, this level in the first years of the new millennium (Goodman 2000). The subject matter has also been relatively stable. 'Pay and conditions', unsurprisingly, have been the main issues, accounting for more than half of all cases in most years. Trade union recognition, redundancy and discipline/dismissal have vied with one another for second place at around 10% of cases, with trade union recognition coming out clearly in recent years, following the introduction of statutory recognition in the Employment Relations Act 1999 (see Chapter 7).

Meanwhile, individual conciliation cases showed a seeming inexorable rise throughout the second half of the period, reflecting the expansion in individual employment rights, changes in the access to rights and attractiveness of remedies, and the changing structure and composition of employment (Dickens 2000). Acas has a duty to offer conciliation when a claim is made to an Employment Tribunal (ET). From 1976 to 1988, the total number of cases was around the 40,000 mark each year. Thereafter, it grew year on year, passing 60,000 in 1991, 70,000 in 1992 and 80,000 in 1995. It passed the 100,000 mark in 1996 and the 120,000 mark in 2000. Only in recent years has the figure fallen back, largely reflecting changes in the operation of ET arrangements (see Chapters 10 and 11).

Although many claims are multi-jurisdictional, there is no doubt that the dominant issue is unfair dismissal (still accounting for more than 40% of cases). Wages Act (unlawful deductions from wages contrary to s.13 of the Employment Rights Act 1996) issues (around 20%) and breach of contract more generally (around 10%) are the next most frequent individual issues.

Two major changes are under way in individual conciliation, the outcome of which are uncertain. One is the implementation of the 'three speed' approach to ET cases under the Employment Relations Act 2002, with the consequential introduction of differential service standards. Conciliation in claims lodged after 1 October 2004 with the Employment Tribunal Service (ETS), such as redundancy, unlawful deduction of wages and breach of contract, will now be limited to a 'short' period of 7 weeks, during which conciliation may be attempted; conciliation in claims such as unfair dismissal will now be limited to a 'standard' period of 13 weeks. All others, essentially discrimination cases, will be 'open' to conciliation until the tribunal hearing.

The other change is the introduction of technology, systems and business processes that will radically change the way information and data flow between Acas and the ETS. Documents such as application and response forms will be received by conciliators in electronic case files. Case notes will be recorded electronically and stored in shared files available instantly to anyone else in Acas with authority to access the information, and there will be automatic prompts to assist conciliators with their case management.

Information and Advisory Services

There has been a significant increase in the demand for Acas' information and advisory activities. Throughout its early years, the main activity of Acas was the in-depth advisory project where senior advisers acted as facilitators to improve the organisational effectiveness and deal with issues and problems that face employer and employees. Altogether, Acas advisers continue to undertake around 400 specific workplace projects each year. They work together with the parties to use joint working and problem solving to examine issues and problems, jointly develop constructive solutions, and where appropriate assist with the joint implementation of agreed solutions (Purcell 2000).

Other means of delivering information and advice have soared. The Acas free help-line has seen a doubling of the number of calls in recent years. In the last operating year, it received nearly 900,000 calls evenly split between employers and employees. The help-line is a key resource for Small and Medium Size Enterprises (SMEs), with the majority of callers working in or for small organisations, many of whom have no personnel or human resource specialist in their workplace.

The help-line advisers deal with calls on every aspect of employment relations. The most frequently-asked questions relate to holiday pay/entitlement, dismissal, sick pay/absence and redundancy/redundancy pay, although identifying the main topics is not entirely straightforward. Employers often ask questions on different subjects relating to a number of different employees. Employees, on the other hand, may ring in about a number of issues, uncertain about what their main problem is. The skill of the help-line advisers is key in disentangling the various problems, identifying the key point, providing the relevant information and, where appropriate, pointing them towards other sources of help and advice, including Acas training and advisory services.

As an integral part of Acas' telephone help-line is Equality Direct – a specialist telephone help-line to provide employers with a simple and immediate answer to any equality query they may have. In 2004/05, the help-line received around 4,800 calls, covering general queries on good practice, discrimination law and equal opportunities.

Acas views training as a major vehicle for delivering information and advice fulfilling its mission and recent years have seen a considerable increase in demand here as well. Two main types are on offer. The first are public events designed to help employers keep up to date with good employment practices and new employment legislation. In 2004/05 Acas ran nearly 3,000 such events, reaching more than 30,000 delegates from a broad range of organisations. Separate events are aimed at small businesses or medium and larger organisations.

The second type involves bespoke training on request in the context of particular issues facing their organisations. Here, Acas advisers work closely with an organisation to train managers and employees to improve their employment knowledge and skills typically in a particular area. For example, it could be a programme designed to combat harassment and bullying or improve information and consultation.

In recent years, Acas has created an easily accessible e-business for the provision of information as well as for learning packages. There has been an exponential increase in the use of its website (which is available at www.acas.org.uk) since the turn of the Millenium. By the end of 2005, each month some 150,000 documents were being downloaded, while the number of unique visitors had increased to 2.5 million, with over 10 million 'hits' per year. Assuming this reflects the known help-line split of employers/employees call ratio, this means that the Acas website is being accessed annually by over one million employers.

Growing requests for information and advice from other countries led Acas to establish an International Department. This, in turn, has made it possible for Acas to play a major role in EU-funded programmes to help new Member States to introduce effective employment relations systems. Indeed, Acas has been involved in no fewer than five of the countries joining the EU in 2004: Hungary, Latvia, Poland, Slovakia and Slovenia. This year, it successfully competed for contracts to engage in major EU-funded projects in Romania and Bulgaria. Typically, involvement means Acas officials spending time in the countries running seminars and conferences. It means that Acas has been gaining further knowledge and experience of what works and does not work in a variety of different situations. This could be invaluable both domestically and internationally – Acas is currently exploring the possibility of major contracts in China and Korea.

MAXIMISING THE CONTRIBUTION OF ACAS

As well as reflecting general labour market and employment relations changes, lying behind the changing balance in Acas' activities has been an on-going debate about how to make the best use of Acas' unique knowledge and experience of employment relations that comes from direct local involvement in workplaces across the country. Critical here were the Government's quinquennial review of Acas in 1999-2000, the comments of contributors to *Employment Relations in Britain: 25 years of the Advisory, Conciliation and Arbitration Service* (Brown & Towers 2000), and the internal *Acas Today and Tomorrow* investigation undertaken in 2001. The latter charted a wider concept for Acas' role summarised in the new mission statement – improving organisations and working life through better employment relations.

A key starting point was the recognition that employment relations did not involve just collective relationships. The motivation and commitment so critical to organisational performance primarily reflect the job satisfaction and emotional reward that *individuals* derive from their work, and both conflict and co-operation are intrinsic to the employment relationship, whether or not a trade union is present. Also, the knowledge and experience possessed by Acas equipped it not just to help to resolve differences between the parties in the workplace or, indeed, help them to avoid disputes. They enabled it to help to put in place the necessary conditions for improvements in productivity and performance, quality and innovation, equality and diversity, work-life balance, skills and development, and public service reform. Moreover, on the basis of these competences, Acas should no longer be content simply to 'run alongside' changes in the world of work (Hawes 2000). Rather, it should be much more up-front in seeking to influence developments in line with its general statutory duty to improve employment relations.

The increase in the demand for information and advice suggests that Acas is on course to deliver the objective of achieving 'first choice' status that *Acas Today and Tomorrow* set the organisation. It also nicely encapsulates the virtuous circle that Acas has been able to create by building on its long-established and highly respected reputation. The reason why the two main customers for information and advice – employees and employers – come to Acas are very similar to those explaining why they come for help to resolve disputes. They want information and advice that are not only accurate and authoritative but also independent and impartial. They do not want to get different answers from different agencies and they do not want to feel they are being used to promote a particular 'cause' or interest. Additionally, many employers value Acas as a source of information and advice because it does not have enforcement powers – many are reluctant to approach the agencies that have these powers because they believe they will get a rights-based instead of a problem-solving response. Many also worry about the possibility of triggering an inspection that could be damaging to their reputation in the eyes of employees and customers.

The direction set in *Acas Today and Tomorrow* has been developed further in the two editions of *Improving the world of work*, which sets out Acas' strategic plans for the periods 2004-2007 and 2005-2008. *Improving the world of work* tries to demonstrate more clearly than Acas has in the past not just how its services fit into the wider policy, social and economic agenda, but also how they can make a unique contribution in the following six areas:

Workplace effectiveness and improved productivity. Priorities here are to help managers to appreciate how improvements in employment relations contribute to increasing productivity and to promote effective information and consultation practice as the basic building block. Initiatives include a national workforce development programme to support managers' appreciation of 'soft' employment relations skills and better work organisation, emphasising the links between good employment relations and improved organisational performance; publicity for and marketing of the 'Acas Model Workplace', which is a diagnostic tool designed to help make workplaces more effective; delivering seminars raising awareness of the Information and Consultation of Employees (ICE) Regulations and targeting advisory projects at helping organisations to reach agreements implementing them; and an advisory booklet on information and consultation specifically for SMEs with fewer than 50 staff that, at present, will not be covered by the ICE regulations.

Micro-businesses and SMEs. Priorities here are to support SMEs during start-up and growth and to encourage SMEs to recognise and value the benefits that good employment relations practice makes to business performance. Initiatives include the proposed development of a subscription service for SMEs ensuring that they receive information automatically; further development of the Acas helpline to offer a more effective and efficient service to users; an extension in the range of training (events and on-line) and products (publications and tools) dealing with employment relations issues for SMEs; the setting up of an SME users' forum to gain a better understanding of the employment relations concerns of small business and to test out new Acas products and services; and much more active collaboration with SMEs and their representative organisations to develop ways of promoting the importance of good employment relations to improved business performance.

Individuals and working life. Priorities in this area are to improve the quality and coverage of information and advice about working life and delivering better dispute resolution of employment rights cases. Initiatives include refinement of Acas procedures for dealing with fixed period and fast track conciliation in the light of the provisions of the Employment Act 2002 and the 2004 Employment Tribunal Rules; the new computerised data links with the ETS to improve the handling of individual conciliation cases; the provision of a mediation service to facilitate the resolution of individual workplace disputes with accredited training to in-house mediators with a recognised award on completion; and collaboration with bodies such as Citizens' Advice Bureaux to ensure that as many individuals as possible are made aware of their rights and responsibilities as employees.

Equality and diversity. Here the priorities reflect the impact on the United Kingdom's workforce of changing demographics such as declining birth rates, more young people going into higher education and increases in longevity, more female labour market participation, more older workers and a more significant role for people from ethnic minorities along with migrant workers. They are to promote the business and wider societal benefits of workplace diversity alongside the equality commissions and other key players. Acas is seeking to improve and expand its capacity to deliver a professional equality and diversity service that is able to inform and support the delivery of the Acas mission. Initiatives include new information, guidance and training packages and seminars dealing with the new disability and age discrimination legislation; the setting up a 'one-stop-shop' equality gateway website; updating of materials dealing with bullying and harassment to include recent legislative changes; a booklet on managing the implications of pregnancy at work; seminars raising awareness of equal pay issues and audits; joint events with the Disability Rights Commission on amendments to disability legislation; updated guidance dealing with sexual orientation in line with the Civil Partnership Act; research on support needs of minority ethnic SME Businesses; guidance on equality and diversity for SMEs; and work with the Home Office and other relevant bodies on the integration of employees entering United Kingdom workplaces for the first time as a result of immigration.

Public services and change management. Here the priority is to work with public service employers and employees to pursue effective change management programmes. Initiatives include on-going dialogue with key policy makers such as the Office for Public Service Reform and the Health, Safety and Productivity Task Force, and the development of existing dialogue with key practitioner groups, such as the National Health Service (NHS) Partnership Forum, and employer organisations and professional bodies such as the new NHS Employers Organisation, Local Government Employers' Organisation and the Chartered Institute of Personnel and Development; a dedicated, charged-for training package in mediation/ alternative dispute resolution targeted initially at the NHS; a suite of training events tailored to the needs of each distinct area of the public sector, initially within the NHS, under a 'managing change and working together' banner; targeted promotional and advisory booklets for each distinct part of the public sector under a 'managing change' banner, initially for local government and the NHS; and forms of 'assisted negotiation' to help the parties to manage change, i.e. making conciliation available before any formal 'failure to agree' is registered.

Regionalisation. Acas is also working with the representatives of locally elected bodies, government agencies and social partners in Scotland, Wales and the English regions to promote the significance of effective employment relations as a key element in regional economic strategies. Acas Wales, for example, is involved in a major 'partnership' project involving the Welsh assembly. Acas Northern and Acas London are now working with Yorkshire Forward and the London Development Agency respectively to deliver major projects in workplace equality and diversity. Acas South East, working alongside SEEDA and other partners, has played a central role in the ground-breaking 'Marine Pooling Project', which has helped to deal with labour supply problems in Southampton shipyards. Acas North West and NWDA recently signed a Memorandum of Understanding committing themselves to working together to promote productive and effective workplaces.

Acas also plays a central role in the Employment Relations Forums that bring together regional social and economic partner organisations to promote the importance of employment relations and its benefits for economic performance and workplace social cohesion, to influential regional and national decision makers. With the debate about United Kingdom productivity and global competitiveness still provoking regular headlines, the forums' role in addressing and finding innovative solutions to the big workplace challenges currently facing United Kingdom businesses and their employees is vital. In 2005, working with partner organisations on the forum's steering groups, Acas brought together representatives from the various forums for the very first time in their history to debate major issues such as these.

Acas has also welcomed the roll-out of the DTI Benchmark Index, seeing this is an excellent opportunity to encourage businesses to use the 'Acas Model Workplace'. The aim will be to raise engagement through these important business support tools and also assist in producing regional analysis of interventions for further use and dissemination at the policy level.

Internally, *Improving the world of work* commits Acas to developing a tailored training programme for its advisers to help them appreciate the full significance of the regional agenda and the important further contribution they have to make. It also means that Acas will be seeking to improve internal knowledge management systems in order to share knowledge, projects and expertise in a more joined-up and focused way. This will give Acas a wealth of data, alongside up-to-the-minute case studies, that will really 'take the temperature' of the nation's workplaces. Acas will publish this regional workplace data in authoritative and regular 'State of the Nation' reports.

MAJOR CHALLENGES

There is a widespread consensus throughout the organisation that the change that Acas is experiencing is unprecedented in its thirty-year history. The intensity of this change is also increasing as Acas faces up to a number of major challenges. To begin with, there are the on-going challenges arising from the strategy begun with the *Acas Today and Tomorrow* review in 2001 to stretch perceptions of Acas from being known as a dispute resolution service dealing with large organisations to being the first port of call for organisations of all sizes and sectors needing information, advice, training and services to help improve their workplace performance.

Getting the 'employment relations matters' message across is a major challenge in itself – 'employment relations', like 'industrial relations', is associated with trade unions and collective bargaining, which are in decline. Many practitioners remain in denial about the realities of the employment relationship – that it involves co-operation as well as conflict; that it is deeply embedded in institutional arrangements that have their origins in work organisation along with management structures and personnel policies more generally. Policy-making is dominated by thinking that prioritises 'markets' – public intervention can only be justified in terms of market failure. It can also be very fragmented. Acas increasingly has to relate to a wide range of agencies sponsored by a number of different departments, each of which is under pressure to meet targets that often have been set in isolation. Areas such as management leadership and skills, attendance, stress and diversity now involve a number of agencies; developments in conciliation are affected by thinking in the Department of Constitutional Affairs as well as the Department of Trade and Industry; and so on (see also Chapter 2).

In the Information Age knowledge management is an on-going challenge, helping to explain why a new Directorate with this portfolio is being created within Acas National. Capturing, analysing and disseminating its unique knowledge of workplace employment relations are critical to Acas maximising its contribution. Time and again the key to the recent success of Acas in promoting the case for employment relations has been the ability to back up the philosophical argument with hard evidence and specific examples. Tight budgets and an emphasis on meeting service delivery targets nonetheless threaten to crowd out time and other resources for the research/knowledge transfer. The objective of encouraging advisers to become 'reflective practitioners', capable of documenting their experiences, is also harder to achieve in practice than it may seem – conciliation and advice tend to prioritise oral over written skills.

Regionalisation presents another set of challenges. Acas regional structure means it is ideally placed to meet the shift in emphasis resulting from the introduction of the Scottish Parliament, the Welsh Assembly and the Regional Assemblies/Regional Development Agencies. Inevitably, however, the increasing tendency for the Acas 'Regions' to make much of the running for the organisation as a whole raises issues about managing diversity. Critically, it means adjusting the 'tight-loose' balance between Acas National and Acas Regions. Regionalisation means a more substantial shift in emphasis in the role of Acas National from 'command and control' to 'servicing and support'. At the same time, however, the Board needs to maintain the high standards and principles that have come to be associated with the need for tighter standards to protect and promote the 'Acas brand'.

Achieving a more appropriate funding regime represents a further challenge. To allow Acas to increase its reach and impact, it has been necessary to introduce a number of charged-for services that enable it to further its mission. Training is the largest area. Wherever possible, the aim is for these initiatives to be self-funding. For this to be practical, however, Acas needs to be confident that a funding regime will be maintained that will enable it to retain income to cover costs without a reduction in grant-in-aid which is the funding Acas receives from government. Here the proposed cuts could mean a stark choice – Acas either considerably scales back on its mission to improve employment relations or considers an alternative funding regime involving a mix of grant-in-aid and income generated from commercial activities. But this raises sensitive issues about independence and impartiality along with charges that Acas is being prepared for privatisation.

On top of these, like the rest of the Civil Service, Acas faces an extremely challenging financial settlement covering the coming three years. The 2005-2006 grant-in-aid means a reduction in resources of 5%; by 2007-2008 that figure rises to 16%. This means an actual cash funding reduction over the next three years from £46m to £45m to £43m. The best estimate is that staff numbers across Acas will have to reduce by around 140, although proposed new activities may off-set some of these. A major 'Futures Programme' has had to be launched re-organising Acas and its use of resources. Implementation of a long-term estates strategy is being speeded up, with most of Acas' out-stations being closed, along with central administration of the arrangements for individual conciliation. Inevitably, this re-organisation has diverted time and energies from meeting the more underlying challenges discussed above.

Coupled with the immediate budgetary situation is the prospect of a review embracing Acas' activities that could mean even more radical changes. This arises from the Government's next three-year spending review. The DTI has announced that, in the light of the much tighter financial constraints, it will need to review the functions that it currently carries out. As part of this, the role of Acas will be reviewed within the broader employment and equality agendas in terms of value for money, meeting the needs of its customers, and strategic fit within the overall programme in the area. The respective roles of Acas and the new Commission for Equality and Human Rights (see Chapter 9) in providing information and advice on employment-related equality and diversity issues will clearly need to be clarified, if there is not to be unnecessary duplication.

These are, then, immensely challenging times for Acas, with its size, shape and future activities uncertain at the time of writing. As it will be arguing to the review, however, it is no accident that Acas has survived thirty years of massively changing economic, political and social change. An enduring feature throughout this period has been the need for the impartial and independent third party information/advice/assistance that Acas has consistently provided. As this chapter has emphasised, demands for Acas services have never been greater. The number of strikes in the United Kingdom may have declined dramatically in recent years as it has in other major industrial countries. But the potential for conflict that is inherent in the uncertainty of the employment relationship has not gone away, as the number of Employment Tribunal cases of alleged infringement of individual rights, and high levels of absenteeism, clearly demonstrate. Also, the complexity of the issues that people in the world of work are having to grapple with means Acas staff are involved in satisfying a substantial and rising demand for information and advice. People are coming to Acas for the very same reasons that they come for help when they are in dispute – they want to know that the advice that are being given is independent and impartial. Crucial here has been Acas' staff extensive practical knowledge and experience of employment relations that comes from direct local involvement in workplaces across the country. What is learnt from one activity has been put to practical use in another. Acas looks like an organisation that you would have to create if it did not already exist.

REFERENCES

Brown, W. & Towers, B. (2000): Employment Relations in Britain: 25 years of the Advisory, Conciliation and Arbitration Service (Blackwell, Oxford)

Dickens, L. (2000): 'Doing more with less: Acas and individual conciliation', in Brown, W. & Towers, B. (2000)

Goodman, J. (2000): 'Building bridges and settling differences: collective conciliation and arbitration', in Brown, W. & Towers, B. (2000)

Hawes, W. (2000): 'Setting the pace or running alongside?', in Brown, W. & Towers, B. (2000)

Purcell, J. (2000): 'After collective bargaining? Acas in the age of human resource management', in Brown, W. & Towers, B. (2000)

Bill Callaghan

THE HEALTH AND SAFETY COMMISSION AND EXECUTIVE

INTRODUCTION

It is over 30 years since the Health and Safety at Work etc Act (HSW Act) created the Health and Safety Commission (HSC) and Executive (HSE) and a role for local authorities (LAs) to implement a new regulatory framework for workplace health and safety in Great Britain. As Chapter 1 of this volume has outlined, the intervening period has been one of massive economic, social and technological change. In some ways, the workforce of 2005 is unrecognisable from that of 30 years ago. Yet, the fundamental aspirations laid down in 1974 remain equally valid today.

The new Act, which largely reflected the recommendations of the 1972 Robens Report, introduced a broad goal setting, non-prescriptive model, based on the view that 'those that create risk are best placed to manage it'. In place of existing detailed and prescriptive industry regulations, it created a flexible system whereby regulations express goals and principles, and are supported by codes of practice and guidance. Based on consultation and engagement, the new regime was designed to deliver a proportionate, targeted and risk-based approach.

The HSW Act also established two new bodies – HSC and HSE – to implement the framework. Having met for the first time on 1 October 1974, HSC is responsible for securing the health, safety and welfare of workers and the public affected by work activity. Its duties include proposing new laws and standards, conducting research and providing information and advice. On the other hand, HSE advises and assists HSC in its functions and has specific responsibility, shared with LAs, for enforcing health and safety law.

While the HSW Act established the regulatory framework, the HSC and HSE were left to fill in the details. Both bodies were products of their time but they were also designed to be flexible; to encompass change. Over the 30 years they have proved themselves robust, responsive and adaptable in a rapidly changing environment. Not only have they reacted and responded to new demands and public expectations but they have also been responsible for pushing the health and safety agenda forward in other directions. In 2005, following a major review of regulators (the Hampton Review), the Government confirmed HSC/E's role as one of seven thematic regulators.

Linda Dickens & Alan C. Neal (eds), The Changing Institutional Face of British Employment Relations 37-47
© *2006 Kluwer Law International. Printed in the Netherlands*

THE HSC/E MODEL

The HSC/E model is unique within Whitehall: it combines two separate and distinct Crown bodies, each with a separate legal personality yet intertwined both by statute and by subsequent administrative developments. In examining the HSC/E model we need to have regard to *both* the involvement of the social partners in the Commission and its advisory committees *and* the relationship between the Commission and the Executive.

The HSW Act does not provide a clear template for how the organisation works in practice. One reading of the Act is to envisage two separate organisations, located in two different buildings, the Commission, with its own staff, having a clear policy focus, and the Executive having a clear enforcement role. In support of this is the fact that the original Bill did not propose the model of a unitary organisation put forward by Robens (1972: Ch. 4). A powerful argument against a unitary model is that trade unionists and employers sitting on the Commission should not interfere in enforcement decisions by the Executive. However it should be noted that this has not prevented other bodies with an enforcement role having a unitary constitution.

Another reading of the HSW Act is that the intention was to create a *de facto* unitary body but to build in a number of checks and balances to prevent the organisation becoming too distant from Whitehall. Thus, the Commission has extensive powers, but these are all subject to Ministerial approval. The HSW Act gives the Commission powers regarding the appointment of the Executive (in terms of the HSW Act literally three people) but is silent about the other members of HSE staff (nearly 4,000). Although the corporate governance is sketchy it is possible to read the Act as creating an organisation with considerable independence but not so independent that it acts completely autonomously. Moreover, the Commission acts as a buffer between Ministers and HSE officials, and this can be seen as one of its most important roles, in keeping Ministers at arms length and so protecting HSE decisions from undue political interference. A further indication of a *de facto* unitary body is Schedule 2, paragraph 13 of the HSW Act, which provides,

> 'The Commission may authorise any member of the Commission or any officer or servant of the Commission or of the Executive to perform on behalf of the Commission such of the Commission's functions (including the function conferred on the Commission by this paragraph) as are specified in the authorisation.'

One indication of how the model was to work in practice was the early decision taken by the Commission to delegate its responsibilities to HSE.[1] This meant that, from early in its existence, HSE was acting not just as an enforcement agency but also as a body

---

[1] Letter from V.G. Munns, Secretary to the Health and Safety Commission, to M. Seals, Secretary to the Health and Safety Executive, 25 November 1976. The letter notes, 'At their meeting on 20 July 1976, the Commission decided to give a formal directive to the Executive under Section 11(4)(a) of the Health and Safety at Work etc Act 1974'. The letter further provides, 'The Commission directs the Executive to do all that is necessary on its behalf in relation to Section 11(1) and (2) of the Health and Safety at Work etc Act 1974 to: (i) prepare proposals for the decision of the Commission; (ii) make recommendations to the Commission from time to time; (iii) carry out the Commission's decisions.'

concerned with advice and research. This broad view of its role has been an essential element in the success of the organisation over the last 30 years. A further example of this dual role is the way the Industry Advisory Committees (IACs) operated until quite recently. The Health and Safety Commission has thirteen IACs, including for Agriculture, Construction and Health Services, and four Subject Advisory Committees, including on Toxic Substances. Membership of these committees was drawn from organisations representing employers and employees. The Confederation of British Industry (CBI) and the Trades Union Congress (TUC) were consulted about membership, but, in addition to HSE providing the secretariat, the Chair of these bodies also came from HSE, typically a senior inspector dealing with the industry concerned.

It would be wrong to suggest that this was a clear model, because the coverage of the advisory committees was patchy; many industries, including ones with strong trade union organisation were excluded, such as chemicals, motors, aerospace and engineering. Nevertheless, the advisory committees illustrated three key dynamics in the organisation: the relationship between employers and trade unions; the relationship between the representatives of the social partners on the HSC and IACs and their peak organisations; and the relationship between the policy arm of HSE and its inspector field force.

The way the HSC/E model developed reflected both the initial challenges faced by the organisation and the institutional structure and strength of trade unions and employers organisations.

Much of the early work of the Commission and the IACs was in developing regulations to implement the broad principles of the 1974 Act. The Single European Act 1986, which provided for qualified majority voting for health and safety matters, was a further stimulus for European Union (EU) legislation, leading to the implementation of the so-called Framework Directive of 1989 and the subsequent daughter directives covering issues such as noise, vibration and display screen equipment. A well-oiled machine developed, and Commission agendas in the 1980s and 1990s were dominated by consideration of draft regulations and guidance or consultation documents proposing regulations and/or Approved Codes of Practice. In addition, the Commission approved sector specific sets of guidance drawn up by IACs.

By any yardstick this was a successful operation. The involvement of the social partners at all stages of the process, through direct consultation, involvement in IACs, and at the Commission meant that regulations proposed by the Commission were practicable and carried the consent of those who were to implement them in practice. A process of bargained corporatism ensured that difficult issues were resolved, and the Commission effectively delivered the support of the TUC and the CBI.

Nevertheless, despite the success of the model in delivering a sound regulatory framework and, more importantly, an improvement in health and safety performance, stresses and strains were beginning to appear. Ministers began to challenge the custom and practice whereby the TUC and the CBI made nominations to the Commission, which were automatically successful. For example, in 1990 the Government appointed the then President of the Electricians, Electrical Technicians and Plumbers' Union (EETPU) to the Commission after the EETPU had been expelled from the TUC. Later, a representative from the Royal College of Nursing, a trade union not affiliated to the TUC, was appointed in 1996. Similarly, in 2000, Ministers signalled that they wanted to see a representative of small firms on the Commission. The independent members of the Commission began to play a bigger role, as Government recognised that the public interest was wider than agreement between the producer group members of the Commission. The first report of the Nolan Committee on standards in public life led to more rigorous and transparent procedures for the appointment of Commissioners.

All these developments were against the background of a decline in both trade union membership, and the coverage of collective bargaining, particularly the decline in national industry wide agreements. It is perhaps no surprise that one of the most successful of the IACs is that for Paper and Board; this is one of the few sectors where there is a formal agreement between the employers' organisation and the trade unions. Moreover, on the employers side, organisations such as the Institute of Directors (IoD) and the Engineering Employers Federation (EEF) have become more influential, and the small firms lobby, although more disparate, has become more vocal.

Behind these institutional factors are the changes in the economy and the labour market discussed in Chapter 1 of this volume. It became clear by 1999, a quarter of a century on from the Act, that a new look was needed at health and safety in this country.

THE REVITALISING CHALLENGE

In 1999, the Deputy Prime Minister, the Rt Hon John Prescott, and the HSC issued a consultation document, *Revitalising Health and Safety* (DETR 1999), and a final joint strategy document was issued in June 2000, entitled *Revitalising Health and Safety* (DETR 2000). The statement reflected on the substantial achievements since 1974, but noted the relatively poor performance on health compared with safety and the fact that safety improvements had plateaued in recent years.

Revitalising Health and Safety had three main elements: these were a set of outcome targets for 2010, ten strategic priorities, and 44 action points. The premise was that the basic structures of the health and safety system in Great Britain were sound, but that, as the title implied, new life and impetus were needed. Nevertheless, there were some radical ideas among the action points, and some have still to be implemented.

The outcome targets were: to reduce the number of working days lost per 100,000 workers from work-related injury and ill health by 30% by 2010; to reduce the incidence rate of fatal and major injury accidents by 10% by 2010; to reduce the incidence rate of cases of work-related ill health by 20% by 2010; and to achieve half the improvement under each target by 2004.

These outcome targets proved to be a major challenge for both the Executive and the Commission. Previously, the organisation had planned and been judged on the basis of measuring inputs and outputs, rather than outcomes. The discipline of thinking in terms of outcomes proved to be arduous, challenging, but ultimately rewarding. An extra stimulus was provided when the Department for Work and Pensions assumed responsibility for the work of the HSC and HSE in 2002, and this led to the introduction of quarterly reports from the Commission and the Executive to DWP Ministers on progress towards the *Revitalising* targets, now incorporated into DWP's Public Service Agreement (PSA) with HM Treasury.

One valuable by-product of the outcome targets was the stimulus given to improving data. The latest *Workplace Health and Safety Survey programme* (WHASS 2005/8) is designed to record health and safety conditions across British workplaces as perceived by workers and employers, and will provide valuable information in addition to the data collected via administrative sources (e.g. under the *Reporting of Injuries, Diseases and Dangerous Occurrences Regulations 1985)* and via the Labour Force Survey. As the data are published on an annual basis, precursor indicators have been developed to inform the quarterly reports.

More fundamentally, the outcome targets have forced the Commission and Executive to be more rigorous in setting priorities. Soon after the publication of *Revitalising Health and Safety,* the Board of HSE and the Commission met at a special meeting to consider the implications. An early outcome was the adoption of 8 priorities – Agriculture; Construction; Falls from Heights; Health Services; Musculo-skeletal Disorders; Slips and Trips; Workplace Transport; and Work-related Stress – chosen on the basis of large numbers of workers covered, high incidence rates, and ability of HSE to make a difference. In particular, these guided the work of HSE inspectors in the Field Operations Directorate (FOD). The priorities did not exclude HSE inspectors looking at other topics and sectors, but, nevertheless, was a clear attempt to impose priorities.

By the Autumn of 2002, it became clear that HSC/E was not likely to meet the outcome targets, particularly the midway targets set for 2004/05. A further stimulus was given by the outcome of the Spending Review for 2002, which gave HSC/E no extra money apart from a ring-fenced sum to implement the recommendations of Lord Cullen's report into the Ladbroke Grove train crash. With strong encouragement from DWP Ministers, the Commission and the Executive developed a new strategy, which was published in February 2004 (HSC 2004). Some of the key themes and challenges of this strategy are set out below, but what were most noteworthy were the development of a clearer strategic focus by the organisation and the lead given by the Commission.

Since the publication of *Revitalising Health and Safety,* the Commission began to develop a new role and form a new relationship with the Executive. DWP Ministers welcomed this process and, in 2004, Ministers set out their expectations of the role of Commissioners in a letter to them. Issues of corporate governance have become more important. A member of the Commission chairs the Audit Committee of HSE, and a Remuneration Committee makes recommendations about the pay of the three members of the Executive.

With the help of HSE's Director General, the Executive have recognised the primacy of the Commission in developing strategy and, in turn, the Commission have recognised the importance of not trying to micro-manage the organisation. So, instead of the Executive presenting papers to the Commission as near final pieces of work, the Executive consult the Commission at an earlier stage. Working and personal relations have improved, and more and more HSE staff recognise the value that Commission members can play in acting as ambassadors, helping to communicate HSC/E's work to external stakeholders, and acting as mentors or as a sounding board.

It would be fanciful to suggest that the constitutional conundrums set out above have been solved, and it is fair to state that not everyone in HSE or HSC is happy with the Commission acting more like a non-executive board and less like a model of bargained corporatism. The involvement of the social partners has not disappeared, but it is taking different forms from those which were typical of the first 25 years of the organisation.

The organisation has adapted its structure to changing circumstances. But has this been reflected in new ways of working? The following two examples suggest that it has.

Against the background of two years of sharply deteriorating safety performance, the Deputy Prime Minister convened the Construction Industry Summit in February 2001. The Chair of HSC chaired the conference, which was attended by the DPM, three other Government Ministers, and senior representatives from all parts of the construction industry, including major contractors, trade unions, architects and designers, and specialist sub-contractors. The outcome of the summit was agreement to a challenging set of targets for improving safety performance, and agreement by each of the main groupings to an action plan. HSE's Chief Inspector of Construction and his team played a key role in stimulating the industry to take action, and in helping them to make commitments at the summit.

The summit process was an early practical example of some of the concepts which were to become embedded in HSC's 2004 strategy statement (HSC 2004). For example, the summit showed the importance of intervening as high up the supply chain as possible, e.g. by engaging the major contractors. It showed the importance of HSE influencing behaviour by companies; it also showed the importance of non-regulatory measures, such as the commitment given to improve training and recognition of skills and competences through the Construction Skills Certification Scheme.

HSE played a key role in monitoring the commitments made at the summit, and accompanied this with carefully targeted enforcement campaigns, inspection 'blitzes' targeted on geographical locations and key hazards. A further summit in February 2005 confirmed that there had been considerable changes in the industry, though progress was still needed, and the latest figures of 71 fatalities in 2004/2005 show that the fatality rate is the lowest on record.

The summit applied new approaches to a traditionally hazardous industry. In contrast, HSC/E's work on stress shows new thinking to a problem that did not feature at all in the 1972 Robens Report: workplace stress, which accounts for 12.8 million working days lost in 2004.

In 2001, the Commission decided not to proceed with a regulation on stress, despite considerable support for such a measure, particularly among trade unions. The Commission recognised that, in contrast to many safety issues covered by regulations, the relationship between action by the employer and the incidence of stress in the workplace was not precise. Nevertheless, the Commission took account of the scientific evidence which showed that certain stressors *tended* to be associated with increased stress in the workplace, such as demands on the individual and the degree of control an individual had over his or her work; other stressors were change, relationships, role and support. The Commission agreed that a set of Management Standards should be developed, which would help both managers and employees analyse the situation in their own organisation and also map their conformity to the standard with the national mean.

The standards were piloted in 22 organisations in the public and private sectors, and were launched in the Autumn of 2004. HSE will take enforcement action if necessary, and one Improvement Notice served on a Hospital Trust for failing to carry out an adequate risk assessment received considerable publicity. Nevertheless, the main focus of HSE work is working with employers – particularly those in the public sector, where the incidence of stress is relatively high – encouraging them to take up the management standards and providing help and guidance.

How HSC/E is Seen Today

HSC/E's work over the last thirty years has won itself many friends. A MORI poll in 2005 shows that the public, and particularly Chief Executive Officers (CEOs), have a relatively high awareness and favourability rating of HSE compared with similar organisations. 83% of CEOs agree with HSE's vision, and 78% think that health and safety benefits their company.

Yet, HSC/E has its critics, many of whom are vocal. Tabloid newspapers regularly carry stories about quotidian and harmless activities, such as playing conkers or paddling in pools, which have been banned because of 'Health and Safety'. The next section explores how HSC should meet the challenge of promoting sensible health and safety, but many see HSC/E contributing to excessive risk aversion and the so-called 'compensation culture'.

The issues are not always as trivial as conkers – railway safety being a case in point. HSC/E assumed responsibility for rail safety in 1990, with staff transferring from the Department of Transport. The background was the rail crash at Clapham in 1988, leading to 35 fatalities and the growing unease about the perceived lack of independence of the Rail Inspectorate under the control of the Department for Transport. Also relevant was the Piper Alpha disaster in 1988, which exposed the dangers of safety in the off-shore oil industry being regulated by the Department of Energy, the same body responsible for economic sponsorship. HSC/E assumed responsibility for the off-shore oil sector in 1991.

The relationship between the railway industry, with its rule-based approach, and HSC/E, with its risk-based approach, was not a happy one, and was tested by four serious (and entirely preventable) incidents: a train passing through a red light at Southall in 1997, another signal passed at danger at Ladbroke Grove in 1999, a broken rail leading to derailment at Hatfield in 2000, and a defective set of points leading to a derailment at Potters Bar in 2002. The view of many in the rail industry was that 'accidents happen', and there was considerable resistance to the actions taken by HSE, including enforcement action. Before 1990, enforcement action was almost unheard of. In January 2004, the Government announced a review of the rail industry, and in July 2004 announced a number of conclusions, including the abolition of the Strategic Rail Authority and the transfer of rail safety from HSC/E to the Office of the Rail Regulator.

HSC/E has a robust relationship with many of the sectors it regulates; it is, after all, an independent regulator and not an industry sponsored body, but the railway industry is the only one in the author's experience where, despite extensive contact, there was a failure to agree on core principles such as 'reasonable practicability', the basis of HSE's requirement that risks should be reduced on an ALARP basis; i.e. as low as reasonably practicable. In contrast, the relationship with the off-shore oil industry was a much more productive one, with HSE working closely with the industry to transform a dated rules-based regime to a more modern risk-based approach.

Despite being a relatively small industry, the railway industry has had a high press and political profile. It has taken up more of the Chair's time than any other industry, and rail industry matters were taking up to one quarter of the Chair's time and that of HSE's Director General between 1999 and 2003.

HSC/E's relations with small firms raise a different set of issues, lack of contact rather than too much. Research carried out for HSE showed that many small firms do not approach HSE for advice and guidance for fear that they might be exposed to enforcement action. Moreover, many small firms saw HSE as an organisation of experts, talking to experts in large organisations. This research has prompted HSC/E to develop sources of advice free from the perceived fear of enforcement. HSC/E has realised that the sometimes baffling language of risk assessment may not be suitable for small firms who want to do the right thing for their staff on health and safety and want simple guidance on what to do.

On the other hand, there are many who think that HSC/E is not tough enough. One critic (Dalton 2000), who had been involved in IAC work from the union side, criticised the HSC/E for adopting a cosy consensus. Pressure groups, such as the Centre for Corporate Accountability, have criticised HSC/E for relatively weak enforcement and excessive discretion. There are *prima facie* grounds to support this critique. Fines for health and safety offences are relatively low, an average of £14,702 in 2003/2004 for all offences. Although harm cannot always be equated with culpability, the average fine of £42,795 for an offence leading to a fatality seems hard to justify when other regulatory offences can lead to much higher fines in the Courts. Many critics argue that fines for health and safety offences are too low for them to have a deterrent effect or act as punishment for careless or reckless behaviour; this has led to calls for other punishments, including making individual directors and employees personally liable and accountable.

Moreover, set against the total number of enterprises, some 1.7 million covered by HSE, it would be difficult to characterise HSE as an intrusive regulator. In 2003/2004 HSE inspectors made 200,000 visits to companies – this led to HSE issuing 6,776 Improvement Notices, 4,438 Prohibition Notices and taking 1,756 prosecutions. Many critics point out that, on average, each workplace in Britain will receive a visit from an HSE inspector once every 10 years, and that HSE only investigates 7% of the incidents notified to it.

The recent report of the Work and Pensions Select Committee (WPSC 2004) encapsulated many of the criticisms of HSE made by trade unions and other campaigning groups. The Select Committee acknowledged that HSC/E was a high quality organisation and that Great Britain has one of the best safety records in Europe. It was, however, concerned about limited progress in reaching the *Revitalising* targets discussed above, and called for a number of measures, including more resources for HSE, more front line inspection (as opposed to increased education, information and advice), and empowering trade union nominated safety representatives to enforce health and safety law, including powers to take prosecutions and issue Improvement and Prohibition Notices. The Select Committee made a number of other recommendations, supportive of many current

HSC/E initiatives, all of them entailing extra resources. No suggestions were made for work to be reduced.

Against the background of critics from both sides of the argument, it would be tempting, but nevertheless complacent, to fall back on the argument that HSC/E has automatically got the balance right. Although the HSC/E model has worked well over the last 30 years, considerable challenges remain, and three of these are explored in the next section.

CHALLENGES

The first major challenge is for HSC/E to maintain and improve public trust and confidence in its role as an independent and respected safety regulator. As the MORI polls show, HSC/E enjoys a high level of public trust and confidence, but the continuation of that trust cannot be taken for granted. Today's public is more questioning and less deferential than 30 years ago, less tolerant of health and safety failures by companies, and also more willing to hold the regulator to account. The establishment of the Food Standards Agency (FSA) in April 2000 set a new standard for regulators: FSA's meetings are held in public and, subject to certain qualifications, its advice to Ministers is also made public. HSC/E was already a relatively open organisation, with much information freely available on its web site, but an important step forward was made in April 2005, when HSC opened up all of its regular monthly meetings to members of the public. In addition, HSC has agreed that its advice to Ministers should also be in the public domain, though, at the time of writing, this had not been accepted by all Government Departments.

HSC/E needs to engage its stakeholders and public more if its decisions on resource allocation are to command confidence and support. More resources for HSC/E, as called for by the Select Committee, would be welcome, but hard choices would still have to be made about how those should be allocated – for example, when considering the work of inspectors, what should be the balance between pro-active work, such as preventative inspection, and reactive work, such as investigation of incidents and prosecutions? At present, the balance is 60/40, with greater emphasis on pro-active work, the argument being that HSC/E's primary function is to help prevent accidents and injuries happening in the first place.

HSC/E also needs to engage the public and politicians on the balance between strict enforcement action and less formal methods of persuasion. HSE has never been just a prosecutor, but HSE and local authorities will have to do more if the choices made about different intervention techniques are accepted as fair and reasonable.

The present Government has taken a number of measures to address the issue of regulatory burdens and 'red tape'. As a modern regulator, HSC/E will need to show the benefits of sound regulation, but also the limits. The achievement of the targets mentioned above will depend on more employers adopting good and best practice, rather than relying on regulatory compliance.

HSC/E will have to do more to engage the public, and be seen to be doing so, if it is to retain public trust. HSC/E must continue to maintain its strong scientific and technical base, but, as many other organisations have found out, trust in the 'expert' view cannot be taken for granted.

This is pertinent to a second challenge alluded to earlier, namely, how to treat risk. A risk free society is neither desirable nor attainable. Yet, how much risk is society willing to tolerate? The moral and financial costs of health and safety failures are immense. But excessive risk aversion has its costs too: Where organisations feel that they must fill out pages of risk assessments before undertaking even simple, low risk tasks, they become mired in bureaucracy. That stands to damage their competitiveness and ability to innovate. At its worst, excessive risk-aversion can also curb our personal freedoms and opportunities. Children, in particular, need to learn how to manage risks, and adventure activities such as rock climbing, sailing and canoeing are an ideal way of doing this. And if rules were imposed which made it more difficult for children to swim, then, surely, the net result will be fewer children able to swim, and more at greater risk in later life. The debate becomes particularly tricky when dealing with extremely low probability but high consequence events. How extensive should residential and commercial development be allowed to take place close to chemical plants and oil refineries? How should we deal with the so-called 'Dread factor', the aversion that society has to certain risks, e.g. cancer-causing chemicals, or large numbers of people being killed or injured in one event? There are no 'right' technical answers to these questions. Probabilistic risk assessment can help, but, ultimately, the choices have to be made. HSC/E can help inform and educate the debate.

A third challenge is how HSC/E continues to cope with the changing world of work and the organisational changes affecting both employers and employees. This chapter has set out how HSC/E has adapted to recent changes. The underlying elements of the HSC/E model remain sound, but further adaptation will be needed.

Almost half of the working population now work in the local authority enforced sector. Moreover, it is the sector with Britain's biggest private sector employers, and the sector with the fastest rate of employment growth. More is being done to engage local authorities in the work of HSC/E, but the relationship is not a perfect one, and local authorities face competing pressures for Environmental Health Officer resources, both locally and from other central government regulators.

A recent development has been the growth of new ways of consulting HSC/E's stakeholders and the public. HSC can no longer rely solely on using a limited number of peak organisations as conduits for consultation. This is particularly true when it comes to engaging small firms; employers may not be a member of a trade association, and employees typically will not belong to a trade union. It is also true about engaging members of the public. Recently, on issues such as gas safety and rail safety, HSC/E has made use of opinion poll research and focus groups to probe public attitudes more deeply.

All of these developments beg the question about the appropriateness of the HSC/E model in the 21st Century. The *de jure* split between the Commission and the Executive is confusing to the outside world (and not properly understood internally in HSE). The case for a unitary model is strong, and it is clear that a national health and safety body set up today would not have the structure set out in the 1974 Act. It is unlikely that a new body would have the same formal tripartite structure, but there is no doubt that any such body would have to find ways of consulting workers and employees, and other interest groups. The case for reform is compelling but not urgent, given other legislative priorities. Moreover, the present legislative structure ought to be flexible enough to cope with the changes in the economy and the labour market.

But the model will be less one of bargained corporatism, one that relies on a hierarchy paradigm, and more one of influencing, one that is based on a network paradigm (Greener 2005). Much of these changes will be seen beneath the level of the Commission and the Board of HSE, and will undoubtedly lead to more complexity in governance. Such a model reflects the fact that different groups have to be engaged on different topics. Of course, there will still need to be a role for the peak organisations, such as the CBI and the TUC, but the continuing success of the HSC/E will depend on how successful it is in engaging a wide range of different and new stakeholders.

REFERENCES

Dalton, A. (2000): *Consensus Kills* (London)

DETR (1999): *Revitalising Health and Safety,* Consultation Document. July 1999 (Department of Environment, Transport and the Regions, London)

DETR (2000): *Revitalising Health and Safety,* Strategy Statement. June 2000 (Department of Environment, Transport and the Regions, London)

Greener, I. (2005): 'Managing through Networks: Public Management and Human Agency'. Paper presented to *Governance without Government Conference,* Cardiff University, May 2005. Available: www.cardiff.ac.uk/carbs/conferences/past.gov05.html

HC WPSC (2004): House of Commons Work and Pensions Committee 2004. *The Work of the Health and Safety Commission and Executive Fourth Report of Session 2003-04 HC 456.* July 2004 (The Stationery Office, London)

HSC (2004): Health and Safety Commission, *A strategy for workplace health and safety in Great Britain to 2010 and beyond* (Health and Safety Executive, Bootle). Available at www.hse.gov.uk/aboutus/hsc/strategy.html

Robens (1972): *Safety and Health at Work: Report of the Committee 1970-72,* Cmnd. 5034. July 1972 (HMSO, London)

Ewart Keep

TRAINING AND SKILLS

An Institutional Patchwork

INTRODUCTION

This chapter differs from the others in this section in three ways. First, it focuses only on England rather than the United Kingdom as a whole. The vast bulk of legislative and administrative powers concerned with employee relations have not been devolved, and remain a UK-wide issue controlled from Westminster and Whitehall. Vocational education and training (VET) is different. In Scotland, and to a much lesser extent Wales and Northern Ireland, VET has long been dealt with differently from England, and with formal moves to national governmental devolution it has become a fully devolved issue controlled by national parliaments or assemblies. As a result, the four UK governments are developing divergent VET systems and, for reasons of space alone, only England can be dealt with here.

The second point of distinction is that, whereas other chapters deal with a single institution, this chapter addresses a constantly shifting system of finance, governance and inspection. There is no single national body that runs the creation and delivery of training and skills policy – there is a complex and evolving patchwork of central government departments, agencies and 'quangos', many with a regional or local focus.

Third, in contrast to much else in this section of the volume, one of the main functions of this chapter is to explain why there is little sign of meaningful social partnership within the area it surveys. As will be suggested below, this absence helps to define the difference of approach to VET between England and most other European Union States.

THE INSTITUTIONS OF VET

In the area of education and training, the past really is always with us. Current concerns about performance in the field of VET are but the latest cycle in a perceived 'crisis' that stretches back a century and a half. Since at least the Great Exhibition and the mid-1850s, commentators and policy makers have gone through phases of concern at the apparent gap between our efforts to invest in the skills and learning of the workforce and that of overseas nations. In the 19th Century the main comparisons were with France, America and Germany. In more recent times, Asian States and the developing world (such as India and China) have been added to the list (see Perry 1976; Institute of Manpower

Linda Dickens & Alan C. Neal (eds), The Changing Institutional Face of British Employment Relations 49-61
© *2006 Kluwer Law International. Printed in the Netherlands*

Studies/Manpower Services Commission/National Economic Development Office 1984; Ainley & Corney 1990; and Brown, Green, & Lauder 2001).

The important point to note is that the longevity of the problem suggests deeply embedded causes. If our weaknesses with VET could be solved through tinkering with the skills supply system, it is surprising that by now success has not attended these efforts. As will be suggested below, many now believe that at least part of the problem is to be found in weak demand for skill, the reasons for which lie within the way our economy is structured and managed.

The Growing Status of VET

One of the reasons for the priority afforded to VET policy, and for the increasingly frantic pace of institutional change that has resulted, is the lengthening list of policy issues and problems that it is believed that more and better skills can tackle. It is widely assumed that higher levels of skill can be used to address relative weaknesses in productivity; boost gross domestic product (GDP); increase international competitiveness; combat poverty and enhance social inclusion; create well-motivated, self-reliant workers; and promote active citizenship. As governments have concluded (for whatever reason) that it is no longer practical and/or legitimate to intervene in other ways within the economic and social spheres – for example, through personal taxation to aid the redistribution of wealth, or through an industrial policy – so the importance of boosting the supply of VET has grown. Expanding VET has been seen as an ideologically neutral form of intervention, and one that commands (at least at a superficial level) support across the political spectrum.

As the salience of VET to economic and social policy has grown, an increasing number of government departments have laid claim to an interest in, and influence over, VET policy. These now include the Department for Education and Skills (DfES), the Department for Trade and Industry (DTI), the Department for Work and Pensions (DWP), the Treasury, and the Cabinet Office. To this cast list can be added the occupants of Numbers 10 and 11 Downing Street and their advisors. It is these actors who determine the overall thrust of VET policy and who design the institutions that plan, fund, deliver and monitor education and training.

Thus VET commands a degree of political salience denied many of the other areas of activity reviewed in this volume. For example, skills are seen by the Treasury and the DTI to be one of the five drivers of productivity, whereas employee relations are not.

The Institutions of VET – Complexity and Change

In the space available, it is impossible to chart in detail the evolution of the English VET system over the past three decades. The only constant has been change, on a massive scale. This has embraced all aspects of the VET system, from responsibility for the design of qualifications to funding systems, to the inspection of publicly-funded adult learning.

During the early 1960s, concern at the failure of a voluntary approach to skill formation led to the introduction (in 1964) of statutory Industrial Training Boards (ITBs), which could raise a compulsory levy on employers in their sector to pay for training. The ITBs were initially designed to be an indirect form of government intervention, with finance coming from industry and control of training remaining in the hands of the employers and trade unions that sat on Boards. All but two of the ITBs were abolished during the 1980s (most in 1981, the rest in 1988) by a Conservative government committed to a wider package of reform of the labour market and labour market institutions. Subsequent New Labour administrations have repeatedly ruled out a return to any blanket legal compulsion on employers to train of the type, for example through compulsory levies.

Experiments with tripartism and social partnership arrangements, embodied in the creation of the Manpower Services Commission (MSC) in 1974, were abandoned by the Thatcher government in 1987. The MSC survived for eight years under Conservative government because it played a key role in designing and implementing schemes to reduce unemployment (particularly youth unemployment via the Youth Training Scheme – YTS). Once the unemployment had peaked and schemes to deal with it were firmly in place, its fate was sealed. In future, the key theme of institution building was to be the creation of bipartite bodies that could cement an effective partnership between government and employers. As we will see, this has proved an illusive goal.

From the early-1980s onward, the VET system entered into a period of non-stop institutional and programmatic reform, the end of which is not yet in sight. One important aspect of this frantic activity has been adherence by government (of whatever political persuasion) to what might be termed a 'Michael Jackson style' school of institution building. Much like the pop star, government has looked in the mirror, not liked what it has seen, and therefore sought to change it, frequently and repeatedly. Thus, since 1981, central government policy makers have been shaking the institutional kaleidoscope in the hope that the next pattern will be prettier than the last.

The results have been a lengthy period of constant revolution, which has amassed a long list of institutional casualties – the National Training Task Force (NTTF), the Manpower Services Commission, Local Employer Networks (LENs), the Skills Training Agency (STA), the National Council for Vocational Qualifications (NCVQ), the Further Education Funding Council (FEFC), the National Advisory Committee on the Education and Training Targets (NACETT), and the Training and Enterprise Councils (TECs). This has meant a limited half-life for major institutions, with associated problems of stability and recognition, not least among employers, parents, students and others who need to use the VET system.

Moreover, despite serial disappointments, those charged with superintending these constant make-overs maintain a firm belief that, 'it's always going to be better next time…'. At each turn it has been announced that the latest institutional remodelling would deliver the desired revolution in attitudes towards training and skills. In some respects, this revolution is still awaited.

The constant underlying and often unacknowledged trend throughout the period has been the growth of direct intervention by the State – in the form of central government and its agencies. The scale of this development is insufficiently appreciated. For example, in 1981 the role of the State in training was relatively minor. Policy was chiefly in the hands of a tripartite MSC, which reported to the Employment Department, but which maintained a significant degree of autonomy from central government. The MSC's involvement in the provision of skills and training was limited to:

- a work experience scheme for the young unemployed (Youth Opportunities Programme – YOP);
- funding a small-scale experimental training scheme for employed young people not undergoing apprenticeship – the Unified Vocational Preparation programme (UVP);
- work experience/training schemes for the adult unemployed, particularly the Community Programme and the Training Opportunities Programme (TOPs);
- the funding of the operating costs of the statutory Industrial Training Boards (ITBs);
- funding and operating a set of government training workshop establishments;
- some low level skills forecasting activity.

The vast bulk of the MSC's spending went on work experience for the unemployed, rather than on skills training. In education, the management of schools and colleges was in the hands of local government, and the largest single direct managerial responsibility held by the then Department for Education and Science (DES) was the running of the schoolteachers' pension scheme.

Since then, within both education and training, central government has extended its influence to a massive degree. In education, the role of Local Education Authorities (LEAs) has been reduced to one of marginal player, while at the same time an 'awesomely centralised' national school curriculum and testing regime has been imposed (Jenkins 1995:121), the qualifications system rationalised and placed under direct State supervision, and semi-autonomous funding councils abolished in favour of much more *dirigiste* bodies. The resulting shift has been characterised as one representing delocalisation, centralisation and nationalisation (Bash & Coulby 1989:17). In the area of skills, tripartism has been abandoned, to be replaced by a range of agencies of central government, delivering training programmes largely designed by ministers and civil servants. In 1981, the role of central government was relatively minor. Today it is paramount.

The System as It Stands Today

A thumbnail sketch of the system as it currently stands is as follows. At the top of the policy food chain stands the Treasury and No.10 Downing Street, who appear to set the over-arching rationale for policy in the field, and to design initiatives that are deemed particularly central to the interests of the Prime Minister and Chancellor. On the next rung down is the DfES, with DWP and DTI in a less central role. DfES designs the detail of most skills policy and supervises the bulk of agencies that deliver its implementation.

As with many of aspects of governmental activity, VET is managed through a set of targets, some set by the Treasury (the Public Service Agreement (PSA) targets), others by DfES or the agencies that work for it. The relationship between many of these targets and real need for skill in the labour market is often extremely obscure.

The central tenets of the government's current skills policy are embodied in the Skills Strategy, and, between the assemblage of central government outlined above and the phalanx of agencies discussed below, sits the Skills Alliance which superintends the progress of the Skills Strategy. This is made up of the departments listed above, the prime delivery agencies, and representatives from the Small Business Council, the CBI and the TUC. The Alliance has two sub-divisions – the Delivery Group (made up of bodies such as the LSC, Jobcentre Plus, and the Higher Education Funding Council for England), and the Social and Economic Partnership (comprising the four government departments, a regional development agency, the CBI, TUC, Small Business Council and the National Institute of Adult and Continuing Education (NIACE). The Delivery Group meets three times a year, the Social Partnership six monthly. The Alliance exists to co-ordinate the delivery of the Skills Strategy, and to monitor progress. It appears to have little formal power, does not establish targets or control spending priorities, and exists to implement a strategy that is already cast in iron.

Beneath this come the agencies and 'quangos', of which there are many. Only the most significant are discussed here. Publicly-funded training is planned and funded via the Learning and Skills Council (LSC), which has 47 local offices – Local Learning and Skills Councils (LLSC). The LSC channels money to further education, VIth form colleges, apprenticeships, and a range of adult learning provision in the workplace and outside. The LSC has no major formal role in policy formation, it proclaims itself to be there to deliver government policy. The members of the national Learning and Skills Council and the LLSCs are all appointed by, and are accountable to, the Secretary of State for Education and Skills. In the language of eighteenth Century politics, they are placemen (and women). They serve solely in an individual capacity.

The arrival of devolution within England, in the shape of the Regional Development Agencies (RDAs) has established another layer of planning and control to the VET system. RDAs have a remit that includes skill and its links to local economic development, and, via what are termed Regional Skills Partnerships (RSPs) RDAs are expected to work with employers and the relevant LLSCs (now organised in regional groupings) to forecast future skill need and plan provision to meet economic development aims.

With national (LSC), local (LLSC) and regional (RDA) levels in place, the remaining requirement for the perfect planning system is a regional focus. It would require a separate chapter to do justice to the twisting and complex narrative that surrounds efforts to establish properly functioning sectoral foci for VET activity. After the abolition of the vast bulk of the statutory ITBs during the 1980s, there followed a succession of attempts to fill the gap left by their disappearance. First came the Non-Statutory Training Organisations (NSTOs), then the Industry Training Organisations (ITOs), which were soon replaced by the National Training Organisations (NTOs). In 2002, the NTOs were abolished by government and replaced by the Skills for Business Network (SBN), to be made up of around 30 Sector Skills Councils (SSCs), superintended by a governmental agency – the Sector Skills Development Agency (SSDA). The SSCs are expected to have a dual role – dealing with skills issues and business development within their sector.

The important point to note is that the succession of changes sketched above has been largely at the behest of, and under the control of, central government rather than employers themselves. Even in an area where employers are nominally in charge, the State often still determines the form and function of activity. Thus, the new Sectoral Skills Councils (SSCs) are supposed to be employer-led, but their overall remit and the shape and size of the network that they are to form has been determined by the DfES, their core activities are State funded, they are licensed by an agency of the State, and many of their key priorities are set by agencies of the State.

In addition to these leading institutions, comes an extensive supporting cast of inspectorial, quality improvement, and curriculum and qualifications design and licensing bodies. Examples include the Adult Learning Inspectorate (ALI), the Qualifications and Curriculum Authority (QCA), and the new body for Quality Improvement in Lifelong Learning.

This system is the mechanism for delivering a complex and shifting array of programmes, learning opportunities and qualifications, some aimed at initial entrants to the labour market, others at adult workers. These include junior, foundation and advanced apprenticeships; Investors in People (IIP), the Employer Training Pilots (ETPs), and Skill Passports.

THE RETURN OF 'MANPOWER PLANNING'

As hinted at above, one of the core functions of this edifice is to plan VET provision. 'Manpower planning' was very briefly and mildly in vogue in the mid- to late 1970s. Thereafter the fashion was for a training market. In the first years of the 21st Century government decided that the best way to avoid skills shortages was to establish an elaborate system that linked labour market forecasting (based on economic modelling), employers' views about the nature and scale of future skill needs, and funding of the VET system. One of the LSC's central functions was to bring this about. The overall aim is to match supply with demand – though what this means in practice is not wholly clear (Keep 2002).

The means to achieve this ambitious objective involves a complex web of overlapping multi-level planning mechanisms that embrace the Treasury's PSA targets, the LSC's plans and targets, 47 LLSCs' plans and targets, 9 RDA Regional Economic Strategies which then plan the skills component via the 9 Regional Skills Partnerships (RSPs). These include input from the SSCs and the relevant LLSCs. At the same time, 30 SSCs, (plus SSDA) will each be producing over the coming years their Sector Skills Agreements (SSAs), which project sectoral needs, identify the training needed to meet it, and to which public funding of VET is meant to be tied.

The belief is that all these plans will somehow 'meet up in the middle'. There is a range of technical problems with such an approach (which space forbids exploration of here), but early indications suggest that the planning system is liable to face substantial tensions. While indicative planning is a useful tool, seeking to match supply and demand is extremely problematic. The interests and needs of the different players do not always coincide, and some resources (talented people and the money to train them) are finite and liable to be the subject of zero sum games (Keep 2002). Moreover, individuals often want different outcomes from employers.

England is unusual, at least in a European context, in choosing to define the needs of the labour market solely in terms of the needs of employers. In other countries, the norm is for social partnership arrangements, and the active involvement of worker representatives in the management of the VET system, to thereby ensure that such needs are conceptualised in terms of the wider requirements of employment and employability rather than the immediate skill demand of employers alone.

EMPLOYERS, TRADE UNIONS AND SOCIAL PARTNERSHIP

In terms of its style of governance, how might the structure detailed above be typified? The government argues that it is at once 'employer-led', but also characterised by social partnership, particularly in relation to the Skills Alliance. What are we to make of these claims?

Social Partnership

There are two problems with efforts to paint the English VET system as one where social partnership matters. First, as suggested above, the role of the Skills Alliance is supervisory and its powers very limited. It in no way replicates the strength of semi-independent policy formation and governance afforded to the tripartite MSC. Second, at all levels beneath it even the vaguest semblance of social partnership structures is absent. Trade unionists serve in limited numbers within a range of bodies and agencies, but in an individual, not representative capacity, and they lack numerical parity with employer representatives.

Employers and Employer Leadership

The saga of sectoral representation within English VET and the oddity of the SSCs as employer bodies are symptoms of a deeper malaise. The gap between the rhetorical expectations created by claims of employer leadership and the reality remains very substantial. Employer involvement in publicly-funded VET is limited, while at the same time employers' own training provision exists largely outside the public VET system. Integration between public and private provision is generally weak. The fate of attempts to revive apprenticeships from the mid-1990s onwards acts as an example of very patchy employer engagement with, and commitment towards, national policy. Despite much talk of apprenticeship as something run by employers, the reality is that it largely remains a government programme, with no more than about 3% or 4% of employers involved, and the vast bulk of delivery (more than 80%) in the hands of training providers rather than

55

individual employers. In many sectors, completion rates remain very low (below 30% in some instances), because firms remove apprentices from the programme before certification is awarded.

It is also very difficult to be clear about the rights, roles and responsibilities of employers. In terms of what public policy might reasonably expect a division of labour to be when it comes to training the workforce, the answer is very vague, as this is an issue that has been fudged and dodged for a long time. For instance, on several occasions in the recent past, task-specific training for adult employees has been identified by government or its agencies as an employer responsibility, yet in 2005 plans are being rolled out for a national system of State subsidy – the National Employer Training Programme – precisely to deliver job-specific vocational qualifications to adult employees with low prior levels of attainment. It is therefore likely that the role of employers, particularly with regards to the funding of VET provision, will continue to be the focus of much debate and some anguish.

Some of these problems stem from the overall weakness and fragmentation of the bodies that represent employers. Our atomised and increasingly patchy system of collective bargaining deprives us of the kinds of relatively powerful and cohesive employer collectivities seen in other EU countries where sectoral and national bargaining persists. They also reflect the fact that the United Kingdom as a whole has a voluntaristic training system – i.e. employers are not compelled by law, except in certain circumstances (such as in relation to food hygiene or health and safety) to offer training to their workforce. Since the abolition of the bulk of the statutory ITBs, responsibility for decisions about the volume and level of training, and who gets access to it, has rested in the hands of managers, with the State lacking any leverage on these decisions other than through exhortation and State subsidy. By contrast, in many other European countries, various aspects of labour market regulation confer rights to be trained on employees, and a duty to support certain types of training provision upon employers.

The Role of Trade Unions

During the 1980s, the Conservative government reduced the role of trade unions within VET. In part this was achieved through its wider policies to diminish union power and influence. The other element was to remove trade unions' rights to be represented within the machinery of VET policy formulation. Since 1997 and the return of a New Labour government, trade unions have been invited in from the cold, but only, it might be argued, as far as the porch.

The chief developments have been the development of the Union Learning Fund (provided by government); the enshrining in legislation of a new type of union representation in the workplace – the Union Learning Representative – with rights to be provided by employers with facilities and time to perform their duties; the development of campaigns such as UNISON's 'Return to Learn' initiative, which aims to engage low-paid public sector workers in adult learning of all kinds; and attempts by the TUC to promote collective bargaining over skills issues among its member unions. The latter has been attended by limited success. Initial results from the 2004 *Workplace Employment*

Relations Survey (WERS) suggest that, in workplaces with recognised trade unions, bargaining over training took place in just 9% of them (Kersley *et al* 2005). Again, the contrast with Europe, where in countries such as Spain and France collective agreements on skills (usually at sectoral or national levels) are significant, could hardly be clearer.

Overall, the main emphasis has been upon unions acting as evangelists for learning to their own membership. Such a role is valuable and worthwhile, but it affords very limited influence to the unions over the wider shape and direction of VET policy. What the government has not been willing to contemplate is affording unions a comparable level of influence and representation within the machinery of VET policy as is given to employers. In this sense, European-style social partnership arrangements, that are common in the governance of VET issues across much of the EU, remain a distant dream for United Kingdom unions. It is a salutary fact that, during the early years of the Thatcher governments, right up until the abolition of the tripartite MSC in 1987, the TUC probably had greater real influence over the design and conduct of VET policy than it does today, after more than eight years of New Labour government. In the absence of meaningful and institutionally embedded social partnership arrangements at all levels of the VET system, and without legal rights to bargain over skills, the unions find themselves operating at the margins rather than the centre of skills policy.

The other huge problem with the role of unions is that it is limited to those workplaces wherein unions have a presence. This means that the potentially beneficial effects of ULRs are absent from precisely those workplaces and workforces (in sectors such as hotels, catering, or contract cleaning) where adult learning opportunities are known to be weakest.

THE PATHOLOGY OF AN OVER-ACTIVE STATE

How are we to explain the overall picture that has so far been presented? There are many approaches that might be assayed, but the one adopted here focuses on the role of the State. Put simply, the problem is that an over-ambitious and over-active national administration has come to 'crowd out' other actors, and to monopolise and centralise control of the VET system in ways that are ultimately likely to prove counter-productive.

Why has this happened? The reasons are complex, but one reading of the problem goes as follows.

The Paradoxes of Weakness and Strength

The weakness of the other stakeholders within the VET system creates a paradox for government. It gives the State great latitude in what it does, as other actors are unable to challenge its priorities. The downside is that the under-development of bodies that might represent the interests of employers means that much that in other countries is done through and by the social partners has here to be undertaken by the State. In many instances, the State's public policy goals exceed the capacity or willingness of other actors to deliver them. In such circumstances, the State feels obliged to step in as substitute.

As suggested above, this situation in part reflects the barriers that confront attempts at building up institutions that can concert, represent and mobilise employer interests around skills. Such efforts have taken place against the unhelpful backdrop of a de-regulated product and labour market, and generally weak employer bodies. This renders the design and maintenance of employer institutions that can deliver collective incentives to train extremely difficult (Streeck 1989).

As a consequence, although the concept of employer leadership within the VET system has been a growing element of government rhetoric, as suggested above, it remains unclear what real influence government is willing to afford employers. In many cases, the role government allots to them is a subordinate one, as recipients of public subsidy and delivery agents for an ever-growing list of schemes and institutions that the government has designed for them.

State intervention in, and funding of, VET is also borne out of weakness on the part of the State, in that it acts as a substitute for other measures that might impact on employers, but which are deemed no longer politically and ideologically unacceptable. This is because the English State's commitment to de-regulation renders unavailable many policy interventions used in other countries, such as training levies, strong trade unions that can block off access to competitiveness through low wages, statutory rights to collective bargaining on skills, strong forms of social partnership arrangement, regulated labour and product markets (such as extensive licence to practice requirements), or an industrial policy that might favour higher skill sectors.

Thus, the political space within which VET policy is developed and directed is delimited by higher order decisions concerning labour market regulation and models of economic management. This produces an interesting result. On the one hand, choices in higher order policy domains dictate the subordinate political space available for VET policy. Ideological 'no-go zones' mean that English VET policy makers find themselves with a very limited room for policy development or experimentation. The firm has to be treated more or less as a 'black box', and this makes attempts to secure change in competitive strategy, product or service specification, work organisation and job design extremely problematic. On the other hand, these prior ideological constraints that limit what lines VET policy might take simultaneously invest VET with greater salience, since they render it one of the few avenues available for legitimate government intervention in the economic sphere.

As a result, government is trapped by the importance it has vested in VET. If skills are so critical to economic success, the State cannot easily be seen to leave their delivery to others, particularly when some of these others, such as employers, appear unable or unwilling to deliver what it is alleged is required.

The Continuity at the Heart of VET Policy

The main reason why the broad thrust of VET policy under New Labour has exhibited many elements of continuity with the policy trajectory developed by Conservative administrations over the preceding seventeen years is because the underlying ideological assumptions have also remained constant. The main intellectual underpinnings have remained constant in the narrow and impoverished fare of de-contextualised forecasts of universal upward trends in demand for skill, and simple readings of human capital theory and market failure.

The main change has been the willing of New Labour to load additional social inclusion and social equity expectations onto VET. Given limited development in the underlying directions of policy intervention, these have simply increased the need for the State to intervene to supply what is required.

ENGLAND – 'ODD MAN OUT' AGAIN

The centralisation of English VET run counter to trends elsewhere in Europe, where, over the last decade in countries such as the Netherlands, Italy, Sweden and Finland, policy has been devolved to local social partnership arrangements, wherein the governmental role is taken up by elected local authorities or municipalities. In Germany, the *länder* have a key role in determining how education and training is conducted, while, in the USA, the role of the federal government is small, with VET policy generally devolved to the level of the individual State and below.

These developments reflect a general on-going trend within the English polity towards a greater centralisation of political power, a diminution in the role and influence of locally elected government, and the substitution of 'quangos' for locally accountable institutions. Other areas that exemplify this thrust included the police service and the National Health Service.

THE FUTURE

In the short term, the current government has indicated that it desires a shift whereby employers (and, to a much lesser extent, other partners like trade unions) will of their own volition do more to deliver public policy goals within a framework set by the State. This is coupled with the dawning of a realisation that the government needs to deploy public training spending to leverage employer investment, and to link public policy interventions with employers' own training efforts.

The success of these moves depends, to some extent at least, on the willingness for the State to come to terms with what a more demand and employer-led system might look like. As this chapter has indicated, at present the State finds itself in danger of being trapped in a situation where it has to do more and more, leaving less and less opportunity or motive for others to play a more active role in the VET system and develop their capacity to act as strong partners.

In the longer term, more broad-ranging change may be needed. After a quarter of a century of policy aimed at expanding the supply of skills (as measured through qualifications), largely at public expense, there has begun to dawn a realisation on the part of some in the policy community that this may be a necessary pre-condition, but on its own is not sufficient, to usher in economic and social transformation. There has also been a gradual acceptance that the United Kingdom's relatively low levels of VET *vis-à-vis* other developed nations may reflect the fact that demand for skill in the economy is relatively limited. As a result, the belief is starting to spread that perhaps training more people and supplying more skills is the easy first stage of the policy process, rather than the end of the story.

How has this change in perception come about? The main answer is that it reflects the slow percolation of research findings into the public domain. Business and skills researchers have evolved considerably more sophisticated models of the relationship between skill and other factors of production, and of the relationship between the supply of, demand for, and utilisation of skill. Of particular importance has been the mounting evidence that higher product or service specification/quality is positively associated with the need for higher levels of skill. These models and a range of empirical findings suggest that significant parts of the economy appear locked in to producing relatively low specification, lower quality goods and services that do not require high levels of skill to deliver them (Keep 2005).

This body of work was taken up by the Cabinet Office's Performance and Innovation Unit (PIU) project on workforce development. The PIU concluded (Cabinet Office Performance and Innovation Unit 2001:74) that:

> 'Workforce development needs to be addressed in the wider context of government and business strategies towards product strategy, innovation, market positioning, IT, human resources policies and so on.'

This analysis has opened the door to a new type of skill policy, whereby the aim is to supply more skills and simultaneously seek to help firms to move up market, become more profitable, increase productivity, develop new markets, organise work differently, and use skills better. Such a policy embraces business support to firms; cluster, network and supply chain development; innovation policy, public support for R&D; and economic regeneration and regional policy. The key goal becomes the engineering of mutually supportive interactions between these different elements.

This kind of policy agenda, which is gradually beginning to be discussed and may become integrated into mainstream thinking, demands a very different approach from one based on boosting skills supply alone. In particular, the kind of transformation being aimed at requires considerable political commitment (at national, regional and local level) and will need 'buy in' from a wide range of actors. This suggests that, for example, the business development role of SSCs may prove to be the key to their potential to produce better outcomes than earlier bodies whose remit was focused on skills alone. At present, traditional skills supply policies are in increasing tension with the kind of broader approach to policy outlined above.

Conceived of more generally, such an approach suggests wider attempts by public policy to influence what goes on in the 'black box' of the organisation and workplace, and holds out the promise of revitalised debate on issues such as work organisation and job design. Lessons from elsewhere in Europe suggest that such issues are best tackled through social partnership models of institution and programme building. Whether this is enough to promote more genuine moves towards social partnership here is open to debate.

REFERENCES

Ainley, P. & Corney, M. (1990): *Training for the Future: The Rise and Fall of the MSC* (Cassell, London)

Bash, L. & Coulby, D. (eds) (1989): *The Education Reform Act: Competition and Control* (Cassell, London)

Brown, P., Green, A., & Lauder, H. (eds) (2001): *High Skills – Globalisation, Competitiveness and Skill Formation* (Oxford University Press, Oxford)

Cabinet Office Performance and Innovation Unit (2001): *Workforce Development Project – Analysis Paper.* Available from the Cabinet Office Web site at http://www.cabinet-office.gov.uk/innovation/2001/workforce

Institute of Manpower Studies/Manpower Services Commission/National Economic Development Office (1984): *Competence and Competition* (NEDO, London)

Jenkins, S. (1995): *Accountable to None* (Hamish Hamilton, London)

Keep, E. (2002): 'The English Vocational Education and Training Debate – Fragile 'Technologies' or Opening the 'Black Box': Two competing visions of where we go next', *Journal of Education and Work*, Vol. 15, No. 4, 457-479

Keep, E. (2005): 'Skills, Training and the Quest for the Holy Grail of Influence and Status', in Bach, S. (ed), *Personnel Management,* 4th edition, (Blackwell, Oxford)

Kersley, B., Alpin, C., Forth, J., Bryson, A., Bewley, H., Dix, G., & Oxenbridge, S. (2005): *Inside the Workplace – First findings from the 2004 Workplace Employment Relations Survey* (Department of Trade and Industry, London)

Perry, P. (1976): *The Evolution of British manpower Policy* (British Association of Commercial and Industrial Education, London)

Streeck, W. (1989): 'Skills and the Limits of Neo-Liberalism: The Enterprise of the Future as a Place of Learning*', Work, Employment and Society*, Vol. 3, No. 1, 88-104

William Brown

THE LOW PAY COMMISSION

INTRODUCTION

The Low Pay Commission appears to have settled into the institutional landscape of the British labour market remarkably smoothly. Created in the immediate wake of the 'New' Labour victory at the 1997 election, the single purpose of the Commission has been to advise on the introduction and maintenance of a National Minimum Wage. The political anticipation of this had been highly contentious. But the issue dropped out of controversy almost as soon as the Wage was implemented. Despite the fact that the Low Pay Commission manages what is arguably Britain's most intrusive labour market intervention, it has come to do this with little public criticism. A newspaper headline that had greeted the introduction of the Wage in 1999 continues to apply: 'Minimum Wage; minimum fuss'.

This paper discusses the context and conduct of the Low Pay Commission (LPC). Other accounts are available of the early life of the Commission and of the National Minimum Wage (Bain 1999; Metcalf 1999a, 1999b; Brown 2000, 2002). This focuses on, at the time of writing in 2005, the comparatively mature operation of the Commission, and discusses the ways in which it has come to deal with an ever-changing labour market. In particular, it discusses how a very self-consciously 'social partnership' institution has developed its own way of operating, with an 'arm's length' relationship with government. The health warning is that the paper is written by a founding member of the Commission; it can make no claims to objectivity.

BACKGROUND

There is nothing new about statutory regulation of wages in Britain. For centuries, Magistrates had been empowered to fix the wages of certain occupations. This had petered out by the early 19th Century. But the years that followed were ones of rapid economic change and of new forms of exploitation. It became increasingly evident that, when there is almost unlimited supply of labour, unregulated wages could be driven down to levels that supported neither common decency nor minimal nutrition. By the end of the 19th Century, Charles Booth estimated that over a third of school age children in London were living below what he calculated to be the physically and nutritionally necessary poverty line. Encouraged by the experience of the Australian State of Victoria,

Linda Dickens & Alan C. Neal (eds), The Changing Institutional Face of British Employment Relations 63-78
© 2006 Kluwer Law International. Printed in the Netherlands

pressure grew to tackle the problem directly through statutory minimum wages. In 1909 Winston Churchill brought in his Trade Boards Act, permitting minima to be established on a national but sectoral basis (Phelps Brown 1965:309). Renamed 'wages councils' in 1945, these comprised equal numbers of employer and worker representatives, with a small number of 'independents' to break deadlocks and represent wider interests (Bayliss 1962). The councils had a small inspectorate with authority to enforce their wages orders, the breaching of which was a criminal offence.

At their peak, in 1953, there were 66 wages councils providing a safety net for around 3.5 million employees – about 17% of the employed workforce – and supported by a couple of hundred inspectors. They covered sectors ranging from the more obvious such as Road Haulage, Baking, and Retail Food Trades, to the more esoteric concerned with, for example, Drift Nets Mending, Corsets, and Ostrich and Fancy Feathers and Artificial Flowers. But for various reasons, not the least being trade union suspicions that statutory minimum wages undermined collective bargaining, the system went into decline. By 1993, when John Major's government abolished all but the Agricultural Wages Board, the coverage was no more than 2.5 million employees. Some sectors that were emerging with large numbers of often highly vulnerable workers, such as industrial cleaning, security, and care homes, were not covered at all. Even for those that were covered, the average 'bite' of the wages councils' statutory rates, expressed as a percentage of sectoral average earnings, had fallen from 50% in 1980 to 43% in 1993. There was evidence of substantial underpayment, perhaps partly because there were derisory penalties in the very rare event of prosecutions (Craig *et al* 1982; LPU 1998).

In 1974, contrary to prevailing trade union opinion, dissatisfaction with this position developed in the public service union NUPE, with the publication of a carefully argued case for what was called a National Minimum Wage by its authors, the general secretary, Alan Fisher and research officer, Bernard Dix. But it was to take twenty years before Rodney Bickerstaffe (successor to Fisher as general secretary of the expanded and renamed Unison) managed to get the proposal onto the Labour Party's electoral platform, with important backing from the M.P. Ian McCartney. Two substantial changes had facilitated this acceptance. One was a greater awareness by a weakened trade union movement that statutory minimum labour standards might actually support, rather than undermine, the floor on which collective bargaining was based. The second was the substantial recent increase in inequality in Britain. In particular, as had been the case a hundred years earlier, there was growing concern that there had been a sharp increase in the proportion of children growing up in poverty.

There have been many factors contributing to the rising inequality of pay in Britain since around 1980. Some are global changes, such as the declining relative demand for less skilled labour: as a result of technological change, and as a result of the increased openness, and increased size, of the international economy. Some are more particular to Britain, such as the decline in trade union membership, the contraction in the coverage of collective agreements, and the abolition of wages councils.

Chart 1 shows how the wages of British employees over 22 years of age fared across the pay distribution in the five years 1992 to 1997, running up to the introduction of the National Minimum Wage.[1]

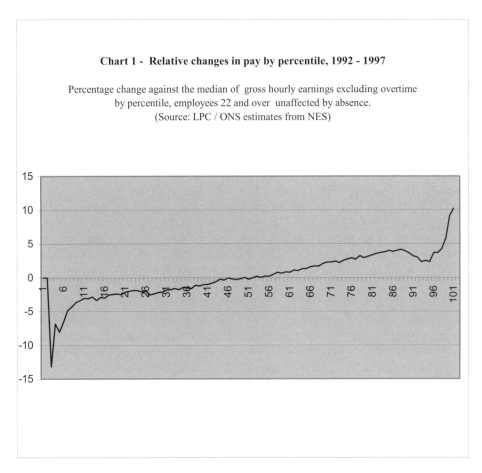

Chart 1 - Relative changes in pay by percentile, 1992 - 1997

Percentage change against the median of gross hourly earnings excluding overtime by percentile, employees 22 and over unaffected by absence.
(Source: LPC / ONS estimates from NES)

It divides the whole employed workforce into hundredths, ranked from the lowest paid to the highest paid, and shows the extent to which the average pay increases received by each of those hundredths differs from the average pay increase of the middle, fiftieth one.

---

[1] The choice of 1997 (April) rather than 1998 (April) allows for the fact that 1998, following the establishment of the Commission, saw significant anticipation by employers of the introduction of the Wage in the following April; many gave unusually large pay rises to their lowest paid employees in order to soften the expected impact of the Minimum Wage in the following year. (For the full analysis, see Butcher, T. 2005).

It is apparent that the lower a worker's earnings were, the poorer the pay increases they received over the five-year period – and that the reverse applied for the relatively well-paid. The bottom and top five or so per cent had the most extreme experience of this.

The implications for child poverty have been substantial. The percentage of children living in households with incomes below 50% of mean income (before housing costs), which had remained fairly steady at around 10% throughout the 1960s and 1970s, rose sharply to above 25% by the late 1990s (Glennerster *et al* 2004:46). Child poverty in Britain, expressed in these relative terms, had become worse than at any time since, at least, the Second World War. Politically, this was seen to be important, because a major policy objective of Gordon Brown's Chancellorship was the reduction of the many adverse social and economic consequences of child poverty.

The government also had a strong financial incentive. As the preceding Conservative administration had discovered, the payment of in-work benefits to working parents on low pay is necessary both to mitigate the effects of child poverty and to encourage parents to move into work who might otherwise become dependent on out-of-work benefits. If, however, there is no floor to wages, there are many employers who are only too happy to offer very low rates of pay and to encourage their employees to maximise their in-work benefits payments. The consequences of the Exchequer in effect subsidising unscrupulous employers as a result of this behaviour were becoming extremely expensive. Between 1988 and 1997 the number of families on in-work benefits rose from around 50,000 to 700,000 and the annual cost to the Exchequer from £200 million to £2,100 million. A statutory minimum wage would force employers to shoulder some of the cost of propping up the finances of low income families.

THE WAGE SETTLES IN

The LPC had pitched its recommendation of the initial level of the National Minimum Wage cautiously, and on the basis of a variety of sources of information, all of which were very imperfect. There were unavoidably contentious projections of what might have been prevailing rates of wages councils, had they not been abolished in 1993. There was the experience of other countries in terms of the relative position in their wage distributions of their own statutory minimum wages – these spanned an unhelpfully wide range. There were data on rates actually paid in the key low wage sectors. Important, if not disinterested, were the views of the trade associations of the most affected sectors on what was affordable. There were also economic modellers' estimates of the effect of different rates on pay differentials and on the macro-economy, all highly dependent upon their models' unavoidably heroic assumptions.

There were also two well-established national sample pay surveys. Unfortunately, for this purpose, they turned out to be seriously flawed. The multi-purpose door-step interviews of individual citizens used by the Labour Force Survey (LFS) proved to be an unreliable source of information both on what people earned and, as important from the point of view of estimating hourly rates, on the number of hours they worked. The LFS tended to underestimate hourly wages. The New Earnings Survey (NES), on the other hand, conceived in the 1960s to monitor incomes policies, used unimpeachable pay-roll data from employers, but was defective in failing to pick up many employees who were not earning enough in a week to meet the threshold which triggers Pay-As-You-Earn income tax payments. These were typically just those low-paid, part-time workers for whom the Minimum Wage was intended. The result was two surveys whose estimates of the incidence of low pay differed substantially. This mattered a great deal since, in the relevant part of the hourly wage distribution, 10 pence difference encompassed around a quarter of a million employees. The Office of National Statistics tackled the problem robustly. As a stop-gap it produced a compromise estimate. But by 2004 it was ready to improve the NES radically, replacing it with the Annual Survey of Hours and Earnings (ASHE). This increased the coverage of the survey of employers and dealt with missing data by imputation and weighting. The bottom end of the labour market will always be characterised by murkiness – cash in hand payments, misrecording of hours, and scrappy records ensure that – but at least those statistics that are available are now providing a more reliable guide.

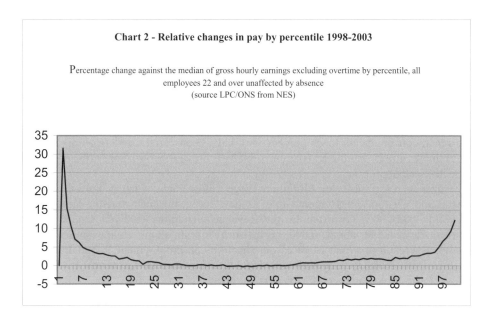

Chart 2 - Relative changes in pay by percentile 1998-2003

Percentage change against the median of gross hourly earnings excluding overtime by percentile, all employees 22 and over unaffected by absence
(source LPC/ONS from NES)

The initial impact of the National Minimum Wage for the low paid has been substantial. Chart 2 indicates, again by percentile, how pay rises differed from the median over the five years up to 2003, after the initial impact of the Wage. The contrast with Chart 1 is notable. Although the top percentiles have continued to do relatively well, those at the very bottom have seen their relative experience transformed. For the lowest ten or so per cent, pay rises have been substantially better than the median. Although there have been other changes in the context of low pay, this transformation is likely to be substantially attributable to the National Minimum Wage. It is also evident that the relative improvement is quite tightly confined to the lowest percentiles, which implies that there has not been a substantial 'knock-on' effect on pay differentials, which had been an early concern.

There have also been substantial consequences for gender equality, since women have been the main beneficiaries of the Minimum Wage. If we take the lowest decile, women's hourly pay as a percentage of men's (aged 22 and over) rose from 80% in 1998 to 85% in 2004. While other factors will have contributed to this, the Commission's own analysis concluded that the Minimum Wage '…has exerted a major influence in narrowing the pay gap at the lower end of the earnings distribution' (LPC 2005: Para 4.24). In summary, the Minimum Wage, thus far, appears to have been working well in the direction intended.

THE LAW AND ITS ENFORCEMENT

How are the institutions underpinning the Wage settling in? Let us start with the 1998 National Minimum Wage Act. This was strong legislation, vastly more so than previous measures supporting wages councils. It had, for example, a broad definition of eligible workers, a requirement of reversal of proof on employers, and it threatened those in breach with substantial penalties. There have been some minor adjustments to the initial legislation, to cover loopholes and inadequate definitions. For example, regulations have been tightened on the payment of arrears by offending employers to workers no longer in employment, as have those concerning the complex matter of piecework pay. The Commission has called for more financially penal treatment of errant employers who delay reparation payments to employees they have been caught under-paying. But the general impression is that the legislation is felt by most of those who are affected by it to be effective and appropriate.

The agency responsible for Minimum Wage enforcement, what is now called HM Revenue and Customs, has entered into its new role with characteristic investigative energy. In 2002-2003, for example, the Revenue's Helpline received around 53,000 enquiries, carried out about 6,000 compliance investigations (many initiated pro-actively), as a result of which 24 cases were heard by an Employment Tribunal, and £3.6 million in wage arrears were identified (DTI 2003). The Revenue's experience with small employers who take chances on tax matters has proved to be valuable.

This is not to say that the Act has never been breached. Far from it. The black economy, cash payment, under-recording of hours worked and collusive illegal behaviour by employers and employees remain very much a feature of the low paid end of the labour market. At time of writing, no criminal prosecutions had been pursued. But, in July 2005, Gerry Sutcliffe, the junior minister responsible, announced that there would a new policy under which particular sectors (initially hairdressing) would be targeted for enforcement and that, separately, efforts would be made '…to identify cases with the aim of identifying a small number of employers for prosecution' (House of Commons 2005). It was felt that some more conspicuous enforcement was called for, *pour encourager les autres*. However imperfect the enforcement process, it is hard to imagine that it could be pursued with more investigative experience, or command more employer respect, than this policing by the Revenue.

THE ROLE OF THE COMMISSION

If one test of the durability of an institution is its capacity to function effectively despite changes in personnel, then that test has so far been passed. The full-time secretariat has seen, in normal Civil Service style, fairly continuous staff turnover without any deterioration of the high quality of support. In 2005, none of the nine secretariat had been with the Commission for more than three years and the Secretary was the fifth in post. Of the nine Commissioners, there had been seven departures and only four of the original members were still present in mid-2005. Adair (now Lord) Turner had replaced Sir George Bain as Chair in 2002. But, so far as these things can be judged, the ethos and sense of common cause among Commissioners seems unchanged after eight years.

It is, perhaps, surprising that this relatively small body should be able to cope with fairly frequent changes in personnel without changing its character and conduct. Part of the explanation probably lies in its very deliberate 'social partnership' construction, with broadly implied roles and 'balance'. There is an implicit expectation that the distinctive employer and trade union backgrounds of six Commissioners will sometimes be evident when it comes to asking awkward questions and testing weak arguments. If they are not to challenge arguments on behalf of their notional constituents, who will? Similarly, the three independents are expected, at least, to ensure that research and its use are rigorous. But all Commissioners act as individuals, drawing on their background experience but not mandated in any way by the organisations they come from. Certainly this is how they behave. Individual positions adopted in arguments on the many issues that come before the Commission are rarely clearly role-related, and it is only on the periodic debate on the recommended level of the Minimum Wage that there is predictable polarisation. Although straw polls sometimes help move discussions along, decisions of the Commission have always been unanimous.

The Commission's work has come to be geared every two years around a major report, which assesses the recent impact of the Minimum Wage and makes a recommendation for the next two years. Usually there has been an interim report on a particular issue – in 2004 it was concerned with the recommendation that there should be a statutory rate for 16 and 17 year olds. As will be discussed below, so far there has been a steady stream of new policy issues, reflecting changes in the labour market, and also of matters raised by government and by particular interest groups. Each year there have been up to ten half-day Commission meetings, one or two over-night 'retreats', and sometimes *ad hoc* meetings or conferences on research. Each year there have been up to ten consultative trips to different parts of the United Kingdom – typically, with three Commissioners and a couple of secretariat – to meet people from three or four different affected sectors at their place of work to discuss their perceptions of current Commission concerns. Finally, as part of the process of preparing for the major reports it has been necessary to have formal hearings in London with the main interest groups.

The most demanding task facing the Commission is that of periodically agreeing on a recommendation for the actual level of the Minimum Wage. As well as the evidence that comes in from interested parties, and from commissioned research, the secretariat carry out a substantial amount of their own investigation, analysis, consultation or other background work that they and Commissioners consider might be relevant. This leads up to the Commission occupying a country hotel for a weekend for structured discussion of key issues. When the proposal of new rates is the main subject, these 'retreats' take the form of initial briefings followed by a series of short meetings both as a whole Commission and in sub-groups. During these, the Chair in effect plays the role of an industrial relations mediator. Supported by the other two independents, he explores the priorities and options of the employer and union members, and cajoles them gradually into converging on an outcome everyone can live with. So far, Commissioners have emerged from these rate-fixing weekends in weary agreement, but it has never been an easy process. The outcomes are set out in Table 1.

Table 1 – Increases in National Minimum Wage, Average Earnings and Prices

Date of NMW increase	*NMW adult rate per hour (workers aged 22+)*	*Increase in NMW since previous NMW setting*	*Increase in average earnings index since previous setting*	*Increase in retail price index since previous setting*
	£	%	%	%
1 Apr 1999	3.60	-	-	-
1 Oct 2000	3.70	2.8	3.1	2.7
1 Oct 2001	4.10	10.8	4.3	2.3
1 Oct 2002	4.20	2.4	3.7	2.3
1 Oct 2003	4.50	7.1	3.6	2.7
1 Oct 2004	4.85	7.8	4.2	2.1
1 Oct 2005	5.05	4.1	n.a.	n.a.
1 Oct 2006	5.35	5.9	n.a.	n.a.

All rates recommended by the Commission have been accepted by the government, although the timing was altered somewhat in the first couple of years. Two years' recommendations have been made at a time, initially to facilitate agreement within the Commission, but later in response to employer requests for adequate notice of Minimum Wage changes. Thus, 1999 and 2000 were decided as a package, as were 2001 and 2002, 2003 and 2004, and, most recently, 2005 and 2006. The 2001 and 2002 recommendations were, as can be seen, quite heavily 'front-loaded', with that for 2001 being substantially larger than that in 2002, but subsequently the loading has been more even.

The initial level of the Wage was set cautiously, partly because of the uncertainties already mentioned about the statistical facts, and also because the Commissioners were aware that the initial shock of the Wage on employers in the unregulated labour market of 1999 would be far greater than that of any subsequent increase. It would never have made sense to fix a long-term rate in relative terms straight away. Both finding an acceptable relative position and allowing the labour market to adjust to it can only be gradual processes. But the Commission were determined that the Wage should 'make a difference' and, with the exception of the increase in October 2002, the recommended increases have been greater than increases in average earnings as a whole. As a result, thus far the Minimum Wage has been gradually moving up the national earnings distribution, thereby increasing the number of workers benefiting.

What has determined these increases? Or rather, what have been the issues at the front of Commissioners' minds as they have edged towards agreement? From the start, the dominant anxiety has been employment. At what position in the national wage distribution might the Minimum Wage start to cause significant job loss, or frustrate job creation? This has been, and continues to be, the central concern during consultations and in the commissioning of research. It was also the prime issue in deciding on the lower 'Development Rate' that was, with considerable internal difficulty, agreed primarily for younger workers. The Commission recommended this lower rate from the 18th to the 21st birthday, but the government has consistently required it to be the 22nd birthday, justifying this variation in terms of vulnerability to unemployment. Employability arose yet again as the main consideration when, in 2004, a minimum rate was recommended for 16 and 17 year-olds. Whatever other issues enter the Commissioners' internal debates, their prime constraint has always been, and continues to be, anxiety about causing job loss.

Considerations other than employment effects have waxed and waned in salience. At the start, when some economic modellers predicted substantial knock-on effects, the potentially inflationary macro-economic impact of the Wage was an issue. Commissioners had two meetings with the Monetary Policy Committee to explain their reasoning on this. But in practice knock-on consequences for the macro-economy proved to be insignificant. International comparisons seemed relevant at first, but as the Wage settled in and experience of it made the Commission more confident, these waned. Close comparison of aspects of statutory minimum wages of different countries is, in any case, made difficult by their diverse labour market institutions and data sources.

The view that the Minimum Wage should reflect the income needs of workers, which has dominated past minimum wage debates in some countries, and features in terms of a 'living wage' in the arguments of some British pressure groups, has never become a major issue for the Commission. This is largely because actual disposable income is so highly determined by family circumstances and the tax and benefit regime. The Commission has had research conducted on the impact of the wage on net family income, but that has not been translatable into discussions of the Wage level. Another concern that loomed large at first but has diminished in the light of experience is whether the Wage might discourage investment in training, especially for young people. The Commission's informed judgement has been that, if anything, having to pay people more may encourage rather than discourage employers to train them, but that, in any case, Britain's training inadequacies have deeper roots.

Considerations that have become more significant as the Wage has settled in, and as anxieties about adverse employment effects have not been realised, have been very practical. Most important has been a concern that compressed differentials may weaken incentives for those paid just above the Minimum Wage. Certainly many employers have argued this with regard to their ability to reward skill, effort, experience, and responsibility. Another emerging concern is enforcement. The higher the Minimum Wage edges in relative terms, the greater the incentive for employers to cheat in some way – by paying in cash 'off the books', or by under-recording working time, and so on. Reflecting another source of concern, the Commission has increasingly kept a keen eye on trends in profit levels, and in company start-ups and bankruptcies. At time of writing, these have shown no adverse signals.

The number of beneficiaries from the Minimum Wage is a question that has always taxed the Commission, not least because it is a natural statistic-of-choice for politicians. Initial estimates were substantially too high, largely because of the problems with the LFS and NES already mentioned. But this does not mean that the Commission ever had an initial target in terms of the number of beneficiaries. The initial estimate was simply the number of beneficiaries implied by the flawed survey statistics once the proposed cautious initial level of the Wage had been decided.

As time has gone on it has become increasingly evident that any estimate of beneficiaries is unavoidably subject to controversial assumptions. For example, it may be that, in the absence of the Wage, the relative position of the low paid would have continued to decline, as it had up to 1998. But how far and how fast? Then again, many employers have got into the habit of anticipating the announcement of Minimum Wage increases due in October by giving earlier increases according to their normal pay round calendar. But the muted response to the relatively small increase of October 2002 suggests that such anticipatory pay increases are, indeed, anticipatory, and would not have been as large without the announcement of the forthcoming Wage. And although knock-on effects are evidently relatively limited, employers undoubtedly raise pay of some employees who are already above the Minimum Wage in order to preserve both internal and external differentials. Indeed, there is good evidence that, for many employers in many industries (and not least the Agricultural Wages Board), the Minimum Wage has become the driving force behind increases in their lowest rates. In brief, any estimate of the number of beneficiaries is unavoidably rough. But, in this spirit, a reasonable estimate might be that, if the Wage were frozen in 2005, then, within a year, at least one and a half million employees would suffer a consequential deterioration in pay relative to all employees. Over a longer period, because the Minimum Wage is being used as a guiding light much more widely, the number would be substantially greater.

Consultation

The consultative visits, which had been essential to the process of initially defining and then setting the level of the Wage, continue to be a crucial part of the Commission's functioning. It is rare that some new insight does not come from an hour's discussion at their place of work with people immediately involved with low paid employment – whether they be concerned with domiciliary care, strawberry picking, dry cleaning, corner shops, packing tights, caravan parks, catering, careers advice, adventure holidays, sandwich making, infant nurseries, or whatever. These people deal on a daily basis with the problem of managing, motivating, affording, competing, and surviving with the Minimum Wage. They may not be statistically representative, but their perceptions have the authority that comes from immediate practical experience, and they are very ready to discuss them. For Commissioners, the shared experience of the visits, and of trying to make sense of what they have seen and heard (and sometimes smelled), continues to be important in generating shared understandings and points of reference. It has become routine at the start of normal Commission meetings to discuss any interesting issues raised by the most recent consultative visits.

In this way, the Commission has been able to pick up on many labour market developments and particular sectoral problems early. Commissioners were, for example, meeting with gang-masters back in 1997, have talked to more subsequently, and thus had a broad understanding of their role in the labour market long before some gang-masters gained national, criminal notoriety in 2004. Another instance of the visits providing early information has been that they have been yielding powerful insights into the way in which new immigrants (legal and illegal), and more recently those from the new EU Member States, have been fitting in at the bottom of the labour market.

Consultative visits have been targeted to help the Commission to gain deeper understanding on which to base their recommendations when new questions have been raised by the Minimum Wage. One example was to do with therapeutic earnings – that is, where people with some sort of disability are encouraged with small incentive payments, when light work is considered to be conducive to their health or recovery. How could such work be defined so that the therapeutic value of it could be protected without denying potentially very vulnerable people the protections of the statutory Minimum Wage? The Commission's definition, derived from discussions with carers and from visits to centres dedicated to the care and rehabilitation of people with learning difficulties, has in part been reflected in revisions to the Government's guidance notes on what constitutes work for Minimum Wage purposes.

A second example arose from the inadequacy of the Minimum Wage regulations' initial definition of piecework. These were, on the one hand, not robust enough to help many manual home-workers, of whom it has been estimated there are up to a million in the British economy, 90% of them women and up to 50% from ethnic minority groups. But, on the other hand, many employers in the clothing industry deemed the Minimum Wage's application to piecework to be terminally crippling to productivity because it denied adequate cash incentives. It took a series of lively discussions with representatives of affected industries to establish the relevant facts (one of which was that the domestic clothing industry needed far more for its survival than a sharp incentive system for production workers) before a clearer and more down-to-earth definition of a 'fair piece rate' entered the regulations.

Quite apart from the information and understanding gained through consultative visits, they provide political credibility to the whole data-gathering process. Pressure groups such as trade associations, disability groups, and regional chambers of commerce value the opportunity to have their more outspoken activists making their case on their home ground. As a matter of policy, if people affected by the Minimum Wage contact the Commission with an interesting new complaint or problem, an effort is made to fit them into a forthcoming visit. It is partly for this reason that the Commission makes an effort to cover most regions each year – it made, for example, six separate consultative visits to Northern Ireland in its first eight years. It matters a great deal to get out, and to be seen to be getting out, of London.

RESEARCH

However insightful the visits are, and however eloquent are the representatives of particular interest groups, it has been essential for the Commission to have dispassionate, representative evidence as well. For each report it has carried out its own postal surveys, with the assistance of trade associations, to elicit responses from many thousand affected employers about the impact of, and their response to, increases in the Minimum Wage. More important, the Commission has become a major commissioner of research. This has ranged from case study fieldwork, through sampled surveys, to the detailed analysis of existing data sources. In all, 74 distinct research projects have been commissioned since 1999, and their findings are summarised in Commission reports. Another round is being competed for at the time of writing. For this work the Commission has been very fortunate in being able to enlist both leading labour market research firms and internationally outstanding industrial sociologists and labour economists. Indeed, it is hard to think of a 'natural experiment' in the social sciences that has received closer academic attention than the introduction of the United Kingdom's National Minimum Wage, and our understanding of the low paid end of the labour market has improved substantially as a result.

The nature of the research programme has changed as the Wage has settled in. The initial concern was with the immediate impact. Appropriate 'before and after' studies were necessarily constrained by the recentness of the event. But if quantitative time-series analyses were not yet possible, more qualitative case study approaches came into their own, while memories of initial adjustments to the Wage were fresh. Much of this work was by people with industrial relations research backgrounds, with their familiarity with interview and case study techniques to explore changing power relationships. Studies were carried out on selected affected sectors (clothing, hospitality, charities, retail, hairdressing, and horse racing, for example) and on selected vulnerable groups, such as young workers, ethnic minorities, people with disabilities, students, rural communities, and employees in small firms. A variety of surveys were conducted, some building fruitfully on existing survey vehicles to detect changing behaviour. Of great value at this stage were studies carried out (with secretariat guidance) by pressure groups and voluntary organisations with unique access to their membership. Citizens Advice Bureaux, which deal with hundreds of thousands of employment rights cases each year, carried out valuable studies of their own casebooks on initial awareness and the impact of the Wage. Other groups contributing included local government researchers, local Low

Pay Units, and organisations concerned with home-workers, the voluntary sector, and with gender equality. More recently qualitative, case study based approaches have been focussed on very specific policy concerns of the Commission, such as training, enforcement, non-compliance, and the employment of 16 and 17 year olds.

The passage of time since the introduction of the Minimum Wage has brought an ever-growing mass of relevant data from a variety of statistically representative surveys. This has brought leading labour market econometricians into the search, with the means to put 'before and after' studies on a sound statistical footing. A particularly potent technique has been the comparison of some aspect of the experience of workers who have been directly affected by the Wage with that of slightly better paid workers, not directly affected, but statistically matched in all other measured characteristics. Recently commissioned econometric studies have explored, among other things, effects of the Minimum Wage on employment, productivity, profitability, the number of hours worked, second job holding, movements in and out of employment, movements in and out of the Minimum Wage, and also the household characteristics of the beneficiaries.

All this work is building up a picture of the impact of the Minimum Wage of growing reliability. It is one of substantial impact, in terms of the numbers of workers affected directly, intermittently, or indirectly. The beneficiaries may not be their household's main income earner, but they are concentrated in the poorest working-age households. Exhaustive enquiry has still failed to give any evidence of adverse employment effects on either primary or secondary jobs. But there is some evidence that, in the service sector, job creation may have been hampered by the Minimum Wage, and it may have led to a slight reduction in working hours. Steering, as the Commissioners must, in a blizzard of anecdotes and speculation, it is hard to exaggerate the guiding value of this growing body of research.

INSTITUTIONAL LESSONS

What wider lessons for labour market regulation might be learnt from the early years of the Low Pay Commission? The National Minimum Wage is a major and apparently effective labour market intervention that has been established with little resistance. The Commission itself has developed a social partnership approach that has won agreement on all aspects of the Minimum Wage, most notably on its level. Its recommendations have been accepted by government, with the trivial exception of whether entitlement to the full rate should start at 21 or 22 years of age. What might account for this apparent success? Are there wider lessons for the national regulation of labour standards?

There are six main features of the Commission that have helped its work. One is that it is a single-issue, and in some ways a simple-issue body. The implied aim of the National Minimum Wage is that it should be an intervention that makes a positive difference to low-paid workers' pay up to a point where it still does not jeopardise their jobs. This is an aim with which all Commissioners can readily identify.

Second, the Commission is sufficiently small for the Commissioners to be able to work closely together, especially through the difficult process of achieving agreement on the recommended level for the Minimum Wage. Regular consultative visits have been important in helping them build close working relationships with each other and with their secretariat.

These consultations are a third important feature. Meeting people throughout Britain who have to work with the consequences of the Commission's deliberations is a fruitful and chastening experience. It probably helps the political acceptability of the Minimum Wage. It certainly helps to keep the Commissioners' feet on the sometimes grim and shifting ground.

However rich the insights gained from consultation, they rarely swing arguments. This is why emphasis must be placed on the fourth feature of the Commission's work: research. Time and again disagreements within the Commission have been resolved by some research on a point of controversy, often no more than a simple quantification. The labour market is so variable, so perverse, so confused, and so subject to myth-making, that without the back-up of sound empirical research, neither the Commissioners, nor the Government, could be confident about the Minimum Wage's effects. Research is the best antidote to myth.

Research is also an important buttress of the fifth feature: the Commission's success in keeping the Government at arm's length. The Commission has now steered the Minimum Wage through the political perils of two general election campaigns. Whether or not all politicians respect research, their civil servants generally do, and the Minimum Wage is research led policy *par excellence*. Whatever the temptation for Government to exercise influence other than through formal evidence, no attempt has been made to do so.

Sixth, is the importance of enforcement. Employers comply more willingly if they can be reassured that they will not be undercut by non-compliant competitors. In the Revenue, the Commission has an enforcer with immense relevant experience. It may not be fully successful in the shadows of the black economy, but it is energetic, ingenious, and generally respected.

These features may have wider applicability for labour market regulatory institutions in the 21st Century: to be small, focused, independent, research active, and to get out and about and talk with, and learn from, the affected public. But uniquely for the British context it is the sixth feature, access to effective enforcement, which is perhaps the most unusual source of strength for the Low Pay Commission.

Over the past thirty years successive British governments have introduced several score statutory labour standards – concerned with equality and fairness of treatment by employers, with parental rights, working hours, working safety, and much else besides. But with the exception of the Minimum Wage, and to some extent health and safety, all these rely on do-it-yourself enforcement. It is up to the aggrieved worker to press for his or her statutory individual employment rights. Indeed, it is the employee's entitlement not only to take such a grievance to an Employment Tribunal, but also to have an Acas conciliator intercede and try to reach a settlement. But in practice these are hollow rights for those with greatest need. For these are the most vulnerable in the workforce, the majority of whom have neither trade union representation nor the self-confidence to challenge their employer.

Almost all other countries have independent labour inspectorates that, to a greater or lesser extent, seek out employers who breach statutory labour standards, and take up cases on behalf of aggrieved employees. Britain's labour market regulation is defective in this respect. The Low Pay Commission's most fundamental lesson for Britain's other regulatory institutions may be the importance of independent enforcement. Can a statutory right be considered truly universal without it? If not, then the National Minimum Wage is arguably Britain's only effective labour standard.

REFERENCES

Bain, G. (1999): 'The National Minimum Wage: further reflections', *Employee Relations,* 21:1, 15-28

Bayliss, F. (1962): *British Wages Councils* (Blackwell, Oxford)

Brown, W. (2000): 'Putting Partnership into Practice in Britain', *British Journal of Industrial Relations*, 38:2, 299-316

Brown, W. (2002): 'The Operation of the Low Pay Commission', *Employee Relations Journal*, Vol 24 (6), 595-605

Butcher, T. (2005): 'The hourly earnings distribution before and after the National Minimum Wage', in *Labour Market Trends*, ONS, October 2005

Craig, C., Rubery, J., Tarling, R. & Wilkinson, F. (1982): *Labour Market Structure, Industrial Organisation and Low Pay* (CUP, Cambridge)

DTI in association with Inland Revenue (2003): *National Minimum Wage – Annual Report 2002/03* (DTI, London)

Glennerster, H., Hills, J., Piachaud, D. & Webb, J. (2004): *One Hundred Years of Poverty and Policy* (Joseph Rowntree Foundation, York)

House of Commons (2005): House of Commons Tenth Standing Committee on Delegated Legislation, 12 July 2005. Draft Minimum Wage Regulations 1999 (Amendment) Regulations 2005

Low Pay Commission (1998): *First Report*, Appendix 5: 'A Century of Statutory Wage Legislation in the UK', Cm 3976 (The Stationery Office, London)

Low Pay Commission (2005): *National Minimum Wage: Low Pay Commission Report 2005*, CM 6745 (TSO, London)

Metcalf, D. (1999a): 'The British National Minimum Wage', *British Journal of Industrial Relations*, 37:2, 172-201

William Brown

Metcalf, D. (1999b): 'The Low Pay Commission and the National Minimum Wage', *Economic Journal*, 109 (453), 46-66

Phelps Brown, E. (1965): *The Growth of British Industrial Relations* (Macmillan, London)

Simon Gouldstone & Gillian Morris

THE CENTRAL ARBITRATION COMMITTEE

INTRODUCTION

The Central Arbitration Committee (CAC) is a statutory body with a wide variety of functions in the area of collective labour relations. It consists of a chairman, deputy chairmen and other members, all of whom are 'persons experienced in industrial relations'; some have experience as representatives of employers, some as representatives of workers. Although members are appointed by the Secretary of State, after consultation with Acas, and Acas is responsible for its staffing and facilities, the CAC operates as a wholly independent body. It is publicly funded and does not charge for the use of its services. Its jurisdiction is confined to Great Britain; in Northern Ireland, a separate body, the Industrial Court, has a parallel role.

The CAC dates back to the Employment Protection Act (EPA) 1975 (see now the Trade Union and Labour Relations (Consolidation) Act 1992, ss 259-265). However, in functional terms it has a longer history, constituting a direct descendent of the Industrial Court, which was established in 1919 to provide a permanent national State-funded facility for settling collective disputes by voluntary arbitration (Amulree 1929; MacKenzie 1921, 1923; Stoker 1920; and Morris 1928). The creation of the Industrial Court was the response to the Whitley Committee's recommendation in its Report on Conciliation and Arbitration in 1918 that a 'Standing Arbitration Council' should be established, and was further evidence of the Government's increasing involvement in industrial relations following the Conciliation Act 1896. The Court was essentially an arbitration body although a later President, Sir Roy Wilson, in evidence to the Donovan Commission did not find it easy to explain why the term 'Court' had been chosen over the possibly more appropriate 'Tribunal'. His view was that the word 'Court', firstly, emphasised permanence, regularity in procedure, consistency in decision-making and impartiality, and, secondly, underlined that it was not subject to Government influence except in so far as Government policy might be embodied in legislation. The Industrial Court was renamed the Industrial Arbitration Board in 1971, no doubt to contrast its functions with those of the National Industrial Relations Court established by the Industrial Relations Act 1971 (see Chapter 1). Over time, the Industrial Court also acquired adjudicative functions, such as jurisdiction under the Terms and Conditions of Employment Act 1959, by which employers could be compelled to observe terms established by collective agreement, and other fair wages legislation.

Linda Dickens & Alan C. Neal (eds), The Changing Institutional Face of British Employment Relations 79-89
© 2006 Kluwer Law International. Printed in the Netherlands

The CAC inherited this hybrid role as arbitrator and adjudicator. In practice, as we explain below, it is no longer called upon to conduct voluntary arbitrations, but its history as an arbitral body has been influential in shaping its ethos that, wherever possible, the parties should be encouraged to seek their own solutions to a problem and that when the CAC is required to make a decision it should have regard to the impact on industrial relations in so doing.

When initially established, the CAC had a wide range of functions in addition to that of voluntary arbitration: claims under the EPA 1975, Schedule 11 that employers were not observing the recognised or general level of terms and conditions of employment in relation to a worker; references under the Fair Wages Resolution and its statutory extensions; disclosure of information for collective bargaining; consideration of claims that mandatory recognition orders had not been observed; and amendment of collective agreements that discriminated between men and women. In effect, it became 'the British collective labour court' in the period 1975-1980 (Davies & Freedland 1993:394-395). The neo-liberal agenda pursued by the Conservative Government elected in 1979 led to the repeal of the majority of these areas of its adjudicatory jurisdiction, until by 1987 it was a mere shadow of its former self, being left to deal only with complaints of failure to disclose information for collective bargaining purposes, a right whose survival could be seen as testament to its ineffectiveness (Gospel & Willman 1981; Gospel & Lockwood 1999).

The advent of a Labour Government in 1997 led to the renaissance of the CAC. This was essentially due to the decision to accord a 'restructured and reinforced' CAC jurisdiction over the newly-established procedure for mandatory union recognition rather than creating a separate 'Representation Agency' as the TUC had initially proposed. At the time of writing, the bulk of the CAC's caseload relates to applications for recognition. There have been 464 such applications between June 2000, when the procedure came into force, and the end of July 2005. As the procedure is multi-stage, each application may involve the CAC in making a number of discrete decisions. The CAC may also be required to adjudicate on the implications of changes affecting a bargaining unit where recognition has been awarded, and on derecognition, although to date there have been very few decisions in these areas.

Jurisdiction over recognition was followed by the grant of adjudicative powers under subsequent legislation providing for new forms of employee representation: in 2000, European Works Councils (EWCs) or other information and consultation procedures in 'Community-scale' undertakings; in 2004, employee involvement in a 'European Company' (or *Societas Europaea*); and finally, in April 2005, information and consultation of employees at national level in undertakings that exceed a specified size. In the latter context, unusually, the CAC has an administrative as well as an adjudicative role; employees have the option of sending a request to establish an information and consultation procedure to the CAC rather than directly to their employer. The choice of the CAC as adjudicator in this context was controversial; some employer organisations fought hard for this role to be allocated to Employment Tribunals on the ground that the CAC's expertise was rooted in a collective bargaining culture that did not embrace non-union employee representation, although the CBI had earlier agreed to the CAC when negotiating the framework of the legislation with the TUC (DTI 2003a).

Under the Information and Consultation Regulations (ICER) 2004 the CAC may be required to decide a variety of questions, including whether there has been adherence to a negotiated agreement or the standard information and consultation provisions (functions accorded to the EAT in the EWC context); Employment Tribunals are confined to their more traditional role of dealing with disputes involving individuals, such as whether an individual has been dismissed or subject to a detriment in contravention of the Regulations or whether time off has been unreasonably refused (see Chapter 11). At the time of writing it is too early to tell whether the encouragement to the parties to agree information and consultation procedures outside the scope of the CAC's enforcement powers will bear fruit; official predictions of the possible CAC caseload in 2006 have ranged from three to 86 (DTI 2004) (but will probably exceed the three applications so far received under the EWC legislation).

The CAC continues to receive complaints under the disclosure of information legislation, although the annual average in recent years has been considerably lower than the 1970s. By contrast, the voluntary arbitration function has effectively died out in practice. References to the Industrial Court were made by the Minister of Labour, and those to the CAC are required to come through Acas. Both the Minister could, and Acas can, act only with the 'consent' of the parties. There were, however, some references made directly to the Industrial Court and the CAC where employers and trade unions were parties to standing arbitration arrangements. The last reference to the CAC for voluntary arbitration was in 1989. This partly reflects a general preference for single arbitrators rather than a board of arbitration as a mode of third party intervention in collective disputes; of the 51 such disputes referred for settlement by arbitration by Acas in 2004-2005, all were referred for settlement by a single arbitrator (see Chapter 3).

Other factors contributing to the removal of this area of the CAC's work have been the reduction in the incidence of industrial action and the decline in national-level collective bargaining and associated dispute-resolution procedures, which regularly involved the CAC and its predecessors. It is also beyond question that the creation of Acas in 1974 had a significant effect on the level of requests to the CAC for voluntary arbitration.[1]

COMPOSITION AND POWERS

The numerical composition of the CAC has oscillated wildly, depending upon the level of demand predicted for its services. In 1976 there were five deputy chairmen, in addition to the chairman, and 25 members; the following year there were 18 deputy chairmen and 63 members. Prior to the introduction of the recognition procedure, by which time its jurisdiction had shrunk to disclosure of information, there were a mere three deputies and eight members (Rideout 2002:7) and its continued existence looked far from certain. The membership expanded significantly in 2000 in anticipation of the predicted caseload

---

[1] CAC *Annual Reports* provide statistics on case-load and information on new developments. The CAC website has published decisions and guidance on various statutory provisions. The CAC Secretariat also holds papers on repealed jurisdictions and a complete collection of decisions of the Industrial Court and its successors.

under the new statutory recognition procedure, and as of March 2004 there were 11 deputy chairmen and 45 employer and worker members. All the new appointments were made following national advertisement of the vacancies, and a selection process which involved identified competencies and an independent assessor. Deputies include academic industrial relations and labour law specialists, practising lawyers, and Employment Tribunal chairmen. Members are all senior industrial relations practitioners, including serving or former union general secretaries and directors of human resources in major companies. The chairman and deputies meet regularly together, and with members, to discuss CAC procedures, and the range of expertise brought by deputies has proved invaluable in this regard. Chairmen of the CAC and its predecessor bodies (a mere six in total) have all been lawyers but the current chairman, Sir Michael Burton, who was appointed in 2000, is the first to hold the office of a High Court judge. The CAC has recently completed a further recruitment round where applications were invited from those with employer experience of smaller organisations and of areas additional to industrial relations, and from those with experience as representatives of workers not exclusively gained as a trade union official.

Members are appointed for a three-year period, but their independence is safeguarded by a presumption of re-appointment other than for specified reasons relating to personal conduct (which must be investigated by a judge and reported to the Lord Chief Justice) or operational or structural requirements of the CAC. They are office holders, who are paid for the services they render on a *per diem* basis. Members are assisted by a secretariat, one of whom will act as the case manager for an individual application or complaint. Case managers act as the contact point for the parties; they may also, for the purposes of the recognition and derecognition procedures, compile reports about union membership and support for recognition from information that the CAC can require the parties to supply to case managers (in default of their agreement to do so) in confidence. CAC staff are civil servants employed by Acas, which is responsible for funding the CAC although the CAC is operationally independent of it.

In performing its functions generally, the CAC is composed of the chairman or a deputy and such other members as the chairman may direct; there is also a discretion to call in one or more assessors to assist it, although at the time of writing neither author is aware of this having been done. Under the Industrial Courts Act 1919 there was a provision for the Minister to appoint to the Court 'one or more women,' and the first President of the Court explained that '[i]f women are, or likely to be, affected, a women member is usually added.' (Mackenzie 1921:5). That provision was not carried over to the CAC. Had it been so, the female members of the CAC would have had a disproportionately heavy caseload, given that at present only four of the deputies and 12 of the members are women. For the purposes of the recognition and derecognition procedures the CAC is specifically required to consist of a tripartite panel. Wherever possible the same panel will deal with an application through all its stages. Members are there to bring their respective areas of experience to the panel, not to act as advocates for either side. Decisions are reached by a majority; if there is no majority, the chairman of the panel decides. All decisions appear as those of the panel/CAC; in contrast to Employment Tribunals, there are no minority decisions. In practice, there is a high degree of consensus within panels.

CAC decisions are generally made public, but have no precedent value. Each panel is formally free to regulate its own procedure but in practice there is a measure of consistency, which is reflected in guidance published by the CAC on which all members have had the opportunity to comment. The freedom of the CAC to regulate its own procedure is another area where the CAC has a strong link to its predecessors. The Industrial Court (Procedure) Rules 1920, issued by the Minister of Labour under section 3 of the 1919 Act, covered, *inter alia*, the ability of the Court to sit in divisions, correct clerical errors in its awards and engage assessors, provisions that bear a striking similarity to those in current legislation (Trade Union and Labour Relations (Consolidation) Act 1992). In 2004, the Labour Government resisted pressure from some quarters for the CAC to be subject to statutory procedural rules.

Decisions are taken on the basis of evidence submitted to the panel by the parties. Documentation is exchanged and the parties are invited to comment on the submissions of the other or others. It is for an individual panel to decide whether to hold an oral hearing on a particular matter. In some contexts, such as the acceptance of recognition applications, the issue can often be decided on the papers; others, such as whether a proposed bargaining unit is 'appropriate,' will generally require a hearing. It is open to the parties to have legal, or any other form of, representation but there is no requirement to do so and there is no power to award costs. In exceptional cases the CAC may itself instruct a lawyer (an *amicus curiae*) to make submissions as to the correct legal position on a matter before it on which the parties may then comment

The CAC has always operated according to the rules of natural justice, which require a fair hearing; an unbiased judge; and evidence being shown to all the parties. Hearings are conducted in as informal a manner as is consistent with clarity and fairness. An application must be supported by such documents as the CAC requires. Beyond that, the CAC has no power to order the disclosure of documents nor can it require the attendance of witnesses, in contrast to Employment Tribunals. However, it can draw an adverse inference from the failure of a party to supply information in the context of membership and support checks under the recognition procedure and under ICER. Speakers and witnesses do not give evidence on oath but they may be cross-questioned where factual issues are in dispute, at the discretion of the panel chair. Hearings are generally held in public, although there is power to hold them in private, e.g. if confidential information is being disclosed. In some contexts the CAC is required to give reasons for decisions, in others not, but even where there is no formal requirement to give reasons, the CAC in its adjudicative role will indicate the considerations that led to its decision (and on the basis of past practice, would probably also do so in its arbitral role were the occasion to arise).

It is a notable feature of the CAC that it has no power to enforce its decisions directly. Where recognition is awarded and the CAC has specified a 'method' by which the parties are to conduct collective bargaining, then in the absence of any contrary agreement by the parties the 'method' has effect as if it were contained in a legally enforceable contract, breach of which is enforceable by way of an order for specific performance, backed up by the contempt remedy, in the courts. In addition, a union awarded recognition by the CAC will be treated as 'recognised' for other statutory purposes such as redundancy consultation and time off work for its members and officials. Under ICER 2004, although the CAC decides whether a negotiated agreement or the standard provisions, as appropriate, have been complied with, only the EAT (see Chapter 12) has jurisdiction to impose a penalty for non-compliance. However, the absence of an enforcement power does not mean that non-compliance with CAC decisions may not have serious consequences for the parties; an employer's failure to comply with a remedial order in respect of its duties relating to recognition ballots, for example, can result in an award of recognition. In addition, where an employer fails to comply with an order to disclose information for collective bargaining purposes, the CAC may, at the application of the union, make an award that takes effect as a term of employees' contracts, displaceable only by a subsequent award under the same procedure, a collective agreement, or by individual agreement to a more favourable term. This term can then be enforced in the same way as any other contractual term. However the absence of the power to impose sanctions directly assists in maintaining the CAC's position as a facilitator of good industrial relations.

THE CAC'S APPROACH TO ITS WORK

The CAC has a general tradition of trying to find a solution consistent with the establishment or maintenance of good industrial relations and to adopt a flexible and problem-solving approach to a dispute, even when it has been accorded an adjudicative role. This is most clearly demonstrated by its approach to the disclosure of information provisions. The statute requires the CAC to refer a complaint to Acas if it considers that it is reasonably likely to be settled by conciliation. The previous CAC Chairman, Sir John Wood, took the view that this could be determined only by meeting the parties and it has become standard practice for the chairman or a deputy chairman, together with an Acas conciliation officer, to do this and to attempt to encourage a joint approach to the problem. This approach has met with considerable success; from 1 February 1977, when the procedures came into force, until the end of July 2005 the Committee had received 522 complaints of which only 13% resulted in a formal decision. ICER 2004 makes explicit provision for Acas involvement where appropriate; here however, unlike disclosure (where the union is required to be recognised), the parties may not have an on-going relationship and the chances of an informal approach being successful may be less.

In recognition cases, by definition, the employer is usually resisting the establishment of an on-going relationship. Tight deadlines within the statutory procedure also reduce the scope for informal contact between the CAC and the parties, although extensions are commonly granted where the parties jointly request this. There are some areas of the statutory procedure where the CAC is given a specific conciliation/mediation role, such as assisting the parties to agree the bargaining unit. In practice, this role has generally been performed by Acas, a division of labour that removes difficulties over the potential need to disclose to the other party confidential information shared with the CAC in the context of a failed conciliation/mediation that may be material to a subsequent decision. However the determination of the principles governing union access to the workforce during ballots has been one area where on occasion the CAC has either facilitated an agreement or, in effect, arbitrated informally between the parties but persuaded them to take ownership of the agreement rather than having it imposed as a decision of the CAC.

This reflects the wider policy of the recognition legislation, which is to encourage voluntary agreement between the parties wherever possible, a policy replicated in the subsequent information and consultation legislation. There is considerable evidence that this policy has been successful; thus, the number of applications or complaints to the CAC does not of itself demonstrate the impact of specific legislation whose existence may act as a spur to voluntary agreement. Finally, in exercising its functions under Schedule A1 of the Trade Union and Labour Relations (Consolidation) Act 1992, in which the recognition procedure is contained, the CAC is explicitly required by paragraph 171 of that Schedule to 'have regard to the object of encouraging and promoting fair and efficient practices and arrangements in the workplace, so far as having regard to that object is consistent with applying other provisions of [the] Schedule in the case concerned'.

JUDICIAL REVIEW

As a body with statutory powers and duties, the CAC is subject to judicial review and this has been a feature of all its statutory jurisdictions. The courts have quashed a very limited number of CAC decisions where there has been an error of law, due sometimes to attempts by the CAC to apply legislation in a way that accorded with industrial realities. This happened most notably in two decisions under the Equal Pay Act 1970. In one, the CAC was found to have erred in amending an agreement it found to be discriminatory on the ground that it did not contain a provision referring specifically to men or women only (*R v CAC ex parte Hy-Mac Ltd* [1979] IRLR 461). In another it was held to have erred in relying upon the Treaty of Rome to support a finding of indirect discrimination when the 1970 Act permitted agreements to be amended only where discrimination was direct (*R v CAC ex parte Norwich Union*, QBD, 8 June 1988). A decision under the disclosure of information provisions was quashed where, *inter alia*, the CAC had included in its award an obligation on the employer concerned to disclose information prospectively, although the court sympathised with the CAC's desire to avoid future disputes about the same subject-matter (*R v CAC ex parte BTP Tioxide Ltd* [1982] IRLR 60). However the courts have, in general, been reluctant to intervene where the CAC has decided factual issues and made decisions in accordance with the industrial relations knowledge and experience of its members, and in 1982 the Court of Appeal warned against reading a CAC award '...which is an award by laymen (*sic*), delivered after argument conducted before the committee by laymen, as though it were an Act of Parliament or as though it were a considered opinion given by the Judicial Committee' (*R v CAC, ex parte BIFU* [1982] IRLR 505, 508, per Lord Lane).

In the context of the recognition procedure, there has been general acknowledgement by the Court of Appeal (and the Court of Session in Scotland) of the expertise of the CAC as a specialist body with whose decisions the courts should be slow to interfere. In a recent decision, the Court of Appeal emphasised the significance of paragraph 171 in interpreting what Parliament intended by the language that it used and structure it provided in Schedule A1, and also recognised the CAC's 'conciliatory general role' and other special features of its jurisdiction (*Ultraframe (UK) Ltd (R on the Application of) v*

CAC [2005] IRLR 641, para.10, per Buxton LJ). This approach has made an important contribution to the success of the recognition procedure. It is noteworthy that, since the entry into force of the legislation on trade union recognition in 2000, the CAC has issued some 500 decisions across all stages in the statutory process, and there have been only eight applications for judicial review. Permission to proceed was granted in six of those applications, and CAC decisions have been wholly or partially quashed in three. The CAC has not, therefore, been impeded by the sort of legal challenges that effectively paralysed the operation of the recognition provisions of the 'Social Contract' legislation (Simpson 1979).

CURRENT AND FUTURE CHALLENGES

The CAC has a distinctive place in British labour relations, being able to operate comfortably in a range of different roles. There is no expectation that it will be granted any major new jurisdictional areas in the foreseeable future, although it is interesting to speculate whether it could one day resume its work in the area of equal pay by examining pay structures and conducting pay audits (see Chapter 9). However, recent legislation has brought some significant new challenges. The Employment Relations Act 2004 made provision for the parties to complain of unfair practices during recognition and derecognition ballots, which came into force on 1 October 2005. These may require the CAC to resolve factual disputes of a kind that it has not been required to resolve before; whether there has been the use of violence, for example. The CAC will be operating against tight time pressures, in what is likely to be a very heated environment, having to decide emotive issues in relation to the conduct of individuals. This may necessitate greater formality in procedures of a kind more usually associated with a court than with an arbitral body. In addition, the CAC may be required to decide issues where there is a greater body of relevant legal precedent. These include whether an individual is an 'employee', what is an 'undertaking' under ICER, and what is 'money's worth' for the purposes of its unfair practices jurisdiction. There may be greater need for the use of an *amicus curiae* where a party is unrepresented. In the context of ICER, the CAC is subject to appeal on a point of law to EAT, which may lead to its decisions being written in a more conventionally legalistic form. These developments carry the risk of the CAC generally becoming subject to a creeping legalism of a kind that has invaded the Employment Tribunals. It may also mean, over time, legal representation coming to be seen as the norm.

Since the advent of the recognition procedure, the CAC has been the target of accusations by employer groups in particular of pro-union bias that are not borne out by the statistics or any other evidence. Employer groups also raised questions over the CAC's suitability to deal with issues under ICER on the basis that members' experience was rooted in collective bargaining, although the decisions the CAC is required to make under ICER are of a similar nature to those in other areas of its jurisdiction. The DTI review of the Employment Relations Act 1999 concluded that '[in] what is potentially a highly controversial area ... the CAC has the general confidence of the social partners'

(DTI 2003b, para 4.15) and that it had 'displayed sound judgment in discharging its duties under the statutory [recognition] procedure' (DTI 2003c, para 4.4).

A major challenge for the future is the preservation of respect for the CAC's role as a problem-solving industrial relations body – its unique strength – in the context of entry into new contentious areas. To date, the CAC and its predecessor bodies have maintained a consistent *modus operandi* although over the years they have been charged with a range of different responsibilities in widely differing circumstances. The Industrial Court was created in 1919 as a permanent body for the resolution of disputes at a time when it was official policy to encourage national level and industry-wide collective bargaining. It was later given adjudicatory powers, such as those under fair wages legislation, to provide for the resolution of disputes that collective bargaining did not, or could not, address. The CAC's position was consolidated as part of the reorganisation of industrial relations machinery in the mid-1970s; at that time its jurisdiction extended almost to the regulatory when it was empowered to determine terms of employment by compulsory arbitration as a sanction under the (then) recognition and disclosure legislation, in addition to its powers to amend discriminatory collective agreements under the Equal Pay Act 1970. Subsequently, as is recorded earlier, many responsibilities were withdrawn, and its workload fell dramatically, due partly to the Conservative Government's desire to reduce trade union power and encourage more individualised pay systems, but also to a cultural shift away from large-scale collective bargaining, a development accompanied by a preference by the collective parties for Acas as a provider of dispute settlement procedures, possibly because the CAC was a body associated in some minds with 'traditional' industrial relations. The renaissance of the CAC took place in a further change in the employment relations climate, with the introduction of a new procedure for mandatory trade union recognition. Independent unions were, for the first time, given the 'right' to be recognised, provided that they fulfilled a number of statutory criteria. The procedure thus located an employment relations issue within an unarguably legal context, and required the CAC to consider a range of novel issues, such as how checks of union membership and support for recognition could properly be conducted. The contemporaneous creation of procedures for union derecognition, which may be invoked by individual workers as well as by collective parties, also brought a significant move away from the CAC's 'traditional' industrial relations functions. A further change is marked by the provisions for information and consultation of employees at national level, which give rights to employees or their representatives but none specifically to trade unions. This, again, represents a cultural, economic and political shift in employment relations to which the CAC will be required to adapt, and which will further test its capacity to maintain its well-established approach to dispute resolution in the face of novel challenges.

REFERENCES

Amulree, Lord (1929): *Industrial Arbitration in Great Britain* (Oxford University Press, London)

Burton, Sir Michael (2001): 'The principles and factors guiding the CAC', *Employee Relations* Vol.24, No.6, p.606

Davies, P. & Freedland, M. (1993): *Labour Legislation and Public Policy* (Clarendon Press, Oxford)

DTI (2003a): *High Performing Workplaces – Informing and Consulting Employees.* Consultation Document, July 2003, pp 7-12 (DTI, London)

DTI (2003b): *Review of the Employment Relations Act 1999.* Consultation Document, February 2003 (DTI, London)

DTI (2003c): *Review of the Employment Relations Act 1999.* Government Response, December 2003 (DTI, London)

DTI (2004): *Regulations to establish a general framework for informing and consulting employees in the UK: Final Regulatory Impact Assessment* (DTI, London)

Gospel, H. & Lockwood, G. (1999): 'Disclosure of Information for Collective Bargaining: The CAC Approach Revisited' *Industrial Law Journal* 28, 233

Gospel, H. & Willman, P. (1981): 'Disclosure of Information: the CAC Approach', *Industrial Law Journal* 10,10

Mackenzie, Sir William (1921): 'The Industrial Court of Great Britain', *International Labour Review,* Vol. III (reprint)

Mackenzie, Sir William (1923): *The Industrial Court: Practice and Procedure'* (Butterworth & Co, London)

Morris, Sir Harold (1928): 'The Industrial Court', *Economica,* March, No 22

Rideout, R. (2002): 'What shall we do with the CAC?', *Industrial Law Journal* 31, 1

Simpson, R. (1979): 'Judicial Control of Acas', *Industrial Law Journal* 8, 69.

Stoker, W. (1920): *The Industrial Courts Act 1919* (Stevens and Sons Ltd, London)

Wedderburn, K. & Davies, P. (1969): *Employment Grievances and Disputes Procedures in Britain* (University of California Press, Berkeley and Los Angeles)

Wood, Sir John (1980): 'The case for arbitration', *Personnel Management* 52

Wood, Sir John (1992): 'Dispute Resolution – Conciliation, Mediation and Arbitration', in McCarthy, W. (ed), *Legal Intervention in Industrial Relations: Gains and Losses* (Blackwell, Oxford)

David Cockburn

THE CERTIFICATION OFFICER

INTRODUCTION

The Certification Officer (CO) is an independent statutory authority with specific functions relating to trade unions and employers' associations. The range of functions performed by the CO includes maintaining lists of trade unions and employers' associations; determining union independence; ensuring annual returns are made, with accounts in prescribed form; supervising union superannuation schemes; investigating unions' financial affairs; ensuring compliance with a range of balloting requirements imposed on unions; overseeing union political funds; supervising mergers, and determining complaints from union members against their unions under different statutes and for certain breaches of rule. These roles involve administrative, investigatory, regulatory and quasi-judicial processes.

Although created in 1975, the origins of the office go back much further and an understanding of the role of the CO requires an appreciation of the social and political evolution of trade unions and of the way the State has increasingly intervened in their internal affairs. Some of the CO's current functions reflect a long-standing legislative philosophy towards trade unions; supporting their autonomy, providing an environment in which they can operate effectively and independently without external interference. Other functions are the product of a different approach; intervening in union internal affairs, laying down standards to which unions are required to adhere. This chapter first outlines the structure of the office and then historically locates the CO before considering its current functions and how they are performed.

STRUCTURE

The legislation which provides for the position of CO is currently the Trade Union & Labour Relations (Consolidation) Act 1992. The CO is appointed by the Secretary of State at the Department of Trade and Industry, after consultation with Acas. The independence of the CO from government has always been guarded jealously by its incumbents. However, since the Human Rights Act 1998, it has been necessary to ensure that the terms of any judicial or quasi-judicial appointment protect the office holder from such interference. Accordingly, the terms of appointment of the CO, which is normally for a period of three years, also provide for automatic re-appointment until the age of 70

Linda Dickens & Alan C. Neal (eds), The Changing Institutional Face of British Employment Relations 91-100
© *2006 Kluwer Law International. Printed in the Netherlands*

in the absence of misconduct, such misconduct to be established following investigation by a judge appointed by the Lord Chief Justice.

Independence is further underlined by the funding arrangements. It is provided by statute that 'Acas shall pay to the CO such sums as he may require for the performance of any of his functions'. It is further provided that 'Acas shall provide … the requisite staff (from amongst the officers and servants of Acas) and the requisite accommodation, equipment and other facilities'. In fact, the Certification Office is situated in the same building as Acas, together with the Central Arbitration Committee (CAC). In the year to 31 March 2004, the net cost of the office was £614,000.

In March 2005, the Certification Office had a staff of ten, the majority of whom work on the collection and analysis of annual returns. The 1992 Act provides for the appointment of Assistant Certification Officers to whom the CO may delegate such functions as he or she thinks appropriate. The appointment of an Assistant Certification Officer for Scotland is mandatory. There is also an Assistant Certification Officer responsible for the running of the office and for taking such decisions as are appropriate in the absence of, or with the authority of, the CO. This is partly because the CO's appointment is on the basis of a three-day working week. A further Assistant Certification Officer has been appointed to conduct those occasional hearings which the CO considers it inappropriate to do himself.

There have been five Certification Officers since 1976. Until the author's appointment in 2001, none had been a lawyer. The others had been former senior civil servants in the Department of Employment or its equivalent.

THE EVOLUTION OF THE ROLE OF CERTIFICATION OFFICER

The position of CO was created by the Employment Protection Act 1975 and the first CO took up post in February 1976. However, the origins of the position lie in the Trade Union Act 1871. Prior to this time trade unions enjoyed what might be described as a precarious legal existence at best. The 1871 Act removed from trade unions their unlawful status at civil law whilst granting certain immunities from legal action. It also gave the Chief Registrar of Friendly Societies the responsibility of compiling a register of trade unions. Registration was to be voluntary and by no means all trade unions chose to register. There were however both symbolic and practical reasons to do so. Symbolically, registration marked the change in status brought about by the 1871 Act, a change in status which seemed more important in 1871 than it does now. The Chief Registrar of the day noted some 12 technical and administrative advantages of registration, ranging from the vesting of property and tax benefits to the amendment of the Libraries Act 1898 so as to make it a criminal offence to create disorder in the library of a registered union.

The definition of a trade union in section 23 of the 1871 Act was made wide enough to include employers' associations, which were also able to register and enjoy the same technical and administrative advantages as trade unions.

The legal foundations of trade unions were further strengthened by the Conspiracy and Protection of Property Act 1875 and the Trade Disputes Act 1906. During this period the number of trade unions which registered with the Chief Registrar of Friendly Societies increased from 173 in 1874, to 448 in 1890, and 598 in 1900 (Chief Registrar of Friendly Societies 1874, 1890 and 1900). By 1910, 77% of all union members were in registered unions, although there were still 615 smaller unions not on the register (Board of Trade 1910).

In the period prior to 1971, the Chief Registrar of Friendly Societies was given two further significant jurisdictions. These both arose out of measures intended to support the activities of trade unions. The Trade Union Act 1913 permitted the use of certain red-circled funds to be used for party political purposes. Secondly, the Trade Union (Amalgamation) Acts of 1917 and 1964 facilitated the mergers of unions by avoiding the cumbersome process of dissolution and reconstitution. Significantly, the Chief Registrar was given not only the role of administering these new processes but also was required to adjudicate upon complaints brought by members that a trade union or employers' association had breached the relevant legislation. The granting of this quasi-judicial role to the Chief Registrar rather than to the courts was not controversial. This may be attributable in part to the antipathy that many unions had for the courts. The Chief Registrar was seen by some as a better alternative.

It is against this background that the impact of the Industrial Relations Act 1971 must be considered. The relatively uncontroversial roles of the Chief Registrar of Friendly Societies were transferred to the newly created Registrar of Trade Unions and Employers' associations. The 1971 Act gave the Registrar of Trade Unions considerably greater power over the content of trade union rules than that of the Chief Registrar. Most significantly, however, the 1971 Act was constructed in such a way that its success was to a large extent dependent upon the registration of the majority of trade unions. For a transitional period all unions on the register of the Chief Registrar were transferred to a new provisional register. However, maintenance on that register was voluntary. While trade union opposition to the 1971 Act was neither as universal nor wholehearted as is now commonly supposed, a policy of deregistration gathered momentum until, by 1973, there were only 20 TUC unions, with a total of about 350,000 members still registered (Weekes *et al* 1975: Chapter 3 and Appendix V). Whilst there is no doubt that deregistration was seen as a tactic to defeat the 1971 Act as a whole, many unions were also opposed to the increased powers of the Registrar in policing the substantive rule changes that the Act required if they were to remain on the register.

The Labour Government of 1974 was pledged to the early repeal of the 1971 Act and, with it, the position of Registrar of Trade Unions. This came about in the Trade Union and Labour Relations Act 1974. For a transitional period, pending the Employment Protection Act 1975, the Chief Registrar of Friendly Societies was called upon to carry out his previous functions.

As noted in Chapter 1, one of the central planks of the Employment Protection Act 1975 was the statutory recognition of trade unions. To achieve recognition, however, a trade union had not only to be on the register of trade unions, but had also to be certified as being independent. A question arose as to who was to determine whether a union was independent. The Act gave this responsibility to the newly created CO, as the successor to the Chief Registrar of Friendly Societies and the Registrar of Trade Unions. It would seem that this name was chosen partly to avoid any linguistic association with the Registrar of Trade Unions and partly because it emphasised the union-friendly aspect of the role, facilitating union recognition. The creation of the position of CO was therefore the act of a Labour Government engaged in extending trade union rights.

Following the fall of the Labour Government in 1979, the role of the CO went through a number of changes. The Conservative administrations of 1979-1997 adopted a piecemeal approach to trade union legislation and the role of the CO was amended six times. Many of the functions that were given to the CO in this period have been retained and will be described in outline below. However, one important role that was introduced in 1980 did not survive, that is the role of making payments to unions of certain balloting expenses (Lewis & Simpson 1981). Unions wishing to receive such payments were required to conduct their ballots in a specified manner. This was seen by many unions as a precursor to the imposition of compulsory ballots, a fear which was fully realised in the Trade Union Act 1984. This measure marked a decisive move away from the position described by Kahn Freund, who noted that, in Britain, 'it has on the whole been common ground that in the dilemma between imposing standards of democracy and protecting union autonomy, the law must come down on the side of autonomy' (Davis & Freedland 1983:274). The task of validating these ballots and making the necessary payments proved to be administratively difficult for the CO and, on occasion, legally complex. It led to a significant expansion of staff and a number of appeals, including one to the House of Lords (*R v Certification Officer, ex parte Electrical Power Engineers Association* [1990] IRLR 398). Although the making of these rebates was phased out in respect of ballots held after 1993, the final payment under the scheme was not made until 2001, a payment of £472 to the Association of Teachers and Lecturers.

A further noteworthy but short lived measure that was introduced during this period provided for funding to be given to trade union members should they wish to take legal proceedings against their union for breach of certain categories of rule. The same measure, the Employment Act 1988, established the position of the Commissioner for the Rights of Trade Union Members (CROTUM). It was the job of CROTUM to determine whether applicants qualified for assistance within the statutory framework. Not surprisingly this non means-tested legal aid scheme proved to be extremely unpopular with trade unions and was repealed by the Labour Government elected in 1997, in the Employment Relations Act 1999. In the same Act, however, the CO was given jurisdiction to determine complaints made by union members of a breach of certain categories of union rules. The categories about which union members can complain to the CO are similar to, but narrower than, those for which legal assistance could be given by the CROTUM. They exclude those rules relating to the authorising of industrial action, the imposition of a levy for the purposes of industrial action, and the application of union assets.

OVERLAPPING JURISDICTIONS

Whilst there are many procedural similarities between the conduct of hearings before the CO and the Employment Tribunals (see Chapter 11), their substantive jurisdictions are mutually distinct. Employment Tribunals adjudicate mainly on employer/employee issues, whilst the CO adjudicates on trade union/member issues. This distinction becomes blurred on just one issue. The statutory right of a union member not to be unjustifiably excluded or disciplined by a union, introduced by the Employment Act 1980, is a right which is enforced by the Employment Tribunal. This can overlap with the right of a union member to complain to the CO about a breach of rules which relates to disciplinary action by the union. In practice, this overlap has caused few difficulties as those who may have a claim under both jurisdictions have generally elected to pursue one or the other. The choice of jurisdiction may be affected by the very narrow meaning given to 'unjustifiable' in the Tribunal's jurisdiction and by the different remedies that are available. An Employment Tribunal can give compensation but cannot make an order equivalent to an injunction, whereas as the CO can make an enforcement order, which has the effect of an injunction, but cannot award compensation.

Although the jurisdictions of the CO and Employment Tribunals are virtually distinct, almost all complaints that can be adjudicated upon by the CO can also be litigated before the County Court or High Court. The legislation deals with this overlap by stating that claimants may choose their preferred forum but, having done so, the right to take proceedings in the other forum on that issue is then lost.

The issues to be determined by the CAC are also generally distinct from those to be determined by the CO. However, in one case, in determining a recognition application, a panel of the CAC found that an organisation was not a trade union even though it had been listed as such by the CO (*BECTU and City Screen Limited*, TUR1/309/2003). There was no appeal.

THE CURRENT ROLE OF THE CERTIFICATION OFFICER

The current role of the CO has four aspects: administrative, investigatory, regulatory and quasi-judicial. These are not distinct, self-contained roles but are rather descriptive of the processes that are required to discharge the various statutory functions of the CO. A more basic breakdown of the functions would divide them into those which impose a supervisory role and those which impose a complaints role.

The supervisory role is generally distinguished by its enforcement mechanism. A union or employers' association which fails to comply with certain statutory requirements supervised by the CO commits a criminal offence and may be subject to prosecution in the magistrates court. The ability to bring such prosecutions is not reserved exclusively to the CO. Any member of the public can do so. In practice, this rarely, if ever, happens and relatively few prosecutions have been conducted by the various Certification Officers since 1975. The preferred means of securing compliance is persuasion, backed by the threat of prosecution. The last prosecution was that of the Anchor Group Staff Association in 2002 for failing to submit an annual return of its financial affairs despite repeated requests and extensions of time in which to do so. The union was found guilty of the offence and fined £1,500. The official of the union responsible for submitting the return was fined £1,000. Costs of over £2,000 were awarded against the union.

There are six functions which might conveniently be described as supervisory in nature, although not all of them may involve the commission of a criminal offence. First, there is the requirement for the CO to maintain a list of trade unions and employers' associations. These lists are entirely voluntary. A union or employers' association must apply for entry on the relevant list and pay a statutory fee. The advantages for a trade union of being listed are that it is an essential pre-condition to making an application for a certificate of independence, it is a requirement to obtaining certain types of tax relief and it grants certain procedural advantages in connection with the devolution of property following a change in trustee. The advantages for employers' associations in being on the equivalent list are not so compelling. However, one benefit of listing shared by trade unions and employers' associations is the protection of that organisation's name. Whether or not a union or employers' association is listed, it must comply with the appropriate regulatory regime. It is for this reason that the CO maintains a schedule to each of the lists. The schedules contain the names of all those unions and employers' associations known to the CO which satisfy the relevant statutory definition but which have not applied for listing. As at 31 March 2005, there were 186 listed unions and 18 unions on the schedule to that list. Similarly, there were 85 listed employers' associations and 79 employers' associations on the schedule to that list. The comparative figures reflect the advantages of listing to trade unions and employers' associations.

A neglected aspect of the work of the CO is the production of the statistics which appear in the Annual Report. These represent a consistent set of statistics going back to 1975 and, in some respects, back to 1871. They chart the fortunes of individual unions and employers' associations, as well as trends across the organisations generally. Since 1999-2000, Annual Reports have been available on the website of the Certification Office (www.certoffice.org), together with the annual returns of individual trade unions and employers' associations submitted from 2004. There is also an e-mail updating and 'decisions service'. By such means, the CO is increasing the transparency of the way in which its statutory functions are discharged.

An obvious trend that can be identified from the Annual Reports of the CO is the gradual reduction in the number of both trade unions and employers' associations. Many of the smallest trade unions are simply ceasing to exist, whilst others are merging to create more viable units. A similar trend can be identified with employers' associations, amongst whom an increasing number is seeking to be removed from the relevant list on the basis that their principal purpose is no longer to regulate relations between workers and employers. Prompted by a decline in national and sectoral bargaining, they are seeking to reorganise themselves as trade associations, removed from any involvement in industrial relations. To be accepted on the relevant list a union or employers' association must satisfy the appropriate statutory definition. This is not normally a difficult matter, but some organisations have been refused – for example, where the organisation has been shown to be no more than a consultative committee, or it has not 'consisted of workers' in the sense required by the statutory definition, while others have not had, as one of their principal purposes, 'the regulation of relations between workers and employers'. Acceptance by the CO on the list of trade unions is deemed to be no more than evidence that an organisation satisfies the statutory definition in England and Wales but, strangely, to be 'sufficient evidence' in Scotland.

Secondly, the CO has the function of certifying a trade union as independent. Independence is to be determined against certain statutory criteria, which exclude any union under 'the domination or control' of an employer. This can be seen as a measure intended to promote effective collective bargaining by excluding 'sweetheart' or house unions from the advantages accorded to independent unions. The principal advantage of a certificate of independence is the ability to apply to the CAC for statutory recognition (see Chapter 7). Other advantages include the ability to apply to the CAC for disclosure of information for the purposes of collective bargaining, the protection of its members from actions taken against them for their trade union activities and the right of its members to seek time off for trade union duties and activities. The fact that an application has been made is publicised in the *London Gazette* or the *Edinburgh Gazette*, as appropriate, and on the website of the Certification Office. This is to enable anyone wishing to object to the application to do so. The granting of the certificate, or its refusal, is conclusive evidence for all purposes that the union is or, as the case may be, is not independent.

Thirdly, all trade unions and employers' associations (whether listed or not) must lodge an annual return with the CO, which must contain certain minimum information and accounts. For example, the annual return of a trade union must state the total number of members, the number of members for whom balloting addresses are held, and the salary of its General Secretary, as well as reporting on its financial status. As noted above, the failure to submit an annual return in proper form is a criminal offence.

Fourthly, the CO has powers to investigate the financial affairs of trade unions and employers' associations. These powers were given by the Trade Union & Employment Rights Act 1993, partially as a result of an unsuccessful prosecution of the NUM by the CO in 1991. The prosecution related to the union's alleged failure to keep proper accounting records and failed following rulings that crucial prosecution evidence was inadmissible. The CO now has power to require the production of any documents relevant to the financial affairs of a union from either the union itself or a third party and to require an explanation of those documents. Should it appear to the CO that there has been certain specified types of misconduct, he or she may appoint an inspector to investigate the financial affairs of the union and report on them. A refusal to co-operate with such inspector is a criminal offence. In fact, only two inspectors have been appointed under these powers since 1993. The CO's preferred practice has been to put any complaint of an alleged financial irregularity to the union and to seek an amicable resolution, only using the various statutory powers if necessary.

Fifthly, the CO has the duty to supervise the establishment, operation and review of trade union political funds. As noted above, this has been an area of responsibility since the Trade Union Act 1913. Trade unions cannot spend money on party political purposes unless such expenditure is from a specifically created and separately maintained political fund. The creation of such a fund requires approval in a ballot of members and, since 1984, its continuation has required renewed approval in review ballots held every 10 years. Any member may claim exemption from having to pay into the political fund.

Sixthly, the CO has responsibility for supervising the merger of trade unions and of employers' associations. This has been an area of responsibility since the Trade Union Amalgamation Acts of 1917 and 1964. Mergers of trade unions can take place either by transfer of engagements or by amalgamation. The draft instrument of transfer or amalgamation must be approved by the CO before the ballot takes place. Should the members vote in favour of a merger, the Instrument of Transfer or Amalgamation is lodged with the CO and a period of six weeks must elapse during which time any relevant member may submit a formal complaint of a breach of the relevant statutory requirements. In the absence of any complaints, the merger takes effect on the date that the instrument is registered by the CO. In dealing with mergers, the staff of the Certification Office have developed a familiarity with rule books and can often alert unions and employers' associations to potential problem areas.

Finally, all unions which have a members' superannuation scheme must maintain a separate fund for this purpose and submit an actuarial report on it every five years to the CO. There are now relatively few unions which maintain such schemes. As at 31 March 2005, only five unions had a total of 12 such schemes between them and only four of these had assets over £250,000.

Apart from the supervisory roles, the CO has a quasi-judicial function in determining complaints brought by trade union members against their unions. The majority of jurisdictions over which the CO can adjudicate are in respect of breaches of statute. A member may bring a complaint that his or her union does not maintain a secure or up to date register of the names and addresses of members. A member may complain that a request for access to any accounting record of the union has not been complied with. A member may also complain that there has been a breach of the various statutory balloting procedures relating to the setting up or maintenance of a political fund or relating to mergers. Perhaps most significant, however, is the jurisdiction to hear complaints about a union's alleged failure to comply with the statutory requirement to hold elections at least every five years for the positions of General Secretary, President and Executive Committee members of a union. Viewed cumulatively, these measures demonstrate the balance that successive governments have struck between trade union autonomy and the imposition of democratic structures on what are essentially voluntary associations.

Since 1999, the CO has also had jurisdiction to determine certain complaints that a union has broken its own rules. Almost all breaches of union rules were previously litigated in the County Court or High Court. The Employment Relations Act 1999 enables union members to complain to the CO that there has been a breach, or threatened breach, of a rule relating to any of the following matters: the appointment or election of a person to, or the removal of a person from, any office; disciplinary proceedings by the union (including expulsion); the balloting of members on any issue other than industrial action; and the constitution of proceedings of any Executive Committee or of any decision-making meeting.

PROCEDURES

The 1992 Act provides that, unless otherwise stated, the CO may regulate the procedure to be followed 'on any application or complaint made to him or where his approval is sought with respect to any matter'. This flexibility is fully exploited to fit the procedure to the issue to be determined. For example, when considering whether to grant a certificate of independence, it has been the practice to arrange site visits to meet with the union representatives and inspect their premises and documentation. Where appropriate, meetings may be arranged with the employers (particularly in a single employer context) and some members of the union. It has also been the practice to seek the views of all interested parties, particularly rival unions, and to obtain the comments of the applicant union on any adverse material that has been gathered.

As to the adjudication process, the CO is required to make such enquiries as are considered appropriate and to give the parties an opportunity to be heard. Any hearing is to take place within six months of the complaint being made, so far as is reasonably practicable. In some cases the parties consent to the complaint being dealt with on the documents, without a hearing. Where there is a hearing, the proceedings are conducted in much the same way as are Employment Tribunals. The process is adversarial, with the claimant having to prove his or her case on a balance of probabilities. Legal aid is not available, although certain expenses can be claimed by claimants and witnesses. Unions are frequently represented by lawyers, but claimants are only occasionally represented. Evidence is not taken on oath. A degree of formality has proved helpful to concentrate argument on the relevant issues and restrict the scope for political speeches or personal acrimony. The CO publishes *Guidance on Procedure*. Should the complaint be successful, the CO must make a declaration and may make an enforcement order requiring, for example, an election to be held or re-run. It is for the successful party to enforce any such order. This is done in the same way as an order of the court. As an equivalent order of the court is an injunction and the offence for not complying with an injunction is contempt, enforcement orders made by the CO are a serious matter.

The Employment Relations Act 2004 introduced a number of procedural changes. It provides, amongst other things, that the CO may strike out a claim or response if it has been brought or conducted in a manner considered to be frivolous, vexatious or otherwise unreasonable. These provisions mirror those already contained in the rules of the Employment Tribunals, and demonstrate a tendency for the legislature to treat complaints to the CO similarly to those made to the tribunals. Indeed, under the scheme made by the Secretary of State for payment of expenses, under section 256(3) of the Trade Union and Labour Relations (Consolidation) Act 1992, the expenses that can be paid by the CO to claimants and witnesses are expressly linked to those paid by Employment Tribunals.

The statutory appeals procedure from a decision of the CO is to the EAT (see Chapter 11). Such appeals are only possible on points of law. With regard to administrative decisions taken by the CO, with no express right of appeal to the EAT, a person with sufficient interest may apply for judicial review.

An Overview

The role of the CO is a product of the development of trade unions in the United Kingdom since the 19th Century. It is therefore not surprising that there is no ready international comparator. Between 1871 and 1971, the predecessors to the CO were perceived as acknowledging the legitimacy of trade unions in return for regulation with a light touch. In the final third of the 20th Century, the regulation of trade unions became politically much more contentious. In this period, the CO became part of the development of specialist 'tribunals' in which easy access was given to individuals to have specific legal rights determined without having to go to court. Learning the lessons of the failed

Industrial Relations Act 1971, there was to be no single measure to reform trade unions, no single Labour Court equivalent to the National Industrial Relations Court and no role for the CO similar to that of the Registrar of Trade Unions. Rather, the functions and jurisdictions of the CO were developed piecemeal, avoiding any involvement with a union's ability to take industrial action.

The extension in 1999 of the CO's jurisdiction to include a limited right for members to complain of a breach of certain categories of rule is consistent with the development of specialist tribunals. The nature of many trade union rule books is such that there are clear advantages in their interpretation being given to a body conversant with the practicalities of running a union. In this way the administrative and supervisory roles of the CO enhance its general expertise in trade union matters and complement its adjudication role. There is nevertheless some scope for conflict between the administrative and adjudication roles of the CO when a union seeks prior administrative approval to a course of action which may or may not be lawful. Whilst the particular union may only be concerned to act lawfully, the CO has consistently refused to give prior approval to any course of conduct which may be the subject of a later complaint by a member. Experience has demonstrated that the administrative functions of the CO can be discharged without straying into such contentious areas.

REFERENCES

Chief Registrar of Friendly Societies (1874): *Annual Report of the Chief Registrar of Friendly Societies 1874* (London)

Chief Registrar of Friendly Societies (1890): *Annual Report of the Chief Registrar of Friendly Societies 1890* (London)

Chief Registrar of Friendly Societies (1900): *Annual Report of the Chief Registrar of Friendly Societies 1900* (London)

Board of Trade (1910): *Report on Trade Unions of the Board of Trade for 1908-1910* (Cd 6109)

Davies, P. & Freedland, M. (1983): *Kahn-Freund's Labour and the Law*, 3rd Edition (Stevens & Son, London)

Lewis, R. & Simpson, B. (1981): *Striking a Balance? Employment Law After the 1980 Act* (Martin Robertson, Oxford)

Weekes, B., Mellish, M., Dickens, L., & Lloyd, J. (1975): *Industrial Relations and the Limits of Law: The Industrial Effects of the Industrial Relations Act, 1971* (Blackwell, Oxford)

Bob Hepple

THE EQUALITY COMMISSIONS AND THE FUTURE COMMISSION FOR EQUALITY AND HUMAN RIGHTS

THE COMMISSIONS

Britain at present has three Equality Commissions with responsibility for combating unlawful discrimination and promoting equality of opportunity: the Equal Opportunities Commission (EOC) dealing with gender equality, the Commission for Racial Equality (CRE) with race equality and the Disability Rights Commission (DRC) with the rights of disabled persons. As from October 2007, there will be a new Commission for Equality and Human Rights (CEHR) into which the EOC and DRC will be merged. The CRE is to join them in the new Commission by March 2009. The CEHR will also deal with three new strands of equality law: religion and belief, sexual orientation, and age.

These Commissions are not exclusively, nor even primarily, labour market institutions. They deal with the public and private provision of goods and services, housing, and education, as well as employment. They are essentially human rights bodies. This is articulated in the Equality Bill 2005, which states (in Clause 3, as considered at the 2nd Reading in the House of Lords on 15 June 2005 – and note that a number of amendments have been made to the Bill since this was penned) that the fundamental duty of the new CEHR is to exercise its functions –

'…with a view to the creation of a society in which –

(a) people's ability to achieve their potential is not limited by prejudice or discrimination,
(b) there is respect for and protection of each individual's human rights,
(c) there is respect for the dignity and worth of each individual,
(d) each individual has an equal opportunity to participate in society, and
(e) there is mutual respect between communities based on understanding and valuing of diversity and on shared respect for equality and human rights.'

Employment is crucial to life chances and participation in society and so, inevitably, the Commissions have been, and the future CEHR will be, concerned to bring about greater equality in the labour market. This has proved to be a complex task. The past and possible future effectiveness of these bodies in bringing about change is not susceptible to easy analysis. This is because of the considerable diversity between and within the

Linda Dickens & Alan C. Neal (eds), The Changing Institutional Face of British Employment Relations 101-114
© *2006 Kluwer Law International. Printed in the Netherlands*

protected groups, and the many factors other than the prohibited grounds of discrimination – such as class, educational opportunities, cultural preferences, and family structure- which cause disadvantage and inequality in the labour market. In this brief chapter it is not possible to do more than describe the ways in which the existing Commissions have exercised their powers of strategic enforcement of anti-discrimination legislation, provided assistance to individuals and sought to persuade labour market actors to change their practices, and then to consider how differently the new CEHR may function.

THE CHANGING FACE OF DISADVANTAGE AND DISCRIMINATION

Any discussion of the Commissions has to be set in the context of the changing position of ethnic minorities, women, disabled persons, and older people in the labour market. During the past three decades patterns of discrimination and social exclusion in society at large have altered considerably, but there continues to be discrimination and disadvantage in the labour market.

Ethnic minorities are no longer 'newcomers' or a 'small minority' as described in the 1975 White Paper that led to the creation of the CRE, replacing the Race Relations Board and Community Relations Commission (Home Office 1975). They now make up 8% of the population. In the first decade of this century they will account for half the growth in the working age population. The United Kingdom is no longer, if it ever was, a society with a 'majority' white and 'minority' non-white population. It is a multi-ethnic, multi-cultural society, with a plurality of communities, including those from the Middle East, Africa and Central and Eastern Europe, as well as those from the Indian sub-continent and the Caribbean. Some of these groups enjoy more power and influence than others (Parekh 2000). The position of ethnic minorities in the labour market is much more complex than it was in the 1960s. However, a persistent phenomenon is that some ethnic minority people are more concentrated than white people in certain sectors and occupations. There are significant variations between different groups: Pakistanis, Bangladeshis and Black Caribbeans experience significantly higher unemployment and lower earnings than whites. Even those minority groups enjoying relative success, such as Indians and Chinese, are not doing as well as they should given their education and other characteristics. There is strong evidence that discrimination plays a significant role. Although overt discrimination is far less pronounced than in the 1960s, institutionalised discrimination – where policies, practices and attitudes have the inadvertent effect of systematically putting ethnic minorities at a disadvantage – remains a serious problem (Cabinet Office Strategy Unit 2003). The perception of growing Islamophobia has also resulted in pressure to deal with religious or faith-based discrimination.

There have been significant changes in the social status of women, and the traditional model of families dependent on the male income has been replaced by many more complex and individual structures since the EOC was established in 1975. Marriage rates have declined, and divorce rates have increased. The proportion of single parent families has trebled over the past three decades. Girls achieve more A-C grades at GCSE and A-Levels than boys, and the proportion of women undergraduates has more than doubled since the 1960s, with women now constituting 52% of those in higher education. In 2005, women made up 46% of the labour market. In the 16-64 age group, two-thirds of women are in employment. However, there are persistent disparities between women and men. For example, nearly half of women (44%) work part-time, while only about one in ten men do so; employment rates are lowest for carers of children and old people, and this affects women disproportionately; four-fifths of skilled tradespeople and process, plant and machine operatives are men whilst at least four-fifths of those in administrative and secretarial and personal service occupations are women; women are underrepresented in many jobs and positions with power and influence. According to EOC research, almost half of the 440,000 pregnant women in Britain experience some form of disadvantage at work simply for being pregnant or taking maternity leave (EOC 2005a). The Equal Pay Act had a marked initial impact between 1970, when it was enacted, and 1975 when it came into force, as employers changed their pay structures in readiness for the new regime. The hourly rates of pay of full-time women rose from 63% to 71% of full-time men's pay between 1970 and 1975. However, women's relative pay was still only 72% in 1983, just before the law was extended to cover work of equal value. Following the introduction of equal value claims, women's rates at first settled at 73%-75%, narrowed to 80% in 1994, but were still only 82% in 2002-2003. EOC statistics also show that the hourly earnings of part-time women workers were still 40% lower than that of male full-timers in 2002-2003, only a slight improvement on the position in 1978.

Public awareness of the disadvantages experienced by disabled people – who make up about 10% of the population – grew during the long campaign for legislation, culminating in the Disability Discrimination Act of 1995 (DDA). After a decade of that legislation, disabled people are still nine times as likely as non-disabled people to be out of work and claiming benefits. Almost half the economically inactive are disabled persons. People with disabilities are more likely than those without a disability to be self-employed or in part-time work. The proportion of disabled people in employment varies according to the type of disability, so, for example, people with mental health problems are less likely to be in work than those with physical or sensory impairments. According to DRC research, more than one-third of disabled people think that they are unfairly treated by employers (DRC 2003). Another group who have raised public awareness of discrimination against them are gays and lesbians; their campaigns were given a boost by the EU Framework Employment Directive 2000/78/EC which included sexual orientation among the new strands of unlawful discrimination that have to be outlawed in the employment field by the Member States.

Finally, there is the phenomenon of the ageing population. The large cohorts of individuals born during the post-war and 1960s 'baby booms' will be reaching retirement between 2010 and 2030. These individuals will have longer life expectancies than earlier generations. In 1951, the average life expectancy for a man was 74.8 years, and for a woman 77.8 years. By 2031, the projected life expectancies are 82.5 years for a man and 85.7 years for a woman. The dependency ratio (the ratio of the number of people over the official retirement age to the working age population) is rising: hence the moves by government, resisted by major trade unions, to raise the retirement age for State pensions, and for public sector occupational schemes from 60 to 65 or beyond. Another key objective of government policy is to increase employment opportunities for workers in the 50-64 age range. For this to happen the tendency towards early retirement, which was pronounced in the 1980s, will have to continue to be reversed. In 1979, 84% of men between 50-64 were in employment; by 1993, this had fallen to 64%. Since 1993 there has been some improvement, but absolute employment rates remain 20% lower for men aged 50-64 than for those aged 25-49, a far larger gap than in 1979 (Brooks *et al* 2002). Older people become detached from the labour market for a variety of reasons, including negative stereotypes, downsizing by offering older workers attractive redundancy packages, and the perception that age discrimination is legitimate. These reasons for discrimination will no longer be acceptable when the EU Framework Directive 2000/78/EC is implemented (by the end of 2006). Action against age discrimination has become an essential feature of EU and UK employment policy. The aim is to increase the participation of older people in the labour force, while at the same time reducing youth unemployment and promoting a skilled, trained and adaptable labour force (Hepple 2003; Spencer & Fredman 2003).

A HISTORY OF BITS AND PIECES

The legislative response to persistent discrimination and disadvantage has been fragmented and inconsistent, reflecting particular pressures at different times. The closest analogy is the 19th and early 20th Century history of factory legislation prior to the unifying Health and Safety at Work etc Act 1974, and the creation of the HSC. This piecemeal development has resulted in five separate statutory regimes (for race, gender, disability, religion and belief, and sexual orientation), with a sixth in prospect when age discrimination legislation comes into force in 2006. A major problem for employers and victims of discrimination is to understand this complicated jig-saw full of inconsistencies and gaps: in 2000 there were 90 regulatory instruments, by 2005 there were 130 (Hepple, Coussey & Choudhury 2000). There are at present three separate Commissions, but, until the new CEHR begins to operate in October 2007, no Commission has responsibility for religion and belief, sexual orientation and age. The powers of the Commissions are similar but by no means identical, and each has chosen to exercise its powers in distinctive ways. Responsibility for the legislation and the Commissions falls under no fewer than five separate government departments, and this complicates the process of reform and modernisation.

The nature and functions of the Commissions were strongly influenced by North American models of administrative enforcement of anti-discrimination legislation. When the Labour Government introduced the first generation of anti-discrimination legislation – the Race Relations Act 1965 – outlawing racial discrimination in public places, a number of pressure groups argued for administrative machinery along the lines of Fair Employment Commissions (FEP) in the USA and Canada, which would rely on education and private conciliation, and only in the last resort on compulsory enforcement (see, generally, Hepple 1970:159-71 and Lester & Bindman 1971:107-49; the case for administrative enforcement was put in detail by Jowell 1965; the report by Street, Howe & Bindman 1967 strongly influenced the 1968 legislation). The main advantages of administrative enforcement were thought to be that strategic action in the public interest would be more likely to change behaviour than ordinary adversarial civil and criminal proceedings, and that a specialised expert body which was independent of government would be free from political pressures and could also investigate complaints against government departments. The Race Relations Board (RRB), established by the 1965 Act, was given power to investigate complaints through local conciliation committees. If the committee failed to settle a complaint by conciliation they reported to the Board. If the Board found that there had been discrimination and it would be likely to continue it could refer the matter to the Attorney-General who could then bring proceedings for an injunction.

The second generation of anti-discrimination legislation – the Race Relations Act 1968 – for the first time made direct racial discrimination in employment unlawful, but placed the main responsibility for enforcement in the hands of voluntary procedures in some 40 industries, with the RRB as only a backstop. The Act retained the two-tier enforcement mechanism of local conciliation committees and the RRB, but the Board itself (rather than the Attorney-General) could now bring proceedings in specially designated county courts (in which the judge sat with assessors) if conciliation failed. However, in the employment field, complaints had to be made to the Department of Employment and Productivity (DEP) which had to send them to 'suitable' voluntary industrial dispute procedures. Only when these had been exhausted, or no such procedure existed, did the RRB have any jurisdiction to deal with the complaint. This cumbersome and ineffective procedure was a compromise agreed by the Labour Government in the face of the concerted opposition from the TUC and CBI who claimed that legal enforcement would undermine the traditions of industrial relations voluntarism (Hepple 1970:175-201). The expectation that reliance on voluntary procedures would stimulate the growth of such procedures to deal with discrimination proved to be illusory. This is not surprising since these procedures were in many cases operated by some of the very people who were likely to be supportive of practices which excluded ethnic minorities. The powers of the voluntary bodies and the Board were also extremely limited. The Board had power to initiate investigations without an individual complaint if they suspected that an individual had been discriminated against, but this depended on specific information and in practice little use was made of this power (McCrudden 1991:12-14).

The third generation of anti-discrimination legislation, namely the Sex Discrimination Act 1975 (SDA), the Race Relations Act 1976 (RRA), and the much later Disability Discrimination Act 1995 (DDA) and Disability Rights Commission Act 1999 (DRCA). marked a major turning point. First, the SDA and RRA imported the American concept of indirect (adverse impact) discrimination, to deal with facially-neutral policies and practices of organisations which have a disproportionate adverse impact on women and ethnic minorities (although, prior to the Disability Discrimination Act 2005, this concept was not included in the DDA, which relied exclusively on the positive duty to make reasonable adjustments for disabled persons). Secondly, all these Acts provided a right for individuals to bring proceedings for compensation for unlawful sex, race and disability discrimination in employment in Industrial (later Employment) Tribunals. Thirdly, they entrusted strategic enforcement in the public interest to the EOC, CRE and DRC. Although the Commissions were empowered to assist individuals, the policy of the third generation legislation was to free them from a responsive complaints-based approach so that they could get on with a broader strategy against discrimination and disadvantage. Organisations were to be persuaded to adopt positive action policies. This promotional work was backed up by the power to issue codes of practice, to conduct formal investigations and to issue enforceable non-discrimination notices. When the DRC was established in April 2000, it was given additional powers to obtain binding undertakings and to require action plans to avoid repetition of unlawful acts.

THE EFFECTIVENESS OF STRATEGIC ENFORCEMENT

The existing Commissions have the constitutions of standard non-department public bodies, with their budgets being set by government and not by Parliament. This means that, despite their independence in policy and operational matters, the Executive exercises ultimate financial control over the scope and extent of their activities. Government is also responsible for appointing the members of the Commissions. Each Commission is composed of between 10 and 15 members with knowledge and experience of racial, gender and disability discrimination respectively. Unlike labour market institutions, they are neither tripartite nor employer- or union-led. In practice, there has usually been a senior CBI and senior TUC member on the Commissions, but these organisations have no formal seats. The Chairs and Chief Executives do not come from labour relations backgrounds. Although employers' bodies and unions are stakeholders, their influence has diminished as NGOs representing ethnic minorities, women and disabled people have become more experienced and assertive. For example, not one of the five members of the Equalities Review Panel set up by the Government in 2005 to examine the causes of persistent equality in Britain has a trade union background, while two come from City institutions. The 'reference group' of 22 stakeholders advising the Panel has only one representative each from the CBI and TUC and one from the Federation of Small Businesses.

The Commissions have been largely successful in their task of setting and raising standards. The principal measures, apart from general publicity, are codes of practice. The legitimacy of these codes was assured by requiring the Commissions to publish a draft, consider representations, and consult employers' organisations, trade unions and other appropriate bodies. The Secretary of State must approve the drafts and lay them before Parliament. Both the CRE and EOC have on occasion had to modify drafts in order to meet government objections. There are currently separate CRE, EOC and DRC codes on race, sex and disability discrimination and equal opportunities in employment as well as an EOC code on equal pay. The codes concentrate on employment processes, for example advertising, selection procedures and monitoring. Their provisions are in some cases inconsistent with each other and have been criticised as out of date and over-elaborate. At the same time, it is clear that significant numbers of employers have been prompted by the codes to review recruitment and selection methods and to take action that has resulted in more employment opportunities for ethnic minorities, women and disabled persons (Coussey 1992:40-43).

The legislators envisaged the use of formal investigations without the need for a complaint by an individual. At first, the CRE believed that it could act as an inspectorate and investigate a specific organisation without any prior evidence of unlawful discrimination, on the basis of general inequality in the industrial sector or occupation or because it was a leading company in the sector. However, in the 1984 *Prestige* case ([1984] I.C.R. 473; McCrudden 1991:67-72), the House of Lords held that investigations into named organisations were not permissible where no unlawful acts were suspected. As a result of this ruling, the Commissions have been restricted to two types of investigation: first, 'belief' or 'accusatory' investigations into suspected unlawful acts by a named person, and secondly, general inquiries (e.g. into chartered accountancy training, by the CRE, and publicly-funded vocational training, by the EOC) which can be carried out without any specific belief that there have been unlawful acts but which cannot be directed at specific named persons and can lead only to a report and recommendations. A belief investigation can lead to recommendations and to the issuing of a non-discrimination notice against which there can be an appeal to an Employment Tribunal. The Commission's powers in belief investigations are heavily circumscribed by procedural requirements, some imposed by the courts such as the need to give the named organisation notice of the proposed terms of reference and the opportunity of a hearing before the investigation starts.

The machinery for investigations and the issuing of non-discrimination notices was described by Lord Denning, in *CRE* v *Amari Plastics Ltd,* as 'so elaborate and so cumbersome that it is in danger of grinding to a halt' ([1982] Q.B. 1194, at 1203). It is small wonder, therefore, that following the restrictive judicial decisions there was a sharp decline in the use of belief investigations by the CRE. The EOC has made even less use of such investigations, conducting only 11 from 1977 to 2005. The last of these was in 1995, since when the EOC has confined itself to general investigations (into pregnancy discrimination in the workplace, gender segregation and modern apprenticeships, and flexible and part-time work). The CRE's experience was that 'employers were more willing to accept advice and introduce widespread change when confronted privately with evidence of inequality, than they were after a public and accusatory investigation' (Coussey 1992:44). The CRE came to see its strongest power as the threat of an investigation and bad publicity as well as relying on 'market leaders' to set the pace of best practice. The CRE's approach since 1989 has been to use formal investigations as a last resort only when attempts to persuade employers and organisations to change potentially discriminatory practices have been exhausted. When an investigation is launched the usual practice has been to negotiate an agreement for changes, and then to suspend the formal investigation while the implementation of the agreement is monitored. This approach has paid dividends with major voluntary changes being recorded over the past decade in organisations such as the RMT Union, the Ministry of Defence (Household Cavalry), the London Borough of Hackney, the Crown Prosecution Service, HM Prison Service and the Ford Motor Co. A useful addition to the powers of the DRC was to reinforce this approach by providing for 'agreements *in lieu* of enforcement action'. These are agreements in which the Commission undertakes not to take enforcement action in return for the named person undertaking not to commit any unlawful acts and to take positive action as specified in the agreement. If the undertaking is breached the Commission may apply for a court order to enforce it. The DRC also has power to require a person who has committed an unlawful act to prepare an action plan for the purpose of avoiding repetition or continuation of the unlawful act.

A limiting feature of third generation legislation is that it relies exclusively on negative duties prohibiting discrimination, rather than positive duties to promote equality. The only exception to this is the duty to make reasonable adjustments for a specific disabled person. Over the past three decades there has been growing recognition that negative duties not to discriminate in the context of adversarial proceedings, induce reactive and defensive attitudes on the part of employers. There is also over-reliance on the 'command and control' activities of the Commissions to detect discrimination and to enforce external standards which organisations have to meet. Most large and medium-sized employers accept that there is a strong 'business case' for equality and diversity, and that the quality of regulation can be improved by bringing into the regulatory process the experience and views of those directly affected. Groups such as trade unions, community organisations and public interest bodies act as watchdogs, educate and inform others, and help individuals to enforce their rights. The key to building regulation on the basis of the self-interests of businesses, and the participation of stakeholders is positive legal duties to promote equality and diversity in the organisation (Hepple, Coussey & Choudhury 2000:56-59). These are the basis of a fourth generation of anti-discrimination legislation being enacted in the first decade of the 21st Century.

The model for this fourth generation of anti-discrimination legislation in Britain is Northern Ireland, where the Fair Employment Act 1989 (FEA) shifted the emphasis from the elimination of unlawful discrimination on grounds of religion or political opinion to the reduction of structural inequality in the labour market whether or not caused by discrimination. Positive duties on employers were introduced to monitor and review the composition of the workforce and to take affirmative action, under the supervision of an enforcement agency. The evidence indicates that this legislation has had a significant impact in reducing inequalities between Catholic and Protestant communities in the workplace (House of Commons, Northern Ireland Affairs Committee, 1999: Paras. 37-53). Another innovation, resulting from the Belfast ('Good Friday') Agreement of 1998, was the enactment of a positive duty on public authorities to promote equality of opportunity, not only between Protestant and Catholic communities, but also between persons of different racial groups, ages, marital status or sexual orientation, between women and men generally, between persons with a disability and persons without, and persons with dependants and without.

This Northern Irish model, which aims 'to make equality issues central to the whole range of public policy debate' (McCrudden 1999) has now crossed the Irish Sea. The Race Relations (Amendment) Act 2000 introduced a duty on public authorities in Britain to have regard to the need to promote racial equality in carrying out their functions, including their function as employers. A similar positive duty in respect of disability is contained in the Disability Discrimination Act 2005, and in respect of gender in the Equality Bill 2005, which is expected to be implemented in this respect in 2006. The statutory duty to eliminate unlawful discrimination and promote equality of treatment can be fulfilled by monitoring workforce composition, consulting with relevant groups, assessing the impact of particular policies and practices upon disadvantaged groups, and by taking remedial action where necessary (O'Cinneide 2002). Unfortunately, many of the public sector schemes currently being implemented in respect of race equality, on the basis of CRE guidance, place too much emphasis on procedures and too little on outcomes. The result has been to generate a large amount of paperwork but, as yet, not much objective measurement of results.

Another effect of the introduction of these positive duties has been to focus recent activity of the CRE on the public sector, with a relatively small division dealing with the private sector where, as yet, there are no positive duties. The new CEHR will inherit all the public sector positive duties. There will undoubtedly continue to be pressure in coming years to extend positive duties to the private sector, in particular in the area of equal pay for women and men (Hepple, Coussey & Choudhury 2000:65-79; EOC 2005b).

ADVICE, ASSISTANCE AND REPRESENTATION

As we have seen, the policy of the legislation since 1975 has been to free individuals complaining of unlawful discrimination from reliance on the regulatory agencies and to give them direct access to Employment (formerly Industrial) Tribunals. A major barrier for individuals is the cost of obtaining advice, assistance and representation. While respondents are generally able to seek the help of in-house or external lawyers, applicants are more likely to use free sources of support such as Citizens' Advice Bureaux, *pro bono* units, trade unions, and the community legal service, or to represent themselves. Those applicants who have legal assistance have a substantially better chance of success than others. The Commissions have the power to provide advice, assistance and representation and where they do so they are likely to provide more effective support than other bodies. This is because they select the stronger cases for representation, they have greater expertise than others, and they provide moral support throughout the earlier stages, thus discouraging withdrawal (McCrudden 1991:204). Their role as enforcement agencies is fundamentally different from that of Acas, which provides conciliation services in discrimination complaints to Employment Tribunals (see Chapters 3 and 11).

There are two categories of case in which the Commissions can give assistance: first, in cases that raise a matter of principle the judicial resolution of which is likely to benefit the disadvantaged group generally, and secondly, those that arise from individual need regardless of broader issues of principle. It is not possible to make direct comparisons between the way in which the three Commissions have exercised their powers in this respect because of the different ways in which they present their statistics.[1] In 2003, the EOC received 142 requests for assistance (about 2% of all sex discrimination and equal pay complaints to tribunals), and granted full assistance in 62 cases, limited assistance in 13 cases and no assistance in 42 cases (53% assisted). In the same year, the CRE received 1,130 requests for assistance (about 36% of all race discrimination cases) but gave full assistance in only 28 of these and limited assistance in 9 cases (3.2% assisted). While the

---

[1] It is noteworthy that in recent years the EOC has not even presented statistics in its Annual Reports. I am grateful to the Research Division of the EOC for the information given in the text about requests for assistance since 2002. The figures are approximate because the calculation year for tribunal complaints is the financial year, and for EOC requests the calendar year.

percentage seeking and granted assistance and assistance has remained fairly steady over the past decade in the case of the EOC, there has been a very substantial decline in the number to whom the CRE grants assistance. This is because of a new legal strategy adopted by the CRE in 2003, which is more in line with that adopted by the EOC since its inception. In previous years the CRE sought to assist everyone who had an arguable case. Since 2003, the CRE has given priority to cases which would clarify points of law or create precedents that may affect large numbers of people, that would help to produce legislative change, or that test the new race equality duty. So far as the 'need' criterion is concerned, the CRE now requires a stronger prospect of success than simply being 'arguable'. Cases which might in the past have been supported directly by the CRE are now more likely to be taken up by Race Equality Councils (RECs), trade unions, or other bodies (CRE 2003). The DRC also applies strategic criteria when selecting cases. In 2003-2004 it helped 655 disabled people with employment cases, taking 30 of these to tribunals and higher courts (DRC 2003-4).

Apart from these formal requests, the Commissions deal with many thousands of enquiries (the DRC help-line alone dealt with 360,000 from 2000 to 2004 and its website has had 1.55 million visits in that period) and give informal advice. In recent years, a number of other agencies have emerged to provide information, support and guidance for employers. These include the Race Relations Employment Advisory Service (RREAS), offered through Acas, to provide advocacy, advice and consultancy services for employers; and Equality Direct (ED) a free, confidential advice service (by telephone and website) on equality designed for small businesses, also provided by Acas. As noted in Chapter 3, Acas services have the advantage of being seen by employers as impartial.

TOWARDS A NEW APPROACH

Over the years the Commissions have published valuable research on ethnic minorities, women and men, and disabled persons in the labour market. They have also, as part of their statutory functions, kept the legislation under review and made many proposals for reform. These proposals have met with a mixed response, being particularly successful in the case of disability and only moderately so in relation to race and gender. Pressure from the Commissions has been complemented by that from NGOs and other private initiatives. The *Cambridge Independent Review of the Enforcement of UK Anti-Discrimination Legislation* reported in 2000 (Hepple, Coussey & Choudhury 2000) that there are two major weaknesses in the present framework. First, it adopts a fragmented, inconsistent and incoherent approach to different manifestations of inequality of opportunity. This makes the harmonisation of legislation and institutions an essential first step to a concerted and integrated approach to social inclusion. The Report proposed a single equality Act and a single Commission. Secondly, the current framework was designed largely to deal with a model of organisations with hierarchical, vertically integrated and centralised bureaucracies. There is a top-down approach which focuses on individual fault-finding and depends on retrospective investigation of an act alleged to be motivated by an unlawful ground of discrimination. In the new age of flatter and flexible organisations equality of opportunity depends not simply on avoiding negative discrimination, but on taking positive action to remove barriers to inclusion, and improving the training and skills of disadvantaged people. The present framework places too much emphasis on State intervention and not enough on the responsibility of organisations and individuals to generate change. This led the Report to advocate positive duties on employers in both public and private sectors to achieve employment equity and pay equity. The Report also proposed a new self-regulatory framework, backed by effective sanctions. Three interlocking mechanisms were envisaged for effective self-regulation. The first is internal scrutiny by the organisation itself; secondly, interest groups must be informed, consulted and engaged in the process of change; and, thirdly, the Commission should provide a back-up role of education, assistance and, ultimately, enforcement where voluntary methods fail.

The Government has, broadly speaking, adopted this new approach although much could still go wrong in the process of implementation. Positive duties have been introduced in respect of the three main strands of discrimination, and the single CEHR will have strategic enforcement powers in respect of all strands of discrimination similar to those of the present DRC – e.g. including the power to require positive action plans and to make agreements *in lieu* of enforcement (see DTI 2004; Joint Committee on Human Rights 2003, 2004; and, for an earlier discussion of options, Spencer & Bynoe 1998). Like the present Commissions, it will be able to assist individuals in equality proceedings, and it will have the added power to intervene in legal proceedings where relevant to the Commission's functions. It will have power to assess a public authority's compliance with the positive duties in respect of gender, race and disability, to make recommendations and to issue compliance notices. The remit of the CEHR will be wider than that of the existing Commissions because it will be required to 'promote understanding of the importance of human rights', 'encourage good practice in relation to human rights', and 'promote awareness, understanding and protection of human rights'. This may be of less importance in employment cases than in the delivery of public services, but it must be noted that the definition of 'human rights' goes beyond the civil and political rights in the European Convention on Human Rights (ECHR). This means that, in the employment field, the Commission may become involved in promotional activities not only in respect of rights such as those to private life, freedom of speech and freedom of association, but also social and economic rights such as those of migrant workers. The CEHR will be able to conduct general inquiries on human rights and to intervene in human rights cases. However, it will have no power to bring stand-alone human rights cases, or to conduct investigations into human rights abuses in individual cases.

The CEHR provides an enormous opportunity to raise the status of the principle of equality, based firmly within a wider culture of human rights. The new Commission is less likely to be seen as representing only sectional interests, in the way the present Commissions have been, particularly since issues affecting white men, such as age and sexual orientation will be included. It can speak with a strong voice and give consistent advice, and can make the connections necessary to tackle multiple discrimination without a duplication of resources. There is, however, a danger that the CEHR will be riven by internal rivalries between different sectional interests. It will have between 10 and 15 Commissioners, who together have experience and knowledge relating to all the strands of discrimination and human rights. There are requirements that at least one Commissioner must be (or have been) a disabled person and that there must be a Disability Committee to whom the Commission's functions are delegated in respect of disability. There is (wisely) no similar delegation of other strands, but the CEHR has power to establish advisory committees. Unfortunately, the Government refused to accept the advice of the parliamentary Joint Committee on Human Rights that the CEHR, unlike the present Commissions, should not be a standard non-department public body, but should have the character of a constitutional watchdog, such as the National Audit Office, accountable only to Parliament and not subject to ministerial dictation or direction.

According to the Secretary of State for Constitutional Affairs and Lord Chancellor, speaking in the House of Lords on 15 June 2005, the Government is now committed to a single Equality Act by 2009, when the CEHR becomes fully operational. Much will depend on the resources made available to the new Commission. But the stage is being set for a challenging new phase in the long struggle for equality and human rights at work.

REFERENCES

Brooks, R., Regan, S. & Robinson, P. (2002): *A New Contract for Retirement* (IPPR, London)

Cabinet Office Strategy Unit (2003): *Ethnic Minorities and the Labour Market. Final Report* (Cabinet Office, London)

Commission for Racial Equality (1977-2003): *Annual Reports* (CRE, London)

Coussey, M. (1992): 'The Effectiveness of Strategic Enforcement of the Race Relations Act 1976', in Hepple, B. & Szyszczak, E., *Discrimination: the Limits of Law* (Mansell, London)

Department for Trade and Industry (2004): *Fairness for All: a new Commission for Equality and Human Rights*, Cm.6185 (Stationery Office, London)

Disability Rights Commission (2003-04): *Annual Report* (DRC, London)

Disability Rights Commission (2003): *Attitudes and Awareness Survey 2003* (DRC, London)

Equal Opportunities Commission (1997-2003): *Annual Reports* (EOC, Manchester)

Equal Opportunities Commission (2005a): *Greater Expectations. Summary final report of EOC's investigation into pregnancy discrimination* (EOC, Manchester)

Equal Opportunities Commission (2005b): 'Pay gap will not close unless new law prompts businesses to act', Press Release 5 July 2005, available at http://www/eoc.org.uk

Hepple, B. (1970): *Race, Jobs and the Law in Britain.* 2nd edition (Penguin, Harmondsworth)

Hepple, B (2003): 'Age Discrimination in Employment: Implementing the Framework Directive 2000/78/EC', in Fredman, S. & Spencer, S. (eds), *Age as an Equality Issue: Legal and Policy Perspectives* (Hart Publishing, Oxford)

Hepple, B., Coussey, M. & Choudhury, T. (2000): *Equality: a New Framework. Report of the Independent Review of the Enforcement of U.K. Anti-Discrimination Legislation* (Hart Publishing, Oxford)

Home Office (1974): *Equality for Women.* Cmnd.5724 (HMSO, London)

Home Office (1975): *Racial Discrimination.* Cmn.6234 (HMSO, London)

House of Commons Northern Ireland Affairs Committee (1999): *The Operation of the Fair Employment (Northern Ireland) Act: Ten Years On,* Fourth Report, Session 1998-99, HC 98

Joint Committee on Human Rights (2003): *The Case for a Human Rights Commission,* 6th Report, Session 2002-03, HL Paper 67, HC 489 (Stationery Office, London)

Joint Committee on Human Rights (2004): *Commission for Equality and Human Rights: Structure, Functions and Powers,* 11th Report of Session 2003-4, HL Paper 78, HC 536 (Stationery Office, London)

Jowell, J. (1965): 'The Administrative Enforcement of Laws Against Discrimination', *Public Law* 119

Lester, A. & Bindman, G. (1971): *Race and Law* (Penguin, Harmondsworth)

McCrudden, C. *et al* (1991): *Racial Justice at Work: the enforcement of the Race Relations Act 1976 in employment* (PSI, London)

McCrudden, C. (1999): 'Mainstreaming Equality in the Governance of Northern Ireland', 22 *Fordham International Law Journal* 1696

O'Cinneide, C. (2002): *Taking Equal Opportunities Seriously: the extension of positive duties to promote equality* (Equality and Diversity Forum, London)

Parekh, B. (2000): *The Future of Multi-Ethnic Britain. Report of the Commission on the Future of Multi-Ethnic Britain* (Chair: B. Parekh) (Profile Books, London)

Spencer, S. & Bynoe, I. (1998): *A Human Rights Commission: the Options for Britain and Northern Ireland* (IPPR, London)

Spencer, S. & Fredman, S. (2003): *Age Equality Comes of Age: Delivering Change for Older People* (IPPR, London)

Street, H., Howe, G. & Bindman, G. (1967): *Street Report on Anti-Discrimination Legislation* (PEP, London)

Janet Gaymer

THE EMPLOYMENT TRIBUNAL SYSTEM TASKFORCE

THE EMPLOYMENT TRIBUNAL SYSTEM

The current Employment Tribunal system consists of three main resources – judicial, executive and preventative. These are the 'pillars' of the current system. Judicial resources are provided by Employment Tribunals in England, Wales and Scotland and by the Employment Appeal Tribunal. Executive and administrative support is provided by the Employment Tribunals Service while the Advisory Conciliation and Arbitration Service (Acas) provides an independent and impartial service to prevent and resolve disputes between employers and employees.

The Employment Tribunal system can trace its roots back to the 1960s following a period (especially in the latter half of the 1950s) when the performance of the British economy and its management were being questioned by those responsible for policy. Three statutes in the employment field marked a change of direction, namely the Contracts of Employment Act 1963, the Industrial Training Act 1964 and the Redundancy Payments Act 1965. Introducing the 1963 Act, Mr John Hare, the Minister of Labour noted:

> 'Voluntary methods are fine, but they are fine only if they are effective. Some progress has been made ... on a voluntary basis in recent years but not nearly enough ... a legalistic approach carries no one very far, but it has its uses especially when the spontaneous approaches of unions and employers are crowned with only patchy success.'

The Contracts of Employment Act 1963 gave to individual employees a statutory right to a minimum period of notice to terminate the contract of employment or receive pay in lieu and required the employer to give written particulars of certain terms of employment. The Redundancy Payments Act 1965 provided that employees dismissed on grounds of redundancy should be entitled to receive a lump sum payment from their employer calculated on the basis of a defined amount of week's pay for each year of service. However, it was the Industrial Training Act 1964 which provided the basis of today's Employment Tribunal system. Section 12 of that Act created tribunals which were empowered to handle all disputes arising under the Redundancy Payments Act 1965 and certain matters under the Contracts of Employment Act 1963, as well as a number of other issues (namely, hearing appeals from the assessment training levy under the 1964 Act; certain appeals under the Selective Employment Payments Act 1966; determining

Linda Dickens & Alan C. Neal (eds), The Changing Institutional Face of British Employment Relations 115-127
© *2006 Kluwer Law International. Printed in the Netherlands*

whether work was 'dock' work for the purposes of the Docks and Harbours Act 1966, and dealing with terms and conditions and compensation for loss of office in local Government and related occupations). At this time, the County Courts (or, in cases exceeding the jurisdictional limits of the County Courts, the High Court) dealt with matters arising out of a contract of employment but, in so far as manual workers were concerned, and the sum involved did not exceed £10, the case might, under the provisions of the Employers and Workmen Act 1875, go to the Magistrates' Courts. As noted in the Report of the Donovan Commission, 'this multiplicity of jurisdictions is apt to lead to waste, to frustration and to delay' (Donovan 1968: Para. 570). In its evidence to the Commission, the then Ministry of Labour invited the Commission to consider whether the jurisdiction of all of the existing Industrial Tribunals should be enlarged. The Ministry noted:

'The nucleus of a system of labour courts exists potentially in these tribunals ... [for] all disputes between the individual worker and his employer ... [and] between trade unions and their members.'

The notion of a labour court was a step too far – albeit that there was, for a brief period in the early 1970s, a specialist court, the National Industrial Relations Court, empowered to hear complaints from individuals, employers and trade unions, which was abolished in 1974, when the Industrial Relations Act 1971 was repealed. Instead, the Donovan Commission's concern remained with the multiplicity of existing jurisdictions and the need to make available to both employers and employees a procedure which was 'easily accessible, informal, speedy and inexpensive' and which gave them 'the best possible opportunities of arriving at an amicable settlement of their differences' (Donovan 1968: Para. 572). Similar virtues had been attributed to administrative tribunals in 1957 by the Franks Committee on Administrative Tribunals and Enquiries, which thought that administrative tribunals generally should possess 'cheapness, accessibility, freedom from technicality, expedition and expert knowledge of a particular subject' (Franks 1957: Para. 406).

There had been a view in the 1970s that ordinary courts were inappropriate for dealing with the resolution of the statutory rights which were being created. As some have commented, a distinction may be drawn between 'administration', which includes voluntary arbitration, and 'adjudication', the judicial method (Schmidt 1969:47). The former method does not make vested rights a matter of principle concern but aims at the adjustment of the relations of the parties with a view to the future. Thus, the parties receive something more than simply a declaration of who is right. There is a 'political' as well as a 'judicial' dimension (Lockwood 1955:336). The Industrial Tribunal System was therefore a form of quasi-court, the intention of which was to avoid the delay, expense and formality normally associated with the court system.

The establishment of Industrial Tribunals marked the first step along the long road to establishing a judicial framework for the settlement of workplace disputes. At the time of their formation, there was no serious parliamentary debate about their constitution and long-term purpose. Commentators have noted that they were the creatures of civil servants and the Ministry of Labour, who were concerned about labour mobility (Wedderburn *et al* 1983:173-8). Moreover, they were perceived differently from courts.

As the then Minister of Labour said during the debates on the Redundancy Payments Bill, in April 1965, the tribunals will be

'organised so as to be easy of access to workers and employers and to provide a speedy means of settling disputes with less formality and expense then might be entailed if disputes were to go to the courts'·

The jurisdiction of Industrial Tribunals had an *ad hoc* appearance, although this changed in 1971 with the establishment of the unfair dismissal jurisdiction, the abolition of selective employment tax in 1972, and changes in the industrial training system which reduced the significance of the levy and levy appeals in 1973. Thus, from the early 1970s, employer and employee disputes came to be seen as the main focus of the work of Industrial (and then Employment) Tribunals. At around the same time (in 1974), third party dispute settlement services, previously provided by the Department of Employment, were transferred to a body which was subsequently to become known as Acas. The Secretary of State declared that,

'so far as the government is concerned, it will not seek to interfere with the activities of the Service' (Weekes 1979:150).

THE EMPLOYMENT TRIBUNAL SYSTEM TASKFORCE

On 26 October 2001, the Secretary of State for Trade & Industry, Patricia Hewitt, announced the formation of the Employment Tribunal System Taskforce. The Taskforce was required both by the Secretary of State for Trade & Industry and the Lord Chancellor to make recommendations on how the services of the Employment Tribunal system could be made more efficient and cost-effective for users against a background of then rising case-loads.

The Taskforce's overall objective was to ensure that the Employment Tribunal system reflected the needs of its users and the changing environment in which it operated. Building on best practice, the Taskforce was required to:

- Identify ways of improving operational efficiency and the scope for improving services, including through electronic business;
- Advise on the need for new investment to meet any revised service objectives and performance measures;
- Consider how to improve liaison between all those involved in the System, including judiciary and the administration; and
- Examine possible improvements to the management of case flow, and of case management.

In coming to its conclusions, the Taskforce was to take fully into account the needs of users (in particular, individual Applicants and small businesses) and the views of the judiciary and staff. The remit of the Taskforce did not cover the primary legislative framework in which the Employment Tribunal system operated or the employment rights they enforced. However, the Taskforce was invited to consider the operational aspects of implementing proposals set out in the 2001 *Routes to Resolution* consultation paper – whose relevant proposals were incorporated into the Employment Act 2002 and included the use of statutory dispute resolution procedures – including operational aspects which could be implemented by secondary legislation. The Taskforce was to pay due regard to judicial independence and devolved responsibilities.

The membership of the Taskforce reflected not only the pillars of the Employment Tribunal system already described but certain user groups. For example, small business was represented by Sarah Anderson CBE. Other representatives of users included Brendan Barber, Deputy General Secretary of the TUC, John Cridland, Deputy Director General of the CBI and Alan Jones OBE, the then Chief Executive of TNT Ltd. The judicial pillar of the system was represented by Colin Milne as President of Employment Tribunals in Scotland and his Honour Judge John Prophet, then President of Employment Tribunals in England and Wales. The Taskforce also had access to advice from Professor Martin Partington CBE.

The Taskforce was required to finish its work and report in Spring 2002. In fact, the report of the Taskforce, entitled *Moving Forward,* was not published until July 2002, although the substantive work of the Taskforce had been completed within the required six months period.

REFORM OF THE SYSTEM AND THE SEARCH FOR WORKPLACE JUSTICE

The appointment of the Taskforce followed a number of initiatives and proposals relating to Employment Tribunals in previous years so that tribunal reform itself had become a growth industry by 2001 when the Taskforce was appointed. The Editor of *IDS Brief* asked, in November 2001 (IDS 2001:697), how the Taskforce fitted in with all these initiatives and proposals, and noted that,

'... the time is right for real change and the opportunities are clear ... the challenge is ... to take the positive lessons that have emerged from the existing tribunal system and other courts and tribunals, in recent years and build on them where possible to ensure that tribunals really do constitute a speedy inexpensive means of work-place justice.'

Meanwhile, other commentators (Financial Times 2001) thought that cost savings were the issue, and quoted the TUC as saying that,

'this is a recognition by Government that going for big bang reform ... is not going to achieve anything very much'.

Certainly, it was true that the System had witnessed a steady increase in applications, which continued to challenge the resources of the System. In 1972, when the right not to be unfairly dismissed was introduced, there were 13,555 tribunal applications. By 1976, when the qualifying period to claim unfair dismissal was six months, the number of applications had risen to 43,066. There was a fall in applications in 1986-1987 to 34,586. In 1989-1990, there were 31,913 applications. This followed the raising of the qualifying period for unfair dismissal to two years. By 1990/1991, there were 43,000 applications, and this had risen steadily until 2001 when there were 130,408 applications.

Other factors which triggered Employment Tribunal reform included a widespread belief that employees were increasingly resorting to litigation to sort out workplace disputes – with particular reference being made to work by Hazel Genn, who had estimated that, between 1992-1997, there occurred 2.4 million serious employment problems (i.e. 500,000 per annum), while, during the same period, there were 429,280 applications to the Employment Tribunals Service (Genn 1999). Also, Employment Law had become increasingly complex, and many business organisations were complaining about over-regulation and burdens on business – pointing, for example, to more than fifty changes in Employment Law during the four years prior to 2001. A number of these concerns were not new.

The Green Paper, *Resolving Employment Rights Disputes – Options for Reform*, issued by the Employment Department in 1994 invited views on a number of issues affecting the operation of the then Industrial Tribunals. The terms of reference for this review were announced by Anne Widdecombe, then Parliamentary Under Secretary of State for Employment, in answer to a Parliamentary Question on 29 April 1994:

'... to review the operation of the Industrial Tribunals with a view to identifying any changes which would help them to cope with an increasing volume and complexity of cases with reduced delays, while containing demands on public expenditure.'

Previously, in 1987, a Committee set up by 'Justice' had also reviewed the procedures, jurisdiction, constitution and expertise of Industrial Tribunals and the Employment Appeal Tribunal, with a view to making proposals for reform. These proposals included the appointment of full-time Tribunal officers, who would assist in preparing the necessary documentary evidence prior to the hearing, and the extension of tribunal jurisdiction in order to include certain contractual claims.

In 1998, the Employment Rights (Dispute Resolution) Act 1998 facilitated the setting up of the Acas Arbitration Scheme (eventually launched in 2001, but not well used), permitted the Chairman to sit alone, emphasised internal procedures in relation to unfair dismissal compensation, and changed the name of tribunals from 'Industrial Tribunals' to 'Employment Tribunals'.

The cycle of reform which led to the Taskforce was formally kicked-off by the consultation document *Routes to Resolution: Improving Dispute Resolution in Britain*. This contained a number of radical proposals in relation to the Employment Tribunal system, which involved placing greater emphasis on the use of internal procedures in order to resolve employment disputes before they reached Tribunals. Employment Tribunals were to constitute a 'back stop' for the enforcement of individual employment rights. A number of the proposals in the paper, in particular those in relation to internal procedures, were incorporated into the subsequent Employment Act 2002.

The consultation document also emphasised the importance of alternative dispute resolution, and sought views on the introduction of a fixed period for conciliation. The thinking behind this latter proposal was that this would focus the minds of the parties on reaching a timely settlement. Some of the proposals, such as introducing a charge for applications to tribunals, did not eventually find favour. Proposals, however, which were subsequently followed through included making completion of the then complaint form ('IT1' – now replaced by the 'ET1') and notice of appearance ('IT3' – now replaced by the 'ET3') mandatory. In its response to the consultation document, dated 8 November 2001, the Government pledged, among other things, to establish a Taskforce to advise on whether and how the Employment Tribunal system could be made 'more efficient, cost effective and user focused to meet the demands it faces'.

At the same time as these developments, another reform initiative which was to have particular effect on the Employment Tribunals Service had been commenced. In May 2000 the Government had commissioned a review of the entire tribunal system led by Sir Andrew Leggatt. The report, entitled *Tribunals for Users: One System, One Service*, was published in March 2001.

The Report covered both the procedures of tribunals (including training and performance) and the wider administrative structure of tribunal systems across Government. Its key recommendations were that:

- Procedures should be fair, economic, speedy and proportionate to the issues at stake. Tribunals should actively manage the progress of cases ensuring that weak cases were weeded out at an early stage. The use of alternative dispute resolution was to be encouraged;
- There was a need for coherent modern IT technology in order to deliver better and more efficient services;
- Tribunals should publish service standards underpinned by arrangements to spread good practice, a range of administrative performance measures, and systems for appraising judicial performance;
- Tribunals should adopt an 'enabling approach' giving the parties confidence in their ability to participate. This would require improved training for tribunal judiciary and staff focusing in particular on the skills needed to implement this approach;
- Users should have access to the information they needed to understand their rights and the tribunal process.

Generally, the Report recommended the establishment of a unified tribunal service to administer almost all tribunals. The service was to be structured in divisions bringing together related tribunal jurisdictions and headed by a judicial president. The role of the Presidents was to be to promote consistency of decision-making and uniformity of procedure and practice. They would be responsible for the composition of the panels to hear individual cases, liaison with a judicial studies board about training requirements, the system for appraising judicial performance and the promotion of more consistent decision-making.

Specifically, in relation to Employment Tribunals, the Report recommended that:

- Employment Tribunals should remain as tribunals but queried whether they should acquire personal injury claims;

- Administrative responsibility for them should move to the Lord Chancellor's Department;
- Unqualified employment advisers should be subject to a licensing system and there should be other safeguards;
- There should be an increase in the number of locations at which Employment Tribunals sat;
- Legal aid should not be extended to Employment Tribunals;
- Costs should not follow the event, but further study on this was needed; and
- An appeal from the Employment Appeal Tribunal to the Court of Appeal should be on the basis of a different test, in order to bring it into line with other courts. In other words, the test should not be 'a real prospect of success on a question of law', but should be by reference to 'cases which raise an important point of principle or practice'.

The recommendations contained in the Leggatt Report were taken into account by the Taskforce in formulating its final recommendations.

In July 2004, in the White Paper *Transforming Public Services: Complaints, Redress and Tribunals* (DCA 2004), a number of the recommendations in the Leggatt Report were followed through. Recommendations for case management reforms, based on the civil procedure reforms, had already been included in new 2004 Employment Tribunal Rules. The White Paper noted that it was not part of the Taskforce's remit to examine the primary legislative framework within which the system operated, and, therefore, did not consider whether legal aid should be introduced into Employment Tribunals in England and Wales, or which department should have responsibility for Employment Tribunals (DCA 2004: Para. 8.3). Despite the tripartite and party-versus-party nature of Employment Tribunals, as opposed to administrative tribunals, the Government accepted that Employment Tribunals should be joined with other tribunals under the Department of Constitutional Affairs. Accordingly, the Employment Tribunals Service becomes the responsibility of the Department of Constitutional Affairs, although Acas remains the responsibility of the Department of Trade and Industry.

THE WORK OF THE TASKFORCE

Patricia Hewitt, the Secretary of State for Trade and Industry, commented in the House of Commons on 27 November 2001 that,

> 'the [Employment] Bill and the work of the Employment Tribunal System Taskforce will help to provide a better Tribunal service to employers and employees.'

In approaching its work, the Taskforce was conscious of the timetable within which it was required to report and the potentially long-term effect of its recommendations. Accordingly, much of the work of the Taskforce necessarily had to be undertaken at a higher level, with a view to indicating those areas which required more detailed consideration in due course. A number of preliminary issues had to be addressed – namely, the extent of consultation and data gathering, the definition of the Employment Tribunal system and answering the question of whether there really was a need for fundamental change in order to ensure operational effectiveness.

Consultation and Data Gathering: As already noted, the Taskforce had a very short period of time within which to complete its work. A process of consultation was needed as was accurate data gathering in order to inform the Taskforce's conclusions. As well as inviting those who had already participated in previous consultation exercises, the Taskforce commissioned a user study from MORI, organised a Consultation Forum, and put in hand a number of face-to-face meetings with interested parties. Some Taskforce members also undertook site visits to tribunals and civil courts.

What is the Employment Tribunal System?: It was important to establish what was meant by the Employment Tribunal system – did this embrace all steps from when an employment dispute arose in the workplace until the final judicial resolution of the dispute after an appeal, or was the Taskforce to focus on the processing of the dispute by Employment Tribunals? A decision was taken to limit the work of the Taskforce to the resolution of employment disputes when they had been formally lodged as claims with the Employment Tribunal, although it soon became clear that the Taskforce's views, for example, on alternative dispute resolution, might have application to dispute resolution outside judicial or statutory processes.

Was there a need for fundamental change?: At an early stage it was decided that there was no need for fundamental change of the current Employment Tribunal system. The original ethos of Employment Tribunals should be maintained, although it was recognised that informality had, in many cases, turned into formality. It was accepted that Employment Tribunals were different because of their unique nature – such as the use of Acas, and the much-valued representation of both sides of industry. This latter observation led to an overall conclusion that the Employment Tribunal system had to operate in an even-handed fashion, whether the user was a well represented senior executive or an unrepresented first-time user. This observation had implications for the Taskforce's subsequent consideration of information technology reforms, and their effect on those who might not be technologically literate.

THE RECOMMENDATIONS OF THE TASKFORCE

In order to give structure to its work, the Taskforce decided that it would review key aspects of the Employment Tribunal system – namely: access, process and procedures, hearing and appeals, and infrastructure and support mechanisms.

Access: The Taskforce reminded itself that the Franks Committee, which reported in 1957, and the Donovan Commission both emphasised the accessibility of tribunals. Sir Andrew Leggett recommended in his review, among other things, that any tribunal system should be 'user friendly'.

In relation to accessibility, issues considered included the obtaining of information about the Employment Tribunal system, the needs of small employers, whether more advice and assistance was needed, and the role of user groups. It became clear that, while much information was available about the Employment Tribunal system – and, in some cases, too much information – there was a need for greater facilitation of access to it. In this respect, the valuable work undertaken by user groups was identified and supported.

Process and Procedures: Under this heading, the Taskforce considered how claims were processed through until the hearing. As well as examining specific aspects of procedure, such as pre-hearing reviews, practice directions, and listing, the Taskforce also considered the role of case management and alternative dispute resolution. In the latter respect, the effect of the fixed period of conciliation for claims to the Employment Tribunal – proposed in the Employment Act 2002 – was of prime concern. Also of concern was the need for issues in cases to be identified at the earliest possible stage.

Hearings and Appeals: The major concern in relation to hearings was to ensure that valuable judicial resources were used efficiently and that hearings were seen to be fair. This approach affected the Taskforce's consideration of how decisions should be delivered and the extent of information which needed to be provided to parties on the conclusion of the hearing. Training was already given to tribunal members, but additional training was not ruled out. The facilities at tribunal hearing centres was an issue for some, and the Taskforce felt it important to establish minimum standards for these, subject to spending restraints.

Tribunal Infrastructure: A number of issues were considered under the heading of tribunal Infrastructure, including the management of Employment Tribunals generally, performance and measurement procedures, and technological needs.

Apart from the need for technological advancement, perhaps the most important conclusion under this heading was the need for greater coherence in the Employment Tribunal system itself. In the course of the Taskforce deliberations, it became clear that the three main independent agencies involved in the Employment Tribunal system – the judiciary, the Employment Tribunals Service and ACAS – were operating in independent but parallel channels. The arrangement of the current Employment Tribunal system was such that, although there was liaison between the three bodies, there were differences in each body's approach to subjects which were the concern of the Employment Tribunal system as a whole – for example in relation to the collation of management information and statistics. There was a need for some mechanism for co-ordinating the work of these three bodies. The Taskforce Report therefore recommended the setting up of an advisory co-ordinating body in order to kick-start this process of greater co-ordination, the achievement of which was to be assisted by the identification of key processes and performance indicators in respect of the System as a whole. Underpinning the creation of the co-ordinating body was a vision for the Employment Tribunal system which was fit for purpose to the 21st Century.

The Taskforce considered that the system should ensure that it could deal with cases in a just, fair and proportionate manner by being:

- even-handed and responsive to the needs of its users;
- accessible and understandable;
- as fast as reasonably practicable;
- reliable, consistent and dependable; and
- properly resourced and organised in an accountable fashion.

This vision did not include a reference to informality, as originally envisaged by the Donovan Commission.

THE GOVERNMENT RESPONSE

Following publication of the Taskforce Report, the Government announced that it would be considering its response, and this was eventually issued on 14 November 2002.

The Government welcomed as a package the recommendations of the Taskforce, and accepted all of the 61 recommendations. In particular, the Government agreed with the overall conclusion reached by the Taskforce that a co-ordinated approach was needed to the planning, monitoring and delivery of a range of system-wide reforms. The Government noted that a number of recommendations required secondary legislation. The aim was to consider how best to incorporate the Taskforce recommendations into business planning over the next three years and the longer term, in order to achieve the greatest benefit for users.

THE FOLLOW THROUGH

The implementation and assessment of the recommendations of both the Taskforce and of Leggatt are on-going. For example, some of the recommendations of the Taskforce have not yet been fully implemented – such as piloting the concept of judicial assistants seconded from the private sector (Taskforce 2002: Para 6.40), and the proposal that a study be undertaken to consider the scope of jurisdiction of Employment Tribunals and the Employment Appeal Tribunal, with a view to widening the extent to which employment-related and discrimination disputes should be dealt with in Employment Tribunals (Taskforce 2002: Para 8.70). By Spring 2006, responsibility for the Employment Tribunals Service should have moved to the Department of Constitutional Affairs and the co-ordinating body proposed in the Taskforce Report may be able to begin its work in earnest. The Government recognised, in the White Paper (DCA 2004: Para. 8.12), that it would continue to facilitate the interest of major stakeholders in the workings of the Employment Tribunal system. The Government proposed that the existing Ministerial Advisory Board should continue, but with a remit to advise the

Senior President and the Chief Executive of the new structure as well as the Secretaries of State for Trade and Industry and for Constitutional Affairs. The paper also recognised the Taskforce's overall recommendations in relation to the Employment Tribunal system, namely:

- Greater co-ordination and consistency of practice;
- The shift in the access of the Employment Tribunal system, so that the emphasis was on early disclosure of information with a view to identifying the issues in disputes and their efficient resolution;
- An emphasis on preventative work, and the identification of, and learning from, best practice; and
- The use of tribunal proceedings as a last resort after all other alternative routes for the resolution of disputes had been exhausted.

WORKPLACE DISPUTE RESOLUTION – PROGRESS OR NOT?

It is premature to evaluate the outcome of the various reforms of workplace dispute resolution which are currently being implemented. However, some trends may be identified – not all of which are encouraging.

First, there is the question of accessibility. The Employment Tribunals Service *Annual Report and Accounts for 2004/05* reported a significant fall in the number of applications registered overall, from 115,042 to 86,181 – a decrease of 25%. Ignoring multiple claims, there was a downward trend in single applications over the last 5 years – namely 16%. The implementation of statutory dispute resolution procedures and the implementation of certain of the new Employment Tribunal Rules have caused initial additional difficulties for Applicants. These have not gone unnoticed by the Employment Appeal Tribunal, which has expressed concern about denial of access to justice where employment rights issues are concerned (e.g. in the 2005 cases of *Richard v U Mole Ltd* and *Grimmer v KLM City Hopper UK*). Even if a claim is permitted to enter the Employment Tribunal system, it is arguable that its early settlement, while saving costs and time, may not finally deliver justice. The Employment Tribunals Service Report for 2004/05 noted that Acas-conciliated settlements were the most common manner of disposal for most types of claim: being the result in over 40% of all unfair dismissal, unlawful deductions, breach of contract, race and disability discrimination and equal pay claims. Also, only 2% of sex discrimination claims, 3% of race discrimination claims, 5% of disability discrimination claims, and 1% of equal pay claims ultimately ended in success before an Employment Tribunal.

Secondly, a more judicial approach to the resolution of workplace disputes may be detected – an increasing focus on who is legally right and therefore increasingly adversarial in tone – despite the rejection by the Leggatt review of the proposals that tribunals should become courts. The absence of legal aid in Employment Tribunals has not impeded the use of legal representation which has been increasing over the years. Employment law itself has become more complex and Employment Tribunals have acquired an increasing number of jurisdictions – now nearly 80 in total. More may come to agree with Munday that 'the belief that industrial law is fundamentally layman's law is a mistaken one' (Munday 1981:149). In addition, proposals such as those made by the Taskforce to encourage earlier elaboration of issues and the greater use of case management inevitably increases the pressure on unrepresented Applicants. The Taskforce recommendation (Taskforce 2002: Para. 5.48) that the application form should remain simple to complete and should have detailed guidance notes to assist users in filling it in may, in practice, prove difficult for some, given the multiplicity of jurisdictions and complexities of employment law today.

Thirdly, the precise role and structure of workplace dispute resolution remain to be resolved. In its most recent *Plan Of Action for 2005/06 – 2007/08* (Acas 2005), Acas notes the decline in collective bargaining, the individualisation of employment relations and the not inconsiderable institutional framework of the Employment Tribunal system and Equality Commissions which have grown up to deal with individual rights appeals, further reinforcing the need for expert impartial information and advice (Acas 2005:6). Acas goes on to set itself an overall aim of shifting the focus from dispute resolution to conflict management – the former largely restricting itself to seeking an effective resolution to the immediate crisis and the latter embracing the wider strategic objectives of anticipating and dealing with issues before they lead to disputes (Acas 2005:8). The question which remains is whether the institutional framework for workplace dispute management should continue to be seen as a place of last resort, dependent upon the vagaries of public financial resources, so that dispute resolution is pushed back into the workplace so far as possible – using, for example, third party assisted dispute resolution. The Government's White Paper on transforming public services notes that conferring the power on all tribunal judges to act as a mediator will be of particular benefit to Employment Tribunals (DCA 2004: Para. 8.6). An alternative approach is to facilitate even greater use of alternative dispute resolution procedures in the workplace with a view to resolving statutory claims at a much earlier stage than at present.

The available machinery for the resolution of workplace disputes continues to be reviewed and, from time to time reformed. This is healthy, although the changing nature of employment relations is such that it is unlikely that a perfect system will ever be identified. In the past, features of this machinery have seemed like a good idea at the time and proved to be of long-lasting effect – such as the use of lay members in both Employment Tribunals and the Employment Appeal Tribunal, their value and importance to tribunal decision making having often been acknowledged (Browne-Wilkinson 1982:70; Jukes 1978:5). A key concern going forward will be to ensure that the aspects of the resolution framework which have worked well are not diluted or sacrificed because of preoccupations about resourcing and losing sight of the overall desirable outcome of any resolution of a workplace dispute which is to deliver a form of acceptable justice.

All the more important, therefore, is it that any framework for the resolution of workplace disputes should take into account the needs and diversity of the Society in which it operates at all times, political, social or otherwise. This requires a recognition that party-versus-party disputes in a workplace context call for a dispute resolution framework which is the product of the views and experience of all of its stakeholders.

REFERENCES

Acas (2005): *Improving the World of Work*. 2nd Edition (Acas, London)

Browne-Wilkinson, The Hon. Mr Justice (1982): 'The Role of the Employment Appeal Tribunal in the 1980's', *Industrial Law Journal*, 11 (June), 69-77

DCA (2004): Department for Constitutional Affairs, White Paper, *Transforming Public Services: Complaints, Redress and Tribunals*. CM 6243 (DCA, London)

Donovan (1968): *Report of the Royal Commission on Trade Unions and Employers' Associations 1965-1968*, [Chairman: Lord Donovan]. Cmnd 3623 (HMSO, London)

Taskforce (2002): Report of the Employment Tribunal System Taskforce, *Moving Forward* (The Stationery Office, London)

Financial Times (2001): 'Team to inspect tribunal reform', 27 October 2001

Franks (1957): *Administrative tribunals and inquiries: report of the Committee* Cmnd. 218 (HMSO, London)

Genn, H. (1999): *Paths to Justice* (Hart Publishing, Oxford)

IDS (2001): *IDS Brief* 697. November 2001 (Incomes Data Services, London)

Jukes, M. (1978): 'Reply: Tribunals – Justice for All?', *Industrial Society* 60 (September/October) 5-6

Lockwood, D. (1955): 'Arbitration and Industrial Conflict', *British Journal of Sociology* 6 (December) 335-47

Munday, R. (1981): 'Tribunal Lore: Legalism and the Industrial Tribunals', *Industrial Law Journal,* 10 (September) 146-159

Schmidt, F. (1969): 'Conciliation, Adjudication and Administration: Three Methods of Decision-Making in Labor Disputes', in Aaron, B. (ed), *Dispute Settlement Procedures in Five Western European Countries* (Institute of Industrial Relations, University of California, Los Angeles) 45-64

Lord Wedderburn, Lewis, R. & Clark, A. (1983): *Labour Law and Industrial Relations: Building on Kahn-Freund* (Oxford University Press, Oxford)

Weekes, B. (1979): 'ACAS – An Alternative to Law?', *Industrial Law Journal* 9 (September) 147-159

Goolam Meeran

THE EMPLOYMENT TRIBUNALS

BACKGROUND AND CONTEXT

When commentators talk about the tripartite nature of the Employment Tribunals, they refer to the composition of the Bench, with a legally qualified Chairman and two Members representing each side of Industry. However, there has always been, in addition, a tripartite relationship between three organisations: Acas, the Employment Tribunals Service ('ETS' – the administration), and the Employment Tribunal judiciary. Whilst the ETS and the judiciary are necessarily bound together in a close, day-to-day working relationship, there is an important link with Acas that has a direct impact on the effectiveness with which the system as a whole operates.

Thirty years after the establishment of Acas, it is as well for all the institutions concerned to re-dedicate themselves to the overriding purpose of this tripartite relationship. Acas has an excellent record of settling over 70% of claims that would otherwise need to be heard by the Tribunals. The recent legislative and procedural changes in the 2004 Regulations and Rules of Procedure, with the emphasis on resolving disputes in the workplace, gives added impetus to the conciliation efforts of Acas.

One of the major recent changes within the system is the fostering of a closer, day-to-day, working relationship whereby Acas receives not simply the claims and response forms, but also case management orders and directions. The effectiveness of co-operation between the judiciary, the administration and Acas is essential if resolution of disputes is to take place at work where they arise. If internal procedures prove to be ineffective, there will be an opportunity at an early stage for the parties, with the assistance of Acas, to explore common ground towards settling differences. This is particularly so where there is an on-going employment relationship; e.g. cases involving discrimination.

JURISDICTION

As is well known, the original Industrial Tribunals (set up by the Industrial Training Act 1964 and renamed in 1996 as Employment Tribunals) were initially granted jurisdiction in a number of manifestly 'administrative' fields – including training levy appeals, certain aspects of 'dock work', and the making of declarations under the Contracts of Employment Act 1963 and the Redundancy Payments Act 1965. This range of jurisdictions fitted broadly within the notion of 'administrative tribunals' as considered

Linda Dickens & Alan C. Neal (eds), The Changing Institutional Face of British Employment Relations 129-144
© *2006 Kluwer Law International. Printed in the Netherlands*

by the Franks Committee in 1957, and generally involved work-related issues arising between individuals and organs of the State.

Table 1. Claims Registered with the Employment Tribunals 2002/03 – 2004/05

	2002-03	2003-04	2004-05
Total claims registered [1]	**98,617**	**115,042**	**86,181**
Nature of Claim			
Unfair dismissal	46,534	46,370	39,727
Unauthorised deduction of wages	39,451	42,524	37,470
Breach of contract	29,635	20,661	22,788
Sex discrimination	11,001	17,722	11,726
Working Time Directive	6,436	16,869	3,223
Redundancy pay	8,558	9,067	6,877
Disability discrimination	5,310	5,655	4,942
Redundancy: failure to inform & consult	3,112	5,630	3,664
Equal pay	5,053	4,412	8,229
Race discrimination	3,638	3,492	3,317
Written statement of terms and conditions	2,753	3,288	1,992
Written statement of reasons for dismissal	1,658	1,829	1,401
Written pay statement	1,117	1,387	1,076
Transfer of an undertaking: failure to inform & consult	1,054	1,321	1,031
Suffered a detriment / Unfair dismissal: pregnancy	1,028	1,170	1,345
Part Time Workers Regulations	500	833	561
National minimum wage	829	613	597
Discrimination on grounds of Religion or Belief	0	70	307
Discrimination on grounds of Sexual Orientation	0	61	349
Others	4,655	6,371	5,459
Total	**172,322**	**197,365**	**156,081**

However, with the introduction, in the Industrial Relations Act 1971, of a right for individuals not to be 'unfairly dismissed', the nature of the jurisdiction took on a different aspect, and marked the beginning of a steady trend towards what is now predominantly jurisdiction in relation to 'party-versus-party' disputes. In consequence of that shift, the modern Employment Tribunals can be clearly distinguished from the majority of other 'tribunals' operating in the United Kingdom – something noted in the report on tribunals prepared by Sir Andrew Leggatt in 2001, and addressed (albeit with some discomfort) in the Government's subsequent White Paper laying the foundations for a unified tribunal system (DCA 2004).

---

[1] A claim may be brought under more than one jurisdiction, or subsequently amended or clarified in the course of proceedings, but will be counted only once.

Table 2. Outcomes of Cases Disposed of by Employment Tribunals 2004/2005

	Total	**%**
Cases disposed	**146,951**	
Withdrawn	43,484	30
Acas conciliated settlements	54,233	37
Disposed of otherwise	10,456	7
Successful at tribunal	26,472	18
Dismissed at hearing (out of scope)	2,146	1
Dismissed at hearing (other reasons)	10,160	7

With a steady stream of new employment rights whose resolution is placed within the jurisdiction of the Employment Tribunals, there are now upwards of 60 distinct grounds of complaint which can be presented for resolution by these bodies – provoking the accusation, in some quarters, that the Employment Tribunals have come to be regarded as something of a 'dustbin' for any new employment-related right devised by Parliament or agreed to within the framework of European Union social policy.

There is also a limited appellate jurisdiction exercised by the Employment Tribunals – the most significant of which involves appeals against the imposition of 'Improvement Notices' or 'Prohibition Notices' upon employers in the context of enforcement measures contained in the Health and Safety at Work etc Act 1974 (see Chapter 4).

Table 3. Cases Appealed from Employment Tribunals to the EAT 2004/2005

	By employers	By employees	All
Cases dealt with at preliminary hearings by EAT			
Dismissed at hearing	38	129	167
Allowed to full hearing	61	119	180
All	**99**	**248**	**347**
Appeals disposed of by EAT at a full hearing			
Dismissed at hearing	132	229	361
Allowed	86	87	173
Allowed and remitted	74	106	180
All	**292**	**422**	**714**
Appeals withdrawn			
Before Preliminary Hearing	46	44	90
Before Full Hearing	87	73	160
All	**133**	**117**	**250**

CONSTITUTION OF TRIBUNALS

The formal provisions as to the constitution of the Employment Tribunals are to be found in the Employment Tribunals Act 1996. In general, cases are heard by a panel consisting of a legally qualified Chairman and two Members, each appointed on a panel representing both sides of industry. Whilst there are now a number of jurisdictions in which a Chairman could sit alone, the vast majority of cases are heard by a fully constituted tribunal of three persons.

However, since the 2004 Employment Tribunal Rules came into force, there has been an increased shift towards various matters being dealt with by a Chairman sitting alone. In addition to the requirement that Case Management Discussions (see below) are always dealt with by a Chairman sitting alone, Rule 18, which provides for so-called Pre-Hearing Reviews (PHRs), envisages that, in the normal case, these hearings will also be held in front of a Chairman sitting alone. Given that a wide range of powers are exercisable at a PHR – including giving judgment on any preliminary issue of substance relating to the proceedings, as well as the ability to strike-out proceedings by way of a judgment or order – this represents, in the view of some commentators, a controversial extension for the areas of Employment Tribunal activity handled without the tripartite representation which goes to make up 'the industrial jury'.

It may be noted that, by virtue of Rule 28(4) of the 2004 Employment Tribunal Rules, where a tribunal is composed of three persons, any order or judgment may be made or issued by a majority – although the incidence of 'split judgments' has historically been very low. In the exceptional case that a tribunal is composed only of two persons – something which is possible with the consent of the parties – and there is disagreement between the two, the Chairman has a second or casting vote.

THE 2004 REGULATIONS AND RULES OF PROCEDURE

The Employment Tribunals (Constitution and Rules of Procedure) Regulations 2004, which took effect on 1 October 2004, introduced a number of fundamental changes to tribunal procedure. The most important change is a new 'pre-acceptance' procedure, which requires Claimants and Respondents to provide certain essential information. Alongside this new procedure has been the introduction of a requirement (eventually brought into force on 1 October 2005) that claims and responses should only be presented on designated forms – the 'ET1', for Claimants, and the 'ET3' for Respondents. The designated claim forms include the relevant mandatory questions, and failure to answer those mandatory questions could result in the Claim or the Response not being accepted.

One of the criticisms that has been made of this procedure is that it has introduced complexity and confusion in a process that had hitherto been simple. The argument in favour of the extended forms is that the parties will have recorded, as early as possible, and while matters are still fresh in their minds, as much of the necessary and relevant information that is required.

When the 2004 Regulations were promulgated, the DTI promised a review at the end of two years. A year after the operation of the 2004 Regulations, there is still insufficient hard statistical data to provide a balanced progress report at the half-way stage. However, industry and the professions are monitoring developments very closely, and the new Regulations are likely to receive some positive recommendations as well as a number of negative comments. The key issue, of course, would be whether or not access to justice for both Claimants and Respondents has been improved or is being denied.

APPEALS

Only a brief word needs to be said about appeals from the Employment Tribunals, since this area is dealt with in Chapter 12 by reference to the work of the Employment Appeal Tribunal.

The right of appeal from a judgment or order of an Employment Tribunal under section 21 of the Employment Tribunals Act 1996 is limited only to appeals 'on any question of law' arising out of proceedings in respect of a designated list of statutes. This, effectively, renders the Employment Tribunal the first and only instance for fact-finding – subject only to challenge on the ground that a finding of fact was 'perverse', in the sense of being a finding which no tribunal, properly directed, could have made on the basis of the material properly before it. For the purpose of assisting in its determination of any such 'question of law', the EAT has been granted effective power (under Rule 30(2)(b) of the 2004 Employment Tribunal Rules) to request that the reasons for a judgment or order are to be provided in written form.

Where an appeal to the EAT is successful, one possible course of action open to the appellate forum is to remit the case to the Employment Tribunal for a (full or partial) rehearing. This will necessitate either the same or a differently constituted panel then to deal with the matter, and the arrangements for the listing and case management of such a remitted case will normally lie in the hands of the Regional Chairman responsible for the Hearing Centre to which the matter has been remitted.

The most recent data indicates that, in 2004-2005, a total of 1,876 potential appeals were presented to the EAT.

THE EMPLOYMENT TRIBUNALS SYSTEM TASK FORCE

The role and work of the Employment Tribunal System Taskforce is considered in detail in Chapter 10. However, it is relevant here to make reference to a number of important recommendations of the Taskforce, and, in particular, to observations concerning:

– The need for more information on forms;
– Increasing time for entering a response;
– A need for greater consistency;
– Digital recording of proceedings; and
– Establishment of a National User Group;
– The introduction of modern IT technology.

The first two of these recommendations touch matters in respect of which there are specific provisions in the 2004 Employment Tribunal Rules. Mention has already been made of the (now mandatory) requirements that specific information be included in the ET1 and the ET3, and it is noteworthy that the array of questions on the designated forms underwent substantial metamorphosis before their eventual (delayed) implementation in October 2005. Meanwhile, the attempt in the 2004 Rules to ensure that equally strict time limits are placed upon Respondents as those applicable to Claimants has proved almost as controversial as was the gross disparity in treatment afforded by the earlier Rules.

Efforts to ensure greater consistency across the System reflect an underlying thrust in the revised 2004 Rules, and have been the focus for a variety of initiatives on the parts of the Presidents in both Scotland and in England and Wales.

On the thorny question of the recording of proceedings, there are self-evident issues of the resources necessary to facilitate such an innovation – an area which is unlikely to be resolved while department responsibility for the Employment Tribunals is in the process of being transferred from the DTI to the Department for Constitutional Affairs.

A few words should be devoted to the Taskforce recommendations in relation to the setting up of a National User Group and the need to achieve greater consistency in tribunal practices.

THE EMPLOYMENT TRIBUNAL SYSTEM NATIONAL USER GROUP

Following the recommendations of the Taskforce, a National User Group was established under the Chairmanship of the President of the Employment Tribunals (England and Wales). The Group is representative of users in England, Wales and Scotland. It meets twice a year, and is a very useful forum for discussing current issues of concern, and exploring ways in which the needs of users can more effectively be met.

To date, the group has met on six occasions. Some of the important issues discussed were:

– The lack of consistency of practice in different Tribunals.
– The use and misuse of Standard Letters and Directions.
– The pros and cons of telephone conferencing.
– The use of the Tribunal's power to award costs.
– The difficulties presented by the 2004 Regulations and Rules of Procedure.

There is much potential in an effective National User Group. In order to keep up the momentum, the representatives of the National User body should ensure that they have an effective network throughout England, Wales and Scotland at a local level, so that matters of concern regarding practice and procedure and any other matter that affect the service to Users, can be dealt with at a local level and, when necessary, be brought to the National Forum.

The Group has, of necessity, to be kept within manageable proportions, and the membership is broadly representative of various interests. However, the importance of

User groups is dependent upon the degree to which there is more effective participation at a local level than is evident, from an examination of the various local user group meetings. A matter of some concern must be the fact that, by and large, attendance at user groups does not fully reflect the needs, and it follows, the concerns of unrepresented parties. However, it is very encouraging to note that the members of the National User Group do have an understanding of the needs and difficulties of under-represented claimants and respondents, and this comes across clearly in the discussions that take place. The Group is very concerned that preliminary indications suggest that the changes in the 2004 Rules raise serious issues regarding access to justice.

CASE MANAGEMENT

Given the complexity of our jurisdictions, and the fact that a substantial percentage of users are unrepresented, there is clearly a need for pro-active case management so as to ensure that the needs of users are met whilst, at the same time, available judicial and administrative resources are used to their maximum benefit.

The current Rules of Procedure make specific provision for case management. Whilst the power to undertake case management had always existed, care was taken during the consultation and discussions on the 2004 Regulations and Rules to ensure that there should be specific reference under the Rules so as to provide clarity to all users, and, indeed, to the Tribunal Judiciary, as to what is expected of them during Case Management Discussions (CMDs). Whilst CMDs may be conducted at any stage, they routinely take place when the file is reviewed on receipt of a Response or, if there is no Response or a Response which has not been accepted, on expiry of the 28-day time limit. If a Default Judgement is not issued, the Chairman will consider what directions, if any, should be given by way of Orders. In some cases, Orders containing directions may be given solely on examination of the file. This is generally where the case is relatively uncomplicated and can proceed to a Hearing without the need for a CMD.

If a CMD is considered appropriate, Orders containing directions may be given by telephone where the point of issue can be resolved without subjecting the parties to the cost and inconvenience of travelling to a Hearing Centre. In other cases, the parties may be called to attend a CMD at a Hearing Centre. This takes place particularly in complex discrimination cases, where there is the greatest need to ensure that the claims and issues are identified with clarity in advance of a Hearing.

In the past, the vast majority of CMDs were conducted by salaried full-time Chairmen. There was an understandable caution about extending the responsibility of CMDs to fee-paid (part-time) Chairmen, some of whom may have had limited experience of Employment Law as practitioners. However, in recent years, the emphasis on recruitment has been from the ranks of practitioners well versed in Employment Law. There is the added concern that, with the increased emphasis on pro-active case management, salaried Chairmen are overwhelmed by the sheer volume of work, particularly in busy regions which have a heavy case-load of discrimination cases. A further consideration is the fact that fee-paid Chairmen were being deprived of the opportunity of acquiring and consolidating much-needed skills in case management. For all these reasons, there has been a shift in policy so as to encourage suitably qualified and experienced fee-paid Chairmen to do CMDs. The decision on whether to assign CMDs to fee-paid Chairmen is that of the Regional Chairman. Such experience is often invaluable to those fee-paid Chairmen who are seeking a salaried appointment.

Much effort has been expended in the last few years on training Chairmen to conduct CMDs. It was necessary to bring about a change in the culture of the organisation so that CMDs are regarded as being very much an integral part of preparing the case for a Hearing.

At a meeting of the National User Group, some concerns were expressed about telephone conferencing, and what seemed to be a disadvantage that unrepresented parties may face. In the course of our training on case management, we ensure that there is a greater level of awareness and understanding of the difficulties a whole range of Users might experience. We take the view that it is for the Chairman to make a judgment as to the most appropriate means whereby a CMD can be conducted – having, of course, regard to the advantages and disadvantages of a telephone conference, as opposed to a face-to-face CMD.

The Taskforce commented on the lack of consistency in the approach taken by various Tribunals. This lack of consistency extended to case management. The degree to which there is a regional variation has been significantly reduced, as a result of the national campaign to identify best practice and to disseminate such practices throughout the regions.

One of our primary concerns has been the long-running, complex discrimination cases where there is an on-going employment relationship. The purpose of pro-active case management is to try to bring these cases forward to a hearing as quickly as possible, so as to avoid further damaging the employment relationship. It will also give the parties a clear understanding of the issues between them, and may possibly facilitate a settlement, either through the auspices of Acas, or by means of any other form of conciliation or mediation.

In complex cases, it may be necessary to hold a lengthy CMD for the purpose of ensuring that there is clarity about the claims and issues in advance of the Hearing. Our experience shows that, by adopting this practice, it enables parties to take a more realistic view as to whether to continue with litigation or to achieve a compromise agreement. It also ensures that the Hearings start on the date and time listed, and that there are more realistic time allocations to complete the Hearing. It is hoped that as a result fewer cases will need to be adjourned part-heard. The most significant saving to the system is that a complex case which is well case-managed will save several days of Hearing, thus saving costs to the parties and to the system. For this initiative to succeed, it requires commitment and application, not only by the tribunal Chairmen and the administration, but on the part of representatives. It is not uncommon for legal representatives to turn up at a CMD without having prepared the case. In the circumstances, they are unable to agree and, where necessary, clarify the claims and issues in the case.

THE 90-DAY TIME LIMIT FOR PROMULGATIONS

There have been concerns about the length of delay in promulgating judgments and reasons, particularly in complex cases. Whilst the majority of such cases are promulgated within 28 days of the conclusion of the evidence, there have been some very worrying examples of delays – many of six, and some as long as fifteen, months. Some delays were clearly avoidable.

On 14 January 2004, all Chairmen were instructed that in cases where delay from the conclusion of the evidence to the promulgation of the judgment exceeded 90 days, a written explanation was to be provided to the President. One explanation for delay in the larger regions is that Chairmen find themselves sitting on one multi-day case after the other, with insufficient time in between to draft their written reasons in a case where judgment was reserved. A possible solution to the problem is to add additional days at the end of a multi-day case so that the tribunal can, if necessary, meet in chambers to reach a decision in the matter, and for the Chairman to draft the reasons. This has helped to reduce delay in many cases.

Where the time limit of 90 days is exceeded, there are, sometimes, good reasons. On other occasions, the explanations are less convincing, and more judicial management effort is expended in ensuring that judgments and reasons are promulgated timeously.

In particularly bad cases, such delays have resulted in complaints to the Lord Chancellor – either directly by a party, or through a party's Member of Parliament. Where there is no satisfactory explanation for the delay, the Lord Chancellor may, after considering any representations by the Chairman, issue a reprimand.

Excessive delay in promulgating judgments and reasons is now a rare phenomenon, but when it does occur it is a matter of much concern.

TRAINING

All Chairmen and members receive comprehensive training. This is not – as with some other areas of the United Kingdom judicial system – conducted directly through the Judicial Studies Board (JSB), but, instead, has, to date, been organised as a specialised facility, through a National Training Panel established by the President of the Employment Tribunals. There is, however, close liaison with the JSB (as appears below) in relation to 'training the trainers', and the move towards a unified tribunal system for the United Kingdom will undoubtedly intensify the rapport between the Employment Tribunals and the JSB.

The President's National Training Panel has concluded that it is undesirable, when training Chairmen and members, to spend a great deal of time and effort in lecturing on substantive law and procedures. These are matters which they should already be familiar with, or should familiarise themselves with, in their own time. Almost all newly appointed Chairmen in recent years are employment law practitioners.

The training courses consist primarily of short presentations, followed by intensive small group studies, dealing with various actual and hypothetical scenarios, conducted by an experienced facilitator. This method of training, for both Chairmen and members, has received general support in the system, and will continue in the foreseeable future.

Members' Training

Newly appointed members are required to attend two compulsory observations before the first day of induction training. After day one of induction training, they are required to do two further observations, and six sittings before day two. There is a gap of about four months between days one and two of training. The underlying rationale for the observations is to give the newly appointed members an insight of what actually occurs in a Tribunal, even if they have, themselves, appeared on behalf of their employers or as representatives of other parties. Being given an insight from the bench is different to an insight as an observer.

The requirement to do two further observations after day one is to enable the new members to observe the practical application of the lessons and principles covered during the first day of induction training.

A further specialist course on discrimination areas of the work is planned for approximately one year after appointment.

New Chairmen

Like members, new Chairmen are also expected to do two compulsory observations before induction training, and two immediately thereafter, before being permitted to sit. The induction training is residential and spread over four days. The Chairmen are given a reading list in advance, and the emphasis is on the practical application of the law by reference to hypothetical and real case histories, discussed in small groups with an experienced facilitator. Formal lectures are kept to an absolute minimum.

The emphasis in the training of both lay members and Chairmen is on the need to ensure that the parties are accorded a fair hearing. Bearing in mind the emphasis on proactive case management, the facilitators are expected to adopt an analytical approach during the small group discussions by constantly raising questions as to what are the claims and issues, and what case management directions would they consider appropriate. We believe that the long-term advantage of emphasising these lessons from the outset is that it will improve the quality of both judicial conduct and decisions, and assisting in attaining a fair hearing for all parties.

The National Training Programme is discussed and agreed by a group of three Regional Chairmen and the President, who meet frequently to discuss not only training needs but also training methodology. Members of the National Training Panel, and all facilitators used on national training courses, have received training by the Judicial Studies Board.

In addition to national training, each Regional Chairman has a Regional Training Panel to advise on training needs and their delivery in the regions. Each region arranges a minimum of two full days training for Chairmen, and one day for members. The National Training Panel makes training material available to the Regional Chairmen.

In addition to the formal training that is offered, many regions have a joint arrangement between the Regional Chairman and the local members, whereby voluntary training is organised several times a year. The members and the Regional Chairman agree on the topic, which is delivered by a Chairman. These events are well attended, and are seen as a joint venture by both members and Chairmen.

The Taskforce identified the importance of more training, and the provision of sufficient funding, to enable a comprehensive training programme to take place. Recommendation 10.41 of the Taskforce Report provides as follows:

> 'Training in the Employment Tribunal system be improved, and that funding levels for training match the best in other leading Tribunals/the Civil Courts.'

The National Training Panel agrees a budget with the administration at the beginning of each financial year. Whilst the amount allocated to training enables us to organise a number of national and regional training courses, there clearly needs to be a greater allocation of funds to ensure that the training provided is more extensive than at present.

Two areas of our jurisdictions frequently come up for criticism by users. The first being discrimination generally, and the second, concerns about the handling of equal pay cases. Given the fact that resources are limited, and not all Chairmen will have the opportunity of dealing with equal pay cases, the National Training Panel decided, as a matter of policy, to embark on a programme of targeted training. Each of the 12 regions in England and Wales was asked to nominate 2 salaried full-time Chairmen, in addition to the Regional Chairman, to attend the first course of such targeted training. Subsequently, there were two further courses. There is now, in every region, a sufficient number of experienced Chairmen who are able to deal with this complex jurisdiction. Many of our fee-paid Chairmen are leading practitioners in equal pay cases. However, given their limited availability for sittings and the need to avoid a conflict of interest, it is, regrettably, impractical to involve them as much as I would like to. This is a loss of much-needed expertise within the system.

As far as discrimination cases generally are concerned, it had been the policy for many years not to permit newly appointed Chairmen to sit on such cases until they had completed refresher training between 18 months to 2 years after appointment. It was assumed that, by this time, they would have gained sufficient judicial experience to enable them to benefit from an intensive course on dealing with discrimination cases.

An examination of the background of Chairmen attending such courses, together with observations made during the courses, caused the National Training Panel to reconsider the practice of an automatic entitlement to attend courses after a given period, regardless of the number of sittings that the individual had conducted. It was decided that, if the underlying basis for the policy not to allow newly appointed Chairmen to conduct such hearings is the need for them to have sufficient judicial experience, it did not make sense to invite Chairmen who had not done sufficient sittings to attend intensive training on discrimination cases.

Accordingly, consideration had to be given to what would be fair and necessary criteria to determine who should be invited to refresher training.

It was decided that there should be a series of criteria including a lower limit of 40 sittings before entitlement to attend the discrimination training course – a change of policy which has not been without its critics. The requirement of 40 sittings is a bare minimum. Given the difficulties in handling such cases, and the importance of these cases to the parties concerned, a strict policy was necessary to raise standards within the system.

The training in discrimination cases is again residential and spread over 4 days, with reading lists in advance, and similar training techniques applied as in the induction course.

Professional Development Training

In addition to the refresher training on discrimination cases, a second refresher course is held approximately two years after 'Refresher 1'. This course deals not only with sensitivity and awareness issues, but also some of the more complex areas of our jurisdiction. As a member of the Tribunals Committee of the JSB, I have a particular interest in ensuring that the JSB modules on equal treatment, suitably adapted from a central part of our training on sensitivity and awareness issues so as to ensure that fair hearings take place. As part of continuing professional development, all Chairmen are required to attend further residential training courses at least once in every three years after completion of the second refresher course. Other specialist courses are also held to deal with particular jurisdictions and issues.

Mediation

Acas performs a very important function in conciliating approximately 70% of cases that are registered in Employment Tribunals. However, there still remain a significant number, mainly of complex multi-day cases, which are not conciliated but which may be amenable to resolution under certain circumstances. It is, sadly, our experience that many large organisations, including local authorities and Government Departments, are involved in long-running litigation where, arguably, neither the claimants nor the employers gain any benefits from such confrontations. They may need to be enabled to see this and act upon it.

It is often apparent to the Chairman – either at a CMD, or early on in a multi-day Hearing – that parties need more assistance than Acas was permitted to give them in order to facilitate a settlement. Tribunal Chairmen can be effective mediators, and should get involved in mediation – not as a substitute for the conciliation efforts of Acas, but complementary to the excellent work done by the Acas conciliation officers.

It is important to promote the idea of mediation in discrimination cases where there is an on-going employment relationship. Far too much damage has been done to industry and to the individuals concerned by protracted litigation in discrimination cases, where often there are no winners, but only losers. It is hoped that by pro-active case management we will, first of all, be able to assist the Acas conciliation officers by sending them a copy of our case management directions so that they are in a good position to approach the parties. If Acas is unsuccessful in its attempts to conciliate, the duty on the tribunal is to ensure that the case is properly prepared for a hearing. However, as a tribunal operating within the reality of industrial and human relations, it is important for us to have regard to the consequences of litigation, not only on the individuals concerned, but also the workplace. If the parties are able to come to a mediated settlement of their case without any particular side being disadvantaged, that would be a far better outcome, particularly if it results in the employment relationship being restored. A successful mediation will often include positive action being taken to repair the damaged relationship and to avoid a recurrence.

The DCA have agreed to sponsor a pilot project involving three regions with a significant number of discrimination cases. A few Chairmen from each region will be identified as potential mediators, and they will be provided with appropriate training to enable them to offer a mediation service to the parties. It is hoped that an analysis of the outcome of these pilots will prove the need for mediation, and the case for Chairmen being involved as mediators.

LISTING OF CASES

The fixed period of conciliation that was introduced by the 2004 Regulations and Rules of Procedure precludes the Tribunal from hearing a case during the fixed period – which is either 7 weeks for a 'short track' case, or 13 weeks for a 'standard track' case. Discrimination cases are not subject to any such fixed period. One of our major concerns in the system has been the delay in listing cases for a first Hearing. We are also concerned about the delays in re-listing cases that go part-heard.

The sending of pre-listing stencils was a practice that was abandoned several years ago in England and Wales, because it took up a disproportionate amount of administrative time without necessarily bringing any significant benefit to the system. With the increase in pro-active case management, and the number of CMDs (whether by telephone or face-to-face), it is hoped that, in the vast majority of cases, particularly those lasting longer than two days, the parties will have been consulted about dates to avoid. Such consultation will take place during the CMD. This should result in fewer applications to postpone because the parties are not ready. It will also eliminate postponement applications which are based on the non-availability of witnesses.

It will be seen that in the year 2004-05, 82% of single cases were listed for a first hearing, and the vast majority were concluded in the time allocated. The delay in re-listing part-heard cases had been a major source of concern amongst the judiciary, the administration, and the users.

For some years now, we have adopted the practice of agreeing the dates of part-heard cases before the parties left the tribunal. This had the advantage of ensuring that the parties' availability is checked before the case is re-listed. It reduces unnecessary applications to postpone, and saves a considerable amount of administrative time in trying to contact the parties. In spite of all these efforts, delays are still at an unacceptable level, and this is partly due to the non-availability of the parties and their representatives of the tribunal panel. It is therefore in the interests of all users for there to be a clear identification of the claims and issues in advance, and a commitment to prepare the cases and to stick to the issues. Part of the training given to Chairmen is to enable them to conduct a hearing in this disciplined way. There is, of course, always the difficulty in conducting a fair hearing whilst exercising legitimate control without a party feeling that they have not been permitted to ask questions or to introduce evidence which, in their opinion, was relevant.

There must be some merit in the argument that, quite often, it is not what the Chairmen says that gives rise to complaint, but the manner in which it is said. Hence, a great deal of emphasis both in the recruitment and selection, and in the training of Chairmen and members, is on inter-personal skills and courtesy. As a former practitioner in Employment Tribunals, I am convinced that some of the attitudes I had witnessed and which detracted from a fair hearing are far less prevalent today.

CASEFLOW

In keeping with progress which has taken place over the past 30 years, a computer-based 'caseflow' system is currently being developed with the active participation of Acas, the Employment Tribunals administration, and the Employment Tribunals judiciary.

The system is intended to replicate electronically the steps presently taken manually. Over the course of time, and in the shorter rather than the longer term, the ETS will move to paperless files. Claim forms, Responses and all written communications will be scanned into the system, processed by case-workers and referred to Chairmen for interlocutory work. Appropriate information will be exchanged much more efficiently between Acas and the ETS. The flow of information between Acas and the ETS should achieve realistic savings, both within the system and to the parties. Great care has been taken to avoid the exchange of information which should properly be withheld.

Caseflow should contribute additionally to the establishment of greater uniformity between the regions and throughout England and Wales and Scotland.

A POLICY ON POSTPONEMENTS

There had been a time in the Employment Tribunals where it was relatively easy to succeed in an application for a postponement, albeit on flimsy grounds. The consideration of an application for postponement is a judicial matter. Each application is considered on its own merits and, when considering such applications, the Chairman's focus is on judicial factors and not administrative. If a postponement is merited, it will be granted without a concern for administrative statistics. The message that has been given to user groups, and emphasised at meetings of the National User Group, is that postponement applications must be supported with grounds. For example, where a witness is unable to attend, the party applying for the postponement must identify the witness, indicate the relevance of the witnesses' evidence to the issue to be decided, the reasons why this witness is unable to attend and, if it was a pre-booked holiday, to provide supporting evidence. Unfortunately, there are still many applications to postpone that do not provide sufficient grounds in support. As a result of the strict policy requiring a case to be made out, there has clearly been an improvement in the standard of such applications, and a well-reasoned case for a postponement has a better chance of being successful.

Sometimes postponements are made on the day of the hearing. Chairmen and members consider such applications with care, since experience has shown that a certain percentage are made for the simple reason that a party may have failed to prepare the case. Occasionally, there are tactical reasons for postponement applications, and whilst such tactics may be regarded as legitimate amongst representatives, they are totally disregarded by the tribunal, which is concerned to deal with merit and not tactics.

An Appraisal Procedure

We are currently piloting a draft competence-based appraisal procedure, which is consistent with the principles of the JSB model. It is to be subject to full consultation with the Council of Employment Tribunal Chairmen. The Judicial Studies Board has agreed to provide appropriate training to Regional Chairmen who will be conducting such appraisals.

Conclusion

The Employment Tribunals today are quite a different creature to the original Industrial Tribunals, set up in 1964. The jurisdictions are extremely complex, and there is far more participation by legal representatives than was envisaged when the Industrial Tribunals were first set up. The absence of legal aid in England and Wales, together with the emphasis that is properly given to the need to ensure that users are enabled to put forward their respective cases without legal representation, has placed a far greater emphasis on the skills and attributes of Chairmen and members than was envisaged. A competency-based approach is now used in the recruitment and selection of both Chairmen and members. It is rare nowadays for Chairmen to be appointed unless they have sufficient knowledge of Employment Law and practice.

The combined efforts of my predecessors and myself have resulted in a change in the culture of the Employment Tribunals. The needs of users are paramount, as is the need to ensure that all concerned are enabled to put forward their cases as easily and as cost efficiently as possible. The language that is used both in correspondence and at hearings ensures that non-lawyers are not disadvantaged. Chairmen and members are recruited as much for their knowledge as their personal qualities. There is an emphasis on inter-personal skills and the ability to communicate effectively. The use of jargon, which causes more confusion than aids understanding, has all but been eliminated in the system. The absence of legal aid places a duty on the whole tribunal to be sensitive and aware of the needs of all the users.

In the last three years, the ETS has consistently recorded a satisfaction rate of approximately 95% in user satisfaction surveys. However, we must continue to strive to work together as a system – i.e. Acas, the ETS, and the judiciary – to assist in ensuring that the policy objective of resolving disputes in the workplace is achieved. Moreover, once a claim is registered with the tribunals, close co-ordination between elements of the whole system is necessary, if the tribunals are not to be clogged up with cases which should really have been resolved without a hearing. There are some matters of concern. Have the 2004 Regulations brought about an improvement in industrial relations and fairness in the workplace? Do both sides of industry feel that the administration of justice in the Employment Tribunal system has improved? A concern that has already been expressed by a number of tribunal users and organisations representing users is that, whilst the Rules introduced some positive changes, there is an overwhelming unease about whether access to justice is being hindered by the complex nature of the Rules and the hurdles which parties need to overcome.

In the next 18 months, whilst the DTI's two-year review is being conducted, the debate on this issue will range far and wide. It must include consideration of the question whether the system should revert to a simple claim and response form of no more than two pages, leaving the Tribunals, through their powers to seek further information, and case management, to ensure that cases are properly prepared for a Hearing.

It is also an opportune moment, whilst celebrating the thirtieth anniversary of Acas, to question whether it makes sense to reduce Acas' budget at a time when the policy expectation is that more emphasis should be given to alternative means of resolving employment disputes. If disputes are to be resolved in the workplace, or, alternatively, without a judicial determination, then, surely, one needs a much-strengthened and properly resourced Acas.

REFERENCE

Leggatt (2001): *Tribunals for Users: Report of the Review of Tribunals* [Chair: Sir Andrew Leggatt], March 2001 (Stationery Office, London)

Peter Clark

THE EMPLOYMENT APPEAL TRIBUNAL

Part I: A Brief History 1976-2002

INTRODUCTION

The Employment Appeal Tribunal (EAT) was established by the Employment Protection Act 1975 (ss.87-88 and Schedule 6) to replace, following a short interregnum when appeals from Industrial Tribunals lay to the Queen's Bench Division of the High Court, the ill-fated National Industrial Relations Court (NIRC), itself set up by the Industrial Relations Act 1971.

In terms of jurisdiction, appeals from Employment Tribunals (formerly Industrial Tribunals) to the EAT lay only on a question of law arising from the lower tribunals' originating jurisdiction under the specified employment protection legislation referred to in s.88(1) of the Employment Tribunals Act 1996 (ETA). That jurisdiction has since been expanded to take account of the increase in employment legislation (s.21(1) ETA), but is still limited to appeals on a point of law. The number of relevant Acts and statutory regulations has also expanded, from six to nineteen. In addition, the EAT has acquired some originating jurisdiction, but, unlike the old NIRC, this is very limited (and, indeed, is being reduced).

Whilst the EAT is described in s.20(3) ETA as a 'superior court of record', it is not a 'court' within the meaning of s.4(5) of the Human Rights Act 1998. In consequence, the EAT cannot make a determination that legislation forming part of its jurisdiction is incompatible with the European Convention on Human Rights (*Whittaker* v *P & D Watson, t/a P and M Haulage* [2002] ICR 1244).

Jurisdiction

The EAT hears appeals not only from Employment Tribunals in England and Wales but also in Scotland. As confirmed in *Davidson* v *City Electrical Factors Ltd* ([1998] IRLR 435), Employment Tribunals are bound by decisions of the EAT wherever it sits. Sittings take place principally in London and Edinburgh. Northern Ireland has no equivalent to the Employment Appeal Tribunal.

In addition to deciding hard-edged questions of statutory construction, the EAT will also consider appeals based on 'perversity' – namely, appeals founded upon the

Linda Dickens & Alan C. Neal (eds), The Changing Institutional Face of British Employment Relations 145-147
© 2006 Kluwer Law International. Printed in the Netherlands

proposition that no reasonable tribunal, properly directed, could reach the conclusion which the particular tribunal reached (*Bastick* v *James Lane (Turf Accountants) Ltd* [1979] ICR 778, approved by the Court of Appeal in *Carter* v *Credit Change Ltd* [1979] ICR 908). However, such appeals should only succeed where an 'overwhelming case' is made out on the perversity ground (*Yeboah* v *Crofton* [2002] IRLR 634).

Constitution

From its inception, the EAT has been based on the tri-partite model of professional judge and lay members drawn from both side of industry. The President of the EAT is a High Court judge appointed by the Lord Chancellor (s.22(3) ETA). In addition, both High Court and, more recently, Circuit Judges sit as nominated temporary Judges.

Historically, lay members were appointed on the recommendation of management and worker organisations (notably, the CBI and the TUC). However, more recently, these appointments have been by way of open competition.

An appeal from an Employment Tribunal Chairman sitting alone will normally be heard by an EAT Judge alone, unless otherwise ordered (s.28(4) ETA).

Practice and Procedure

Prior to the current Practice Directions issued by Burton P. (first on 9 December 2002, and then on 9 December 2004), the practice of the EAT varied under different Presidents. In general, appeals were either listed for a Preliminary Hearing in order to determine whether the appeal raised an arguable point of law, or went straight to a Full Hearing with both parties present. They were not rejected on paper.

The time for appealing is 42 days from the date of the Employment Tribunal Judgment or Order in question (*Hammersmith and Fulham LBC* v *Ladejobi* [1999] ICR 673, approved by the Court of Appeal in *Gdynia American Shipping Lines* v *Chelminski* [2004] IRLR 725). That time limit will only be extended in exceptional circumstances (*United Arab Emirates* v *Abdelghafar* [1995] ICR 65, approved by the Court of Appeal in *Aziz* v *Bethnal Green City Challenge Co Ltd* [2000] IRLR 111). The initial decision as to whether time may be extended lies with the Registrar, with a right of appeal to a Judge.

Historically, parties have not been permitted, save in exceptional circumstances, to raise new points of law not argued below (*Kumchyk* v *Derby CC* [1978] ICR 1116, approved by the Court of Appeal in *Glennie* v *Independent Magazines (UK) Ltd* [1999] IRLR 719). Nor will a party be permitted to adduce fresh evidence on appeal unless the test set out in *Ladd* v *Marshall*, [1954] 1 WLR 1489, is satisfied.

Papers have always been pre-read by the members of the division hearing an appeal. The practice of lodging skeleton arguments gradually took hold and is now mandatory.

Costs orders in the EAT have traditionally been rare, due to the limited circumstances in which they may be ordered, but are now – as can be seen from the recent case of *Salinas* v *Bear Stearns International Holdings Inc.* [2005] ICR 1117 – becoming more frequent. Successful appeals result in the decision of the Employment Tribunal being reversed, or the case being remitted to the same or a different Employment Tribunal for rehearing in whole or in part (s.35(1) ETA). The approach to the issue of whether remission should be to a differently constituted tribunal has recently been set out in *Sinclair Roche & Temperley* v *Heard* [2004] IRLR 763.

A further appeal lies to the Court of Appeal (or, in Scotland, to the Court of Session), either with leave (permission) of the EAT or those Courts (s.37(1) and (2) ETA). Thereafter, appeals lie to the House of Lords with leave. Cases may also be referred by the EAT to the European Court of Justice for preliminary rulings under Article 234 of the Treaty Establishing the European Community.

Sir Michael Burton

THE EMPLOYMENT APPEAL TRIBUNAL

Part II: The EAT 2002-2005

Since 1993, the EAT has been governed by the Employment Appeal Tribunal Rules (SI 1993, No.284, amended in 2001). In 1996, Sir John Mummery, the then President, issued a Practice Direction, which enshrined the body of practice which had been developed and honed over the first twenty years of the EAT's existence. The changes over the past three years have now been reflected in the 2004 amendments to the EAT Rules, and by two further Practice Directions, first in December 2002, to implement the effect of the changes introduced in practice as from October 2002, and then in December 2004, once they had bedded in, to adjust to the amended Rules, which had also reflected those changes. The following provides a brief summary of those changes, together with some reflections upon their effect.

The EAT Team

There is now a regular cadre of EAT judges in addition to the President – both visiting judges from a select band of nominated High Court judges, and a very experienced group of Circuit judges (led by the two resident such judges, Judges Clark and McMullen), which has meant we have been able to surmount the removal, as a result of the decision by the House of Lords in *Lawal* v *Northern Spirit Ltd*, [2003] ICR 856, of almost the entire team of recorders. The experience and diligence of that cadre of judges, and their keenness to work with the changes and to do much more work on paper and out of court than had previously been the case, have, together with the determination and enthusiasm of the EAT Registrar and her staff and the willing co-operation of the lay members, facilitated fundamental change at the EAT.

The Sift

The most significant change has been the introduction of the 'Sift', which means that every notice of appeal is now considered on paper by a judge, very shortly after presentation. In order to assist proper consideration of the appeal, the Rules now require that the notice of appeal must be accompanied not only by the Employment Tribunal judgment or order appealed against, but also by a copy of the claim form ('ET1') and the response ('ET3'), or an explanation as to why they are not available; and information must be provided as to whether there is an outstanding application to the Employment Tribunal for review. The judge now considers the papers and has available to him a new

Linda Dickens & Alan C. Neal (eds), The Changing Institutional Face of British Employment Relations, 148-58
© *2006 Kluwer Law International. Printed in the Netherlands*

document called a Sift sheet and a selection of various draft standard orders which the judge can adopt or adapt. If the cases are ordered to go forward to a preliminary hearing ('ph') or a full hearing ('fh') the judge will include on the Sift sheet a short summary of the nature of the case, for inclusion in the 'Sift Bulletin' (see below). On the Sift, the judge has four options:

1. ***An order for a stay*** (making sure that there is a final date by which the papers must be restored for further consideration). This option, introduced when the Sift was implemented, was entirely new. There may be a stay for the following purposes:

    a. *Until the outcome of a review*, if one has been applied for (see above); or to give the *opportunity* for the would-be appellant *to apply for such a review* (albeit out of time – the ordinary 14 day time limit for a review is likely already to have expired given that the time limit for an appeal is six weeks).

        There will be cases where, if there is any merit at all, an application for a review would appear far more appropriate than an appeal: e.g. where there are allegations of material errors of fact in a judgment, or apparent inconsistencies in a judgment, or the appellant wishes to rely on fresh evidence. Irrespective of the expiry of any time limit, the Employment Tribunal, on such a reference to it, can decide to review a judgment of its own initiative (Rule 34(5), ET Rules 2004).

    b. *For the provision of reasons*, or further reasons, by the Employment Tribunal, if the appeal is in whole or in part 'a *Meek* appeal', based upon alleged inadequacy of reasoning or findings (*Meek* v *City of Birmingham*, [1987] IRLR 250).

        The Employment Tribunal is requested to indicate whether it had such reasons or further reasons or made such findings, and if so what they were, without adducing any further evidence (always being free of its own initiative to review its decision if it were so minded). This is not a remission, as at an fh when the Employment Tribunal's decision is quashed, but a referral back, and the appeal remains live, though stayed. This course is now known as 'a Burns/Barke referral', in that it was first described and explained in *Burns* v *Consignia PLC (No.2)*, [2004] IRLR 425 (approved by the Court of Appeal in *Barke* v *SEETEC Business Technology Centre Ltd*, [2005] IRLR 633). Such a referral order is made with caution and will always provide both parties with liberty to apply on paper on notice to vary or discharge it. It can also be made at a ph. It has been adopted on approximately one hundred occasions since its inception after October 2002.

    c. *For further information* if the appeal is in whole or in part based on allegations of bias or misconduct by the Employment Tribunal below, unless it already looks sufficiently arguable to be sent forward, with appropriate directions (see below) to a ph or fh.

During such a stay, the 'Paragraph 11 Procedure' (see below) will be operated, and there may be provision in the order for the operation of the EAT/Acas Protocol (see below).

Such appeals, after being stayed, may never go any further, as the cases may be reviewed by the Employment Tribunal, or there may be satisfactory answers given by the Employment Tribunal or they may be compromised or conciliated. If and when they return to the EAT, they will be resifted, and may then be dealt with under Rule 3, or sent through to an fh (or perhaps a ph).

2. *Rule 3 of the EAT Rules*

This (an effective strike out) was rarely, if ever, activated before October 2002. Since then, it has been regularly used as an option on the Sift. Rule 3 has now been amended to reflect what we had in fact started to do even prior to the rule changes:

a. Prior to its recent amendment, a Rule 3 direction could only be made by the Registrar, so the judge on the Sift could only make a recommendation to the Registrar, which the Registrar was then required to reconsider. The direction can now be given on the Sift by a judge, with reasons.

b. Prior to such rule change, Rule 3 could only be operated in respect of an entire notice of appeal and not, as is so often appropriate, so as to eliminate some obviously insupportable grounds, while preserving others: and a quasi-consensual route had to be adopted to achieve this. Since the amendments, Rule 3 can be operated in respect of the whole or any part of a notice of appeal.

c. Prior to the rule change, the trigger for consideration under Rule 3 was as to whether the EAT had jurisdiction to hear the appeal (of course it being a given that the EAT only had jurisdiction in respect of points of law). Many apparently hopeless appeals could be so interpreted. The amended Rule, however, has now specifically authorised operation of Rule 3 where the notice of appeal (in whole or in part) '*discloses no reasonable grounds for bringing the appeal*'.

d. After a Rule 3 direction, a party can seek renewed consideration of such appeal either by submitting a fresh notice of appeal within Rule 3(8), within a specified time limit, in which case the appeal will be resifted and/or he can apply under Rule 3(10) for reconsideration. In practice, prior to the rule change such an application was always heard in open court by a judge; and that has now been enshrined as a right in the amended Rule 3(10).

3. *Full Hearing (FH)*

Prior to the introduction of the Sift, it happened only rarely that an appeal would be sent straight through to a full hearing, but where the appeal appears arguable this is now regularly done, accompanied by an order containing detailed directions, making use of a standard Sift fh order. As discussed above, there is a series of such standard orders now available (both on the Sift and indeed after a ph), into which I have sought to include (at least as options) all the orders which may need to be considered, thus alleviating the absence of a ph and avoiding, in all except rare cases, any need for an Appointment for Directions. Thus, on the Sift, a category will be assigned – 'P' (for President), 'A', 'B', or 'C', depending upon complexity or importance – and a time estimate will be made by the Sift judge, but with notice to the parties that they must speedily indicate if and when they disagree. This has made listing much easier. There is also provision for other matters: for any cross-appeal (which will need to be separately sifted), for orders in respect of the 'Paragraph 7 Procedure' or the 'Paragraph 11 Procedure' (see below), in respect of any application for fresh evidence, and for the timing of service of bundles of documents and of authorities (now made the responsibility of the parties), and of skeleton arguments and chronologies.

4. *Preliminary Hearing (PH)*

Perhaps the most dramatic effect of the Sift was the end of the automatic ph in almost every appeal. The effect of this had been that, because almost every case had such a ph, the courts were clogged with cases which either did not need a ph, because they were capable of being sent straight on to an fh with appropriate directions, or could have been disposed of under Rule 3, or, possibly, by the mechanism of the stay. Lay members' and judges' reading time and court time was being taken up, and parties' costs were being wasted, by cases which, when called on for a ph, were simply nodded through to an fh, or could have been disposed of summarily. The ph is now reserved for those cases about which, on the Sift, a judge feels genuine doubt as to their arguability, or perhaps cases which do not appear obvious candidates for Rule 3 and may, on being sorted out, disclose a nugget of argument. In respect of what is now a substantial minority of cases, the ph, as now operated, can be of considerable value:

    a.   The respondent is obliged immediately after the Sift to activate any cross-appeal. This ensures that there can be a ph of both appeal and cross-appeal, far more satisfactory than the previous system where a cross-appeal could end up being ph'd separately from, and subsequently to, the appeal. A possibility is that both or neither could go through, if they are considered together.

b.   More significantly, the respondent is usually obliged (or in some cases simply entitled) to put in 'concise written submissions in response to the Notice of Appeal, dedicated to showing that there is no reasonable prospect of success for all or any grounds of any appeal' *(*EAT Practice Direction, para.9.8*)*. An *inter partes* ph is rare (and would be an additional costs burden for the respondent), but, in this way, even at an *ex parte* hearing the EAT will have the gist of the respondent's response, which may lay to rest a false impression or a misunderstanding as to what occurred or did not occur, or was or was not argued, below – there may be a 'killer point'.

c.   If an amendment is suggested at the ph, which may often happen if there is fresh representation of the appellant (e.g. by ELAAS), then this may be similarly unfounded, and yet the respondent will not have had an opportunity to address it in submissions: and so any permission to amend would be given on the basis that the respondent could apply on paper on notice, disclosing any 'killer point' sufficient to rebut the new way in which the case has been put on the basis of the new amendment, to vary or discharge the order and thus perhaps dispose of the appeal.

d.   There can be discussion at the ph of the orders which, if the appeal had been sent through on the Sift straight to an fh, would have been included on the standard order. The judge will ordinarily now only deliver a judgment if the appeal is, in whole or in part, dismissed: it is the content of the order which thus becomes significant, which the judge is now under a personal responsibility to confirm, once it has been drawn up by the associate.

Similarly to the Sift sheet, the judge will complete after the ph, as in relation to a Rule 3(10) hearing or an fh, a Hearing Topic Sheet, which will include a short summary of the case, and this summary will be included in the weekly 'Hearing Bulletin' (see below), as well as being incorporated at the outset of the transcript of any judgment the judge gives at the hearing, if it is subsequently transcribed, or in any reserved judgment.

'Oral sift'

There may be cases in which an appeal is 'sifted orally'. This will arise if it can be seen on the papers that the appeal relates, for example, to a refusal of an adjournment of an imminent Employment Tribunal hearing. On occasion, the arguability of such an appeal has been resolved on an *inter partes* telephone hearing, from the Employment Tribunal at which the hearing was to take place, arguability usually dictating the result.

TWO SPECIFIC PROCEDURES

The Paragraph 7 Procedure

This is entirely new and is contained in Paragraph 7 of the EAT Practice Direction. The old system of Notes of Evidence (requests by one party or the other for the notes taken by the Chairman of the Employment Tribunal to be transcribed and made available for the appeal) was wholesale – made in a large number of cases and often in respect of all or most of the witnesses: time consuming – it could and did delay the listing of the appeal by as much as six months: and pointless – very often in the end the substantial transcripts so provided went into the appeal bundle and were hardly if at all consulted, and, indeed, were often only required to prove a negative; i.e. that such and such evidence was *not* given. The Paragraph 7 Procedure now directs the parties to seek to agree what is in fact required, which may only be a statement to the latter effect, or perhaps an agreed note of some small part of the evidence. If the procedure is followed, then any disagreements can be resolved, and it may be that both sides' differing notes can be put forward, or that some limited request for information, or for a short note relating to identified matters, will be made to the Employment Tribunal Chairman.

The Paragraph 11 Procedure

This is now a distillation into Paragraph 11 of the EAT Practice Direction of the guidance of Lindsay P. in *Facey* v *Midas Retail Security*, [2000] IRLR 812, in an appeal where there is an allegation of bias or misconduct by the Employment Tribunal, particularly the Chairman. A system, governed by timetables, is now incorporated by way of standard order, made either on the Sift or on a preliminary hearing (unless the matter has been dealt with under Rule 3), dedicated towards obtaining affidavits from the parties and comments from the Employment Tribunal Chairman and members. Warnings have now been incorporated into the Practice Direction, and into the EAT orders made, that a party who makes such an allegation is at risk as to costs; together with a reminder that appeals which are in fact in respect of a complaint about effective case management by an Employment Tribunal will not be favourably considered.

EAT/ACAS PROTOCOL

Mediation is not an easy option for the parties before the EAT, largely because of the normally costs-free nature of the jurisdiction. We have the benefit of the experienced services of Acas, which has until very recently wholly concentrated upon the first instance Employment Tribunal. Acas has now agreed that, originally for a trial period which has now been extended, they will be willing to consider referrals for consideration at the appellate level. The Protocol between Acas and the EAT, reached in December 2004, and subsequently amended and extended in August 2005, provides not only for the specific involvement of Acas where a case is stayed on the Sift to allow investigation or particularisation of allegations of bias or misconduct by the Tribunal (see above): in such a case, because of the particular difficulty of resolving such a dispute at a hearing, and the fact that very often such allegations simply mask or reflect an underlying unhappiness with the result, the assistance of Acas may be invaluable. But there may now also be included in any Sift or ph order a provision requiring papers to be sent to Acas, and for the parties to co-operate with Acas with a view to possible conciliation; but in those circumstances without imposing any stay, which might delay the hearing of the appeal, unless and until there is some real prospect of success for the conciliation.

LISTING

A combination of all this has enormously speeded up and facilitated Listing. The primary reason is of course the far lesser number of preliminary hearings requiring to be listed, freeing up court time for the resolution of fhs. But there are additional factors:

a. The existence of the Sift with its effective choice of track, and laying down of directions and timetables. The case can now be listed straight after being sifted;

b. The time estimate given at the time of the Sift;

c. The absence of the persistent delays caused by requests for Notes of Evidence;

d. The fact that the associates, to whom appeals have always been specifically allocated, have now been freed up from the burden of preparing bundles, and can and do accept the responsibility for overseeing their own appeals. Thus, they can chase up the parties to comply with time limits to ensure that the papers are complete well in time for the hearing: and can facilitate the new procedure, whereby the appeals in which there are breaches of an obligation to deliver skeletons etc. are listed for mention and to secure compliance, prior to the appeal, before a judge, rather than non-production or late production resulting in adjournments and post-hearing recriminations. Associates are finding, particularly in relation to litigants in person, of whom the EAT has a large number, that because cases are being brought on speedily, they are spending far less time having to deal with 'irate or distraught or pernickety customers';

e. The greater flexibility of hearings for judge alone, which is the case for a Rule 3(10) hearing and is now regularly enforced where the decision below was by a Chairman alone (s.28(4) ETA);

f. The offering of 'hearing windows' to Counsel, advocates and litigants within which the appeals, save for the most complicated, must be heard: leavened with co-operation to allow so far as possible for the convenience of the advocate, in order to facilitate not only the first choice of the client, but also the preference, if at all possible, for the advocate who appeared below.

The existence of the Sift Sheets and the weekly Sift Bulletin (containing the Sift judge's summary of the nature of the cases sifted through) has facilitated the co-ordinated listing of similar cases, and the appointment, where appropriate, to a category or class of similar cases of an assigned associate and indeed an assigned judge. The Hearing Topic Sheets and weekly Hearing Bulletins serve a similar purpose, of making sure that judges and associates are informed about what cases are going through the system, and have enabled us to co-ordinate hearings of similar cases: such as those involving non-economic loss, rolled up holiday pay, and post-employment discrimination, and those requiring to be stayed pending a decision in the Court of Appeal and/or the House of Lords, if appropriate, such as the recent decisions on holiday pay and the Working Time Regulations in *Commissioners of Inland Revenue v Ainsworth* [2005] ICR 1149.

JUDICIAL TIME

The time of the judges and lay members, in the light of all this, is being much more efficiently used, being concentrated, so far as court time is concerned, on fhs of appeals which have a realistic prospect of success. There has always been an emphasis at the EAT on time for pre-reading. Now, although the parties have assumed the responsibility for the preparation of the bundles, there is a limit of 100 pages, and if they need to go over that, they will only be given permission by the Registrar to do so if they provide an 'essential reading list' (EAT Practice Direction, Para. 6.3). Fewer judgments are being delivered, both because of the reduction in the number of hearings as a result of the drop in phs but also because, if a case goes through on a ph, there is not usually a judgment given. In any event, not all judgments are transcribed – only those for which a specific request is made by a party, or where the judge considers a transcript is required: this is a very considerable saving of clerical time – on average only approximately 65% of judgments are transcribed, whereas previously every word of wisdom (or otherwise) was religiously produced in transcript. The new summaries at the outset of every transcript (see above) are, I believe, of considerable value to the profession.

The collegiate spirit of the EAT has always been manifest in relation to the excellent relationship between the judges and the lay members, but this has now been further developed, and the opportunity for the pooling of information increased, by the introduction of a weekly meeting of the judges sitting at the EAT and a termly meeting for all EAT nominated judges. For a time we have had six courts sitting in London (with two or three in August and September), now reduced to five: plus our court in Edinburgh, sitting on average one week a month, presided over, until his promotion, by Lord Johnston, and now by Lady Smith.

Sir Michael Burton

(1)   A calculation has been carried out by the Registrar's staff of the approximate number of phs 'saved', or avoided, since the official recognition of the Sift (although, in practice, it had been in operation for a few weeks before that) by the Practice Direction of 9 December 2002. Between that date and 31 July 2005, it is reckoned that approximately 3,000 phs have not taken place, which would have taken place, because they have been dealt with by one of the other options made available on the Sift, as described above. That judicial time – the time of both judges and lay members – and the preparation by the associates for such phs, has been able to be diverted to dealing with other, more fruitful, matters, so far as the judges are concerned by dealing with a good deal of matters on paper (always with liberty to the parties to apply), but in particular to the reduction, and subsequent elimination, of the waiting time for full hearings.

(2)   The total figures between 9 December 2002 and 31 July 2005, by way of breakdown of orders made on the Sift, are as follows:

Full hearings	1,031
Preliminary hearings	1,204
Rule 3	1,546
Stays	621

It can be seen, therefore, that there is still a reasonable quantity of phs, which, as discussed above, can have some value – not only in dealing with doubtful cases, but in streamlining cases which are to go forward (at any rate, in part). However, the bulk of cases have been dealt with either by sending them through to an fh, with appropriate directions, or disposing of them as unsupportable.

(3)   Of those 1,546 cases in which Rule 3 was activated as a result of the Sift, 457 (less than a third) have been referred back to open court as a result of an application under Rule 3(10); and, of those, 109 (less than a quarter of that third) have, as a result of a Rule 3(10) hearing, been referred forward to a ph or fh. It can be seen that the large majority of those whose appeals were considered by a judge and rejected, with reasons, has accepted that decision, and the large majority of those who wished reconsideration under Rule 3(10) has not persuaded a judge on a re-hearing in court that there was anything arguable in their appeal. Anyone unsuccessful on Rule 3(10) has the opportunity to appeal to the Court of Appeal (with permission) – although, as at the time of writing, there is no indication of any material number of successful challenges.

(4)   The result is that what was a waiting time for the fh of an appeal of up to 18 months, or sometimes 2 years, and an average of a year or more, has been reduced and finally eliminated, so that cases are now heard, at least where there is no ph, and in the absence of some reason for delay, within 3 months of presentation of the appeal, and even where there is both ph and fh, well within 6 months. There has been no material

change in the volume of appeals from the EAT to the Court of Appeal (or in the number of successful appeals).

(5)   Disposal of appeals was calculated prior to December 2002 by reference only to disposals at phs and fhs. Now, of course, there are the other methods of disposal, arising out of the other options available on the Sift, particularly the Rule 3 option, and they are naturally reflected in that calculation. The figures for the total number of appeals presented and for the total number of disposals (as so calculated) in each financial year between 1998 and 2005, together with the figures for appeals outstanding at the end of each year, all as provided by the Registrar and her staff, are set out below. It can be seen that there has been a sharp rise in the number of appeals disposed of (out of a fairly constant number of appeals presented) and a very sharp fall in the number of outstanding appeals.

Year	Appeals presented	Appeals disposed of	Outstanding at year end
1998-99	1,741	1,323	1,147
1999-00	1,707	1,334	1,224
2000-01	1,869	1,608	1,152
2001-02	1,833	1,442	1,195
2002-03	1,938	2,272	716
2003-04	2,084	2,376	597
2004-05	1,876	2,142	351

THE FUTURE

The future is Leggatt – or, at least, Leggatt substantially amended (Leggatt 2001).

The Presidents of the Employment Tribunals – H.H.Judge Goolam Meeran (the England & Wales President) and Colin Milne (the Scottish President) – and I have spent a great deal of time in negotiations with the Department of Constitutional Affairs, as well as holding discussions with Brooke LJ and Carnwath LJ (as successive prospective Senior Presidents of Tribunals), and with presidents of other tribunals, over our future within or alongside the proposed unified tribunal system, as to which the publication of a draft Bill has been anticipated for some time, but will obviously not now be ready for enactment in April 2006, as was originally planned. The signs are now good for the future of the EAT (and, indeed, the Employment Tribunals), in that it is intended that we remain, in substance, outside the new tribunals system, as a '*separate pillar*', in parallel with the administrative tribunal system, but sharing and pooling not only ideas but resources, premises and administration. Importantly, it seems clear that we will be retaining our own Rules and Practice Directions, and the particular expertise of the specialist judges and vastly experienced lay members. In consequence, as we approach the 30th anniversary of the institution of the EAT, which will be celebrated in April 2006, all of the relevant stakeholders – judges, lay members, staff, practitioners and users –

would seem to be of the opinion that the EAT is in good shape to meet the challenges of continuing high profile change.

As we approach the thirtieth anniversary of the institution of the EAT in April 2005, I think we can all feel, judges, lay members, staff, practitioners and users, that the EAT is in good shape.

REFERENCE

Leggatt (2001): *Tribunals for Users: Report of the Review of Tribunals* [Chair: Sir Andrew Leggatt], March 2001 (Stationery Office, London)

List of publications in this series

STUDIES IN EMPLOYMENT AND SOCIAL POLICY

1. W. Beck, L. van der Maesen and A. Walker (eds.): *The Social Quality of Europe*. 1997. ISBN: 90411 0456 9
2. F. Pennings: *Introduction to European Social Law*. 2001. ISBN: 90411 1628 1
3. R. Blanpain, M. Colucci, C. Engels, F. Hendrickx, L. Salas and J. Wouters: *Institutional Changes and European Social Policies after the Treaty of Amsterdam*. 1998. ISBN: 90411 1018 6
4. Vai Jo Lo: *Law and Industrial Relations: China and Japan after World War II*. 1998: ISBN: 90 411 1075 5
5. A. Den Exter and H. Hermans (eds.): *The Right to Health Care in Several European Countries*. 1998. ISBN: 90 411 1087 9
6. M. Biagi (ed.): *Job Creation and Labour Law from Protection towards Pro-action*. 2000. ISBN: 90 411 1432 7
7. W. Beck, L.J.G. van der Maesen, F. Thomése and A. Walker (eds.): *Social Quality: a Vision for Europe*. 2000. ISBN: 90 411 1523 4
8. J. Murray: *Transnational Labour Regulation: The ILO and EC Compared*. 2001. ISBN: 90 411 1583 8
9. R. Blanpain and C. Engels (eds.): *The ILO and Social Challenges of the 21st century*. 2001. ISBN: 90 411 1572 2
10. M. Biagi (ed.): *Towards a European Model of Industrial Relations?* 2001. ISBN: 90 411 1653 2
11. J. Clasen (ed.): *What Future for Social Security? Debates and Reforms in National and Cross-National Perspective*. 2001. ISBN: 90 411 1671 0
12. A. Numhauser Hennings (ed.): *Legal Perspectives on Equal Treatment and Non Discrimination*. 2001. ISBN: 90 411 1665 6
13. R. Blanpain (ed.): *Labour Law, Human Rights and Social Justice*. 2001. ISBN: 90 411 1697 4
14. M-C. Kuo, HF. Zacher and H-S. Chan (eds.): *Reform and Perspectives on Social Insurance: Lessons from the East and West*. 2002. ISBN: 90 411 1819 5
15. P. Foubert: *The Legal Protection of the Pregnant Worker in the European Community*. 2002. ISBN: 90 411 1842 x
16. M. Biagi (ed.): *Quality of Work and Employee Involvement in Europe*. 2002. ISBN: 90 411 1885 3
17. F. Pennings: *Dutch Social Security Law in an International Context*. 2002. ISBN: 90 411 1887 x
18. T. Carney and G. Ramia: *From Rights to Management: Contract, New Public Management and Employment Services*. 2002. ISBN: 90 411 1889 6
19. R. Blanpain and M. Colucci: *European Labour and Social Security Law, Glossary*. 2002. ISBN: 90 411 1905 1
20. I.U. Zeytinoğlu (ed.): *Flexible Work Arrangements. Conceptualizations and International Experiences*. 2002. ISBN: 90 411 1947 7
21. J. Berghman, A. Nagelkerke, K. Boos, R. Doeschot and G. Vonk (eds.): *Social Security in Transition*. 2002. ISBN: 90 411 1969 8

22. R. Blanpain: *The Legal Status of Sportsmen and Sportswomen under International, European and Belgian National and Regional Law.* 2003. ISBN: 90 411 1980 9

23. R. Blanpain and M. Weiss (eds.): *Changing Industrial Relations & Modernisation of Labour Law, Liber Amicorum in Honour of Professor Marco Biagi.* 2003. ISBN: 90 411 2008 4

24. J. Malmberg (ed.), B. Fitzpatrick, M. Gotthardt, S. Laulom, A. Lo Faro, T. van Peijpe, A. Swiatkowski: *Effective Enforcement of EC Labour Law.* 2003. ISBN: 90 411 2160 9

25. M. De Vos (ed.): *A Decade Beyond Maastricht: The European Social Dialogue Revisited.* 2003. ISBN: 90 411 2163 3

26. M. Seweryński (ed.): *Collective Agreements and Individual Contracts of Employment.* 2003. ISBN:90 411 2190 0

27. R. Blanpain, M. Van Gestel: *Use and Monitoring of E-Mail, Intranet and Internet Facilities at Work. Law and Practice.* 2004. ISBN: 90 411 22 66 4

28. A.C. Neal (ed.): *The Changing Face of European Labour Law and Social Policy.* 2004. ISBN: 90 411 2312 1

29. E. Sol and M. Westerveld (eds.): *Contractualism in Employment Services: A New Form of Welfare State Governance.* 2005. ISBN 90 411 2405 5

30. F. Pennings (ed.): *Between Soft and Hard Law – The Impact of International Social Security Standardson National Social Security Law.* 2006. ISBN 90 411 2491 8

31. L. Dickens and A.C. Neal (eds.): *The Changing Institutional Face of British Employment Relations.* 2006. ISBN 90 411 2541 8